Entrepreneurship in Asia:

Social Enterprise, Network and Grassroots Case Studies

Japanese Management and International Studies
(ISSN: 2010-4448)

Editor-in-Chief: Yasuhiro Monden *(Tsukuba University, Japan)*

Published

Japanese Management and International Studies – Vol. 11

Entrepreneurship in Asia:
Social Enterprise, Network and Grassroots Case Studies

editors

Stephen Dun-Hou Tsai
National Sun Yat-sen University, Taiwan

Ted Yu-Chung Liu
National Pingtung University, Taiwan

Jersan Hu
Fu Jen Catholic University, Taiwan,

Shang-Jen Li
Meiho University, Taiwan

 **World Scientific**

NEW JERSEY · LONDON · SINGAPORE · BEIJING · SHANGHAI · HONG KONG · TAIPEI · CHENNAI

Published by

World Scientific Publishing Co. Pte. Ltd.

5 Toh Tuck Link, Singapore 596224

USA office: 27 Warren Street, Suite 401-402, Hackensack, NJ 07601

UK office: 57 Shelton Street, Covent Garden, London WC2H 9HE

Library of Congress Cataloging-in-Publication Data
Entrepreneurship in Asia : social enterprise, network and grassroots case studies / [edited] by
Stephen Dun-Hou Tsai (National Sun Yat-sen University, Taiwan), Ted Yu-Chung Liu (National
Pingtung University, Taiwan), Jersan Hu (Fu Jen Catholic University, Taiwan), Shang-Jen Li
(Meiho University, Taiwan).
    pages cm. -- (Japanese management and international studies, ISSN 2010-4448 ; vol. 11)
   Includes bibliographical references and index.
   ISBN 978-9814612210 (alk. paper)
   1. Entrepreneurship--Asia--Case studies. 2. Social responsibility of business--Asia--Case studies.
I. Tsai, Stephen Dun-Hou.
   HB615.E63343 2015
   338'.04095--dc23

                             2014030772

British Library Cataloguing-in-Publication Data
A catalogue record for this book is available from the British Library.

In-house Editors: Lum Pui Yee/Chitralekha Elumalai

Typeset by Stallion Press
Email: enquiries@stallionpress.com

Printed in Singapore

Japan Society of Organization and Accounting (JSOA)

Assistant Managers
Satoshi Arimoto, Niigata University, Japan
Hiromasa Hirai, Takasaki City University of Economics, Japan

Mission of JSOA and Editorial Information

For the purpose of making a contribution to the business and academic communities, the Japan Society of Organization and Accounting (JSOA), is committed to publishing the book series, entitled *Japanese Management and International Studies*, with a refereed system.

Focusing on Japan and Japan-related issues, the series is designed to inform the world about research outcomes of the new "Japanese-style management system" developed in Japan. However, as the series title suggests, it also promotes "*International Studies*" on the interface of managerial competencies between Japan and other countries that include Asian countries as well as Western countries under the globalized business activities of Japanese companies.

Research topics included in this series are management of organizations in a broad sense (including the business group or networks) and the accounting that supports the organization. More specifically, topics include business strategy, business models, organizational restoration, corporate finance, M&A, environmental management, operations management, managerial & financial accounting, manager performance evaluation, reward systems. The research approach is interdisciplinary, which includes case studies, theoretical studies, normative studies and empirical studies, but emphasizes real world business.

Each volume contains the series title and a book title which reflects the volume's special theme.

Our JSOA's board of directors has established an editorial board of international standing. In each volume, guest editors who are experts on the volume's special theme serve as the volume editors. The details of JSOA is shown in its by-laws contained in the home-page: http://jsoa.sakura.ne.jp/english/index.html.

Editorial Board

Contents

Preface

Toward the Construction of Entrepreneurial Society

The importance of entrepreneurship in sustaining the prosperity of society is commonly recognized, and thus how to build up an entrepreneurial society has become a significant issue for most countries in the world. In order to display the different and maybe unique experiences of stimulating and fostering such creative momentum in Asia, the present collection thus invites the contributors from Taiwan and Japan to share their exploration and understanding of the issues in entrepreneurship, particularly regarding social enterprise, network and grassroots entrepreneurial stories.

Holding the similar belief with Berglund *et al.* (2012), we conceive entrepreneurship as a societal rather than an economic phenomenon. Relating society and social change to entrepreneurship adds some further dimensions on entrepreneurship studies (Steyaert & Katz, 2004). Social entrepreneurship is regarded to be able to shed a light for aiding the disadvantaged minority by its function bringing about maximization of social value. In this vein, social enterprise is one significant and substantial development to notice. To promote and ensure the flourishment of social enterprise, our contributors engage themselves with exploring different strategies of market entry and resource acquisition that determine diverse social entrepreneurial models, and trying to advance the social impact measurement for social enterprise (see Chapters 1 and 4). Moreover, to investigate the social aspect of innovation and their benefit to the whole society, the potential of frugal innovation and the multiple innovations of social technologies for social value creation are further examined in Chapters 2 and 3. We believe these discussions could be helpful and inspiring for those who would like to involve in social enterprise and social entrepreneurship, and more or less demonstrate the endeavor of societal entrepreneuring in Taiwan.

Perhaps embedded in the unique Asian cultural climate, the construction and building of relation and network in different aspects is constantly to be key issue for the substantial development and performance of business in Asia. In the discussions in Chapters 5–7, our contributors, respectively, look into the importance of commitment in the construction of reliable relation in the case of "one network organization related to the publication business of the not-for-profit academic society in Japan"; the external effects of network as meta-organization to the member companies in the case of Kyoto Shisaku Net; the benefits brought by the formation of community of practice through the establishment of teachers training system in the case of BS Supplementary Education Group in Taiwan. We could see the different features of network and its diverse functions in its becoming upon the substantial entrepreneuring of enterprises in these chapters.

Based our continuous care about the entrepreneurship in Asia, we found that wealth creation is not the only reason to start up a new venturing; seeking autonomy and authoring can be the alternative aims of entrepreneurship (Rindova *et al.*, 2009). We believe that there are some people who start up a business for supporting their unique lifestyles and values, their imagination of better world and different social visions, rather than pursuing money, especially in cultural and creative industry. Those entrepreneurs have their distinctive visions and thinking on their business and entrepreneurial actions, and their business and actions also reflect their unusual personal value, belief and thought vice versa. In those grassroots entrepreneurial stories in Japan, Taiwan and Mainland China shared in this collection, we can see different conceptions of business/entrepreneurship and its connections to social change, which goes beyond the mainstream economic discourse, and draws more attentions to the issues of being and becoming entrepreneur, who ultimately being the very dynamic of the construction of entrepreneurial society. We hope this collection could show another perspective of entrepreneurship, emphasizing the ontological connection between *entrepreneuring* and the dynamic of societal change.

Stephen Dun-Hou Tsai & Ted Yu-Chung Liu, 2014

References

Berglund, K., Johannisson, B., & Schwartz, B. (2012). *Societal Entrepreneurship: Positioning, Penetrating, Promoting.* Cheltenham, UK & Northampton, MA, USA: Edward Elgar Publishing.

Rindova, V., Barry, D., & Ketchen, D. J. (2009). Entrepreneuring as Enmancipation, *Academy of Management Review*, 34(3), pp. 477–491.

Steyaert, C. & Katz, J. (2004). Reclaiming the Space of Entrepreneurship in Society: Geographical, Discursive and Social Dimensions, *Entrepreneurship and Regional Development*, 16, pp. 179–196.

About the Editors

 **Stephen Dun-Hou Tsai** is a Professor in the Department of Business Management at National Sun Yat-sen University, Taiwan. He served as a Visiting Scholar of the College of Management & Economics at Växjö University in Sweden, the Judge Institute of Management Studies at University of Cambridge, UK, and Stanford University, USA. His current research interests mainly focus on the development of societal entrepreneurship, the methodology of narrative inquiry, and the reconceptualization of entrepreneurial education. He has published numerous academic journal articles in international journals such as *Journal of Management Inquiry, Journal of Management Studies, and Organization Studies.*

Contact Stephen Dun-Hou Tsai via dhtsai@bm.nsysu.edu.tw

 **Ted Yu-Chung Liu** (PhD, University of East Anglia, UK) is an Associate Professor, at National Pingtung University, Taiwan, and was a Visiting Scholar at University of Illinois, Urbana-Champaign, USA, Adjunct Assistant Professor at National Chengchi University and National Sun Yat-sen University. He is the holder of the Oversea Researcher Students Awards UK, National Science Council (NSC) Outstanding Specialty Award 2011. Current research interests mainly include on the methodological issues of narrative enquiry, the epistemological issues of entrepreneurial learning, and the ontological issues of entrepreneurs' subjectivity and identity. He is particularly interested in *Foucauldian* and *Deleuzian* thinking and implications, philosophy of curriculum, critical pedagogy, and

culture studies in education. He is a member of Philosophy of Education Society of Great Britian (PESGB), Philosophy of Education Society of Australasia (PESA), and has published many articles and books both in English and Chinese. Recent published books include *If Our Days Are Marbles: Ten Lessons of Happiness in Teaching and Learning in Taiwan Community Universities (2012)*, *The First Course on Narrative Enquiry (co-author with Stephen Dun-Hou Tsai, 2011)*, *Re-imagination of Pedagogy: Deleuzian Thinking and Philosophy of Education (2010)*, *Post-structuralism and the Exploration of Contemporary Pedagogy: Return to the Worldy Realities (2009)*.

Contact Ted Yu-Chung Liu via tedycliu@gmail.com

Jersan Hu is a Professor in the Department of Business Administration at School of Management, Fu Jen Catholic University (Taiwan). His study topics for the past decade focus on the constructing of global resources configuration, strengthening of competitive capabilities via inter-organizational learning in accordance with evolution of network strategy, and promoting of industrial status in value network through resources integration of Taiwan companies. Since 2009, because of the economical distortions caused by financial tsunami, he began to inquire the blind points of capitalism-based social institution. His research interests had shifted to social entrepreneurship, social innovation, and social enterprise management-related topics.

Contact Jersan Hu via 074986@mail.fju.edu.tw

Shang-Jen Li (PhD, National Sun Yat-sen University, Taiwan) is an Assistant Professor and Director of hospitality management at Meiho University, Taiwan. He has conducted a post-doctoral research project in Linnaeus University, Sweden, focusing on the study of family business.

Current teachings and research interests mainly lie on strategy management, entrepreneurship, family business research, narrative inquiry method, franchising, and chain store management. Now he devotes efforts on establishment of theory of entrepreneuring organization as well as study of SME family business in Asian and Chinese society.

He is a recipient of Honorable Mention Dissertation 2011, SME Administration, Ministry of Economic Affairs, Taiwan, ROC. His articles are published in Chinese as well as in English Journals: *Sun Yat-sen Management Review, Journal of Entrepreneurship Research*, and *The Journal of Global Business Management*. Emerging research ideas are also presented and discussed at international conferences, such as ICSB 2011, ECEI 2006, BAI2008, AAOM, etc.

Currently, by focusing on narrated life-story, he tries to develop life story approach in order to contribute more in-depth and insightful implications on family business study.

Contact details:

Department of Hospitality Management, Meiho University
23, Pingguang Rd., Neipu, Pingtung County, Taiwan, ROC
Phone: +886 8 779 9821 ext. 6606
E-mail: x00010180@meiho.edu.tw

List of Contributors

Satoshi Arimoto
Niigata University

Tzu Yang Chang
Fu Jen Catholic University

Jersan Hu
Fu Jen Catholic University

Jung-Chih Hung
National Sun Yat-sen University

Gautam Kamath
Fu Jen Catholic University

Ming-Rea Kao
Wenzao Ursuline University of Languages

Anthony Kuo
Fu Jen Catholic University

Chien Hsien Lee
Fu Jen Catholic University

Chih-Yu Lee
National Sun Yat-sen University

Leemen Lee
Fu Jen Catholic University

Shang-Jen Li
Meiho University

Shelley Hui-Yin Lin
National Sun Yat-sen University

Ted Yu-Chung Liu
National Pingtung University

Yasuhiro Monden
University of Tsukuba

Akira Sawamura
Niigata University

Stephen Dun-Hou Tsai
National Sun Yat-sen University

Meng-Chen Wu
National Sun Yat-sen University

Naoya Yamaguchi
Aoyama Gakuin University

Zong-ying Zhou
Fu Jen Catholic University

1

Market Entry and Resource Acquisition Strategies for Social Enterprises

Jersan Hu
Fu Jen Catholic University

Leemen Lee
Fu Jen Catholic University

Zong-ying Zhou
Fu Jen Catholic University

1. Introduction

Over the recent decades, the overall economic and business performance, in Taiwan, has been marked by a moderate growth. The gross domestic product (GDP) has increased from 9.7 billion in 2000 to 14.098 billion TWD in 2010. The monthly average wages have increased from 41,861 to 45,771 TWD over the same period. Paradoxically, the number of low-income households has increased steadily, from 66,000 to 93,000 households, or a population growth of 156,000 to 223,000 over the same period. The population ratio rose from 0.7 to 0.97% which is in contradictory given the overall positive economic development. This shows that the job opportunities and salaries levels were not proportionately beneficial to all social layers. Knowledge-intensive works were offered higher income rewards than others while the unemployment level grew with the increasing number of job seekers. The income-increase for the affluent class substantially exceeds that of the low-income groups, leading to the polarized development in which "the rich get richer, and the poor get poorer." The ambition of improving people's living through the developing of a socially just economy did not materialize. Instead, there has been a more pronounced and unbalanced allocation of resources across the social structures.

The poverty that emerged during the economic development process is distinct from the extant concept of poverty; the phenomenon is similar to what is stated in Dixon *et al.* (1998): "a form of global poverty is taking shape through the social economic effect of capitalist globalization, affecting every corner of the world," including poor work, unemployment, and resource gap within the disadvantaged groups, coupled with the relative poverty caused by rising living costs and misallocation of social wealth. This is distinctive from the traditional definition of economically disadvantaged groups of the "aged, disabled, ailing, and minors." In the era of knowledge economy and globalization, the disadvantaged population in the "new poverty society" may see their situation worsen gradually. As the mid-age unemployed workers or single-parents are also the sources of income for their households, their being unemployed not only affects their health insurance payment, the financing of the education of their children, but also affects the employment of their dependents, thus creating a ripple effect on the society.

Some social groups cast their hope on the government institutions and the businesses. The social mechanism in capitalism encourages businesses to offer products and create employment for profit. However, business operation has its blind spots which are the pursuit of profit-maximization, private capital returns, rational cost-benefit analysis, while downplaying the effects of individual or social structure factors of employment. The needs of low-income populations and those in rural areas are neglected, resulting in the phenomenon of "market failure" (Hu & Chen, 2009). The weak business performance is also attributable to the government's public resource distribution or social policies. Hence, "government failure" occurs because of the bureaucracy in the complexity of the policy making, and the rigidity of regulations often hinders the delivery of public welfare.

In order to make up the gap of public welfare insufficiency, market failure, and the "voluntarism failure" resulting from the limited donations to non-profit organizations (NPOs), a new type of "self-sufficient organization which blends social service value and management capacity" — social enterprise — is thus extolled with the expectation of meeting the neglected needs of the society. The OECD (1999) stated that social enterprise is equipped with the unique functions of innovative social institutions, including (1) social enterprise takes the form of a business, keeps an autonomy distant from the state, yet deliver the behavioral value of social service; (2) social enterprise provides employment, advances needs in social service, and makes up the market exclusion and discrepancy in social welfare supply as a result of rapid economic development; (3) other than the managers, the members of a social enterprise include its volunteers and funders. Volunteers can assure the non-profit nature of the enterprise and strengthen the trust of government and customers upon social enterprise. However, since social organizations or enterprises serve the disadvantaged market, it is difficult to attract business resource, and also bears risks in venture development which are higher than regular commercial ventures. The unfavorable conditions that social entrepreneurs face should be taken into account in order to design a more adaptive entrepreneurial model or market entry mode. Hence, this study focuses on exploring various social entrepreneurship models that overcome the difficulties in market development and resources mobilization. Hopefully, the study may contribute to make up for the over-emphasis of commercialization in entrepreneurship theory and the insufficiency of the literature on social entrepreneurship.

2. Theoretical Background

2.1. *Opportunity seeking in social entrepreneurship*

Zahra *et al.* (2009) believed social entrepreneurship is the action and process of discovering, defining, and exploiting opportunity. Peredo and McLean (2006) found the following features of social entrepreneurship: social entrepreneurship is an individual or a group of individuals who (1) exercise excellent methods and their combination to create social value; (2) recognize and take advantage of the opportunity to create social value; (3) practice innovation; (4) accept and bear risk; and (5) are not discouraged by the limitation of current resources.

Dees (2001) pointed out that the difference between a social entrepreneur and a business entrepreneur is that a social entrepreneur focuses on the social mission. When a social entrepreneur finds and evaluates an opportunity, social mission is the vital evaluation criteria. The context of social entrepreneurship Dees recognized includes: a social entrepreneur plays the role of a change agent in social sector; the mission he adopted is to create and maintain social value; he pursues the new opportunity to accomplish his mission; he integrates sustainable innovation, adapts and learns in the process, would not be limited to existing resources, possesses a strong sense of responsibility of creating outcome; in operation goal, social entrepreneurship values non-monetary social value or social service far more than regular businesses, and before management challenges, it also bears more expenses in social responsibility than commercial organizations.

Haugh's (2007) model of non-profit venture creation includes six stages: (1) identifying opportunities; (2) articulating ideas; (3) owning ideas; (4) mobilizing stakeholders; (5) exploiting opportunities; and (6) reporting to stakeholders; it emphasizes recognizing social needs and encouraging people in discovering venture opportunities. Bornstein (2007) conceives social entrepreneurs as "transformative" forces, that is, "People with new ideas to address major problems who are relentless in the pursuit of their visions, people who simply will not take 'no' for an answer, who will not give up until they have spread their ideas as far as they possibly can." However, this model lacks the insights of practical social venture action and management system design.

Guclu *et al.* (2002) stated the two stages in social entrepreneurship: the first stage is "generating promising ideas" and is followed by "developing promising ideas into attractive opportunities." Even in the first stage, the "promising ideas" are not readily available; it takes the personal (social) experiences of the entrepreneur to identify social needs and the various social assets that can be harnessed to address those social issues. Following the new concepts that emanated from promoting social change, the balanced perspectives in valuing social needs and problem-solving capacities have also emerged. The second stage emphasizes the theory of transforming "promising ideas" into social impact that social value, and then design the operating model and business strategy accordingly. Guclu *et al.* highlighted that what social entrepreneurship needs are a concrete business philosophy, a managerial system, and social resources to fuel the social venture.

2.2. *Resources integration in social entrepreneurship*

The establishment backgrounds of social enterprises may be different, but they may be classified into two main categories: (1) commercial ventures by philanthropic organizations (NPO for profit) and (2) commercial business enterprises with social purposes (PO for social purpose). Personal experiences and background of the entrepreneur will certainly delineate the social assets and social needs realization of the venture organization. To strengthen the business operation capacity or to effectively identify social needs, entrepreneurs must strive to acquire the lacking social venture resources. A social venture, just like any regular business, not only requires resources like operating capital, facilities, technologies, and management, when identifying social needs and devising solutions to social problems, it also needs to involve resources that identify more with social engagement. Kretzmann and McKnight (1993) called it "neighborhood assets map," which stresses the necessity of social enterprises' need of diverse forms of social institutions and assets, especially social assets.

Social capital is a capacity of managing resources; it enables businesses to acquire, integrate, reorganize, and transfer resources (Blyer & Coff, 2003); or a capacity of actualizing business goal through the intangible resources of social relationships. Yang (2007) believed that there are four features in social capital: (1) basic features emphasize the strength, contact frequency, and the chains among individual staff members in the organization's social relationship; (2) specific features emphasizes the content of interpersonal (including colleagues, friends, and association members) relationship, e.g., identification, attitudes, including trust, respect, trade, obligation, cooperation, and expectations to collaboration; (3) generalized features emphasize the relationship between the individual and the general public (the strangers), including acceptance of collective norms, abiding common rules, and the trust on strangers; (4) the last feature is the structural features of social relations, including the concentration of relationship within specific social groups.

Lin (1999) believed that the resource owned by the social entrepreneur is related to the entrepreneur's social status or social structure positioning. The entrepreneur's initial social status positioning has a significantly positive correlation with the social resources available to the venture. Also, the entrepreneur can obtain and utilize better social resources to enhance the success rate of the venture. This demonstrates the impact of the entrepreneur's social status, social relations, and work experience on venture mobility.

Westlund (2003) classified external social capital into three categories: (1) production-related capital, including the contacts with suppliers, product users, and R&D collaborators; (2) environment-related capital, including the contacts with local/regional environment and policy makers; (3) market-related, including trade mark and customer relations.

Although academics still have divergent definitions of the attributes of social capital, a common understanding is that, unlike the commercial business resources, more extensive and functional resources are the *sine qua non* resources to address the specific social problems that social enterprises face.

3. Method

Based on the challenges entrepreneurs face in identifying market needs and operation resource required, this study takes as its research subjects the social enterprises with distinct venture processes and resource acquisition approaches. Proceeding with in-depth case studies and cross-case comparisons, the aim of this study is to induce the market entry modes and resource acquisition strategies in the case of social entrepreneurs.

3.1. *Multiple case comparisons*

The case study approach can be classified into four research design combinations: based on its context situation and the clarity of theory context, there are embedded theory verification and holistic theory exploration; based on the expected degree of theory generalization, there are single-case or multiple-case approaches (Yin, 2003). This study aims to thoroughly observe the venture process (models) and resources portfolio of social enterprises under various resource conditions. To provide evidence of the various venture models, this study adopted the corresponding cases to build a generalized theoretical framework; therefore, this study employed multiple case — based (embedded) theory as its research tool.

The study, through comparison of various venture processes, aims to reach the double objectives of learning the causal or narrative analysis of the case firms and building the generalizability of various behavior models (Hammersley & Gomm, 2000). This kind of knowledge is a form of generalization, not scientific induction but naturalistic generalization, arrived at by recognizing the similarities of objects in and out of context and by sensing the natural variations of happenings. It is both intuitive and empirical (Stake, 2000).

3.2. *Selection of cases*

The three requirements of the research sampling are: first, they must represent an authentic entrepreneurship not a transformation of an established business. Second, social utility or social service must be upheld as one of their goals. Third, the entrepreneurship or entry in business modes for each case must be distinct from the others. This study selected a sample of nine social enterprises. Through interviews and observation, we have concluded that these case firms not only met the previous three requirements, their operations designs have also reached a sufficient level of stability thus making them the adequate examples for studying the differences in social entrepreneurship/venture process.

The industry and the capital input of the nine firms selected are described in this section. The nine cases constitute to some extent a general picture of the social enterprises in Taiwan (Table 1). Most of these firms are traders of traditional products or traditional service providers, produce farming and sales, as in case firm 2; food and beverage production, as in case firms 1, 4, 6, and 7; community care and cleaning, as in case firm 9; service industry, as in case firm 3; case firm 8 is the only one in the media communication industry. From the perspective of industrial capital (labor, land, technology and equipment, and capital), the most needed is technical labor, as in cases 1, 3, 4, 7, and 9; followed by operating system, as in cases 2, 3, and 8; next would be land or community, as in cases 2, 5–7, and 9.

3.3. *Data collection*

This study probes into the entrepreneurial experiences of the nine cases with the inquiries include: the social service philosophy of the firm, the target group, the motives underlying their specific entrepreneurial choices and paths, how the social entrepreneurs integrate business management and social service, the business challenges in the venturing process, how relevant are the entrepreneur's prior experiences or expertise, what kinds of social or business knowledge the entrepreneur pick up later on. The approaches to obtaining data include lectures, interviews, and on-site observation.

(1) Lectures

In managing Taiwan Social Enterprise Innovation and Entrepreneurship Society, since 2009, the leading author began a series of Social Entrepreneurship Workshops and had the privileges of inviting outstanding social entrepreneurs to give lectures on their personal experiences in the field. Up to March 2011, over 30 firms presented their ventures according to the preset key issues, i.e., the issues this study addresses. Questions pinpointing the key issues were raised in the lectures.

(2) Interviews

The authors conducted interviews with the entrepreneurs and/or the executive directors of the nine social enterprises. The length of the interviews ranged from 1.5 to 2 hours. All interviews were recorded and transcribed for analysis.

Table 1. Business characteristics of the cases

Social enterprise	Entrepreneurial initiative	Business items and scope	Social purpose
1. Children-Are-Us Bakery	Children-Are-Us Foundation invested in bakeries and cafeterias, brought in trainers for job and service skill training, and expanded the number of stores.	Pastry production, chain-store outlets, cafeterias.	Empowering mentally challenged people through job skills development and employment for contact and social inclusion.
2. Li-Ren Organic Chain Store	Bliss and Wisdom Cultural Foundation, based on the concept of life education, invested in the sales of organic produce. The business was commissioned to the group members and expanded its chain operation.	Organic vegetable certification, purchase, distribution, and chain store sales service.	Promote organic agriculture; "cherish life" philosophy; provide safe produce.
3. Victory Gas Station	Victory Potential Development Center for the Disabled teamed with China Petroleum Corp., Taiwan and trained the physically challenged people to operate certain gas stations.	Gas station service and management.	Empowering the physically challenged people with job opportunities and the venture opportunities of being an operator at a gas station.
4. Sunny Kitchen	In addition to in-house food service, Sunny Kitchen (Restaurant) also promotes "meals-on-wheel" in the community and trains other food service providers in management skills and meal delivery service.	Vegetarian meals, community diners serving quick meals.	Meals-on-Wheel service for senior citizens in the community; train and hire disadvantaged women; assist other food service providers in management to increase employment for the disadvantaged.

(Continued)

Table 1. (*Continued*)

Social enterprise	Entrepreneurial initiative	Business items and scope	Social purpose
5. Geng Xin Lian Yuan	The main engagement is after school care; also offer community childcare and meals served to parents with limited financial resource (free meals if necessary); parent–child education; and other revenue generating ventures.	After school care for primary and middle school students; managing vegetarian restaurants; hand-made food production and sales.	Care for children from disadvantaged families in after school learning, meal service, and parent–child relationship building; community service; traditional cultural education.
6. ASUS Bakery	ASUS Company invited Children-Are-Us Bakery to operate the company's in-house bakery and café, providing competitive wages and benefits to the employees with disabilities from Children-Are-Us Bakery.	Beverages, bread, quick meal preparation, and dining service.	Empowering people with disabilities; providing Children-Are-Us Bakery operation location and ensuring their revenue.
7. Rejoice Community Supported Agriculture Group	Rejoice engaged farmers in growing wheat by contract; hired mentally challenged youth in bread making and flour products; then sell the products in communities at very competitive prices.	Contract farming of wheat; flour product manufacturing; low cost bread sales.	Guarantee farmers income; employment for disadvantaged women; provide low cost bread for community.

(*Continued*)

Table 1. (*Continued*)

Social enterprise	Entrepreneurial initiative	Business items and scope	Social purpose
8. The Big Issue (Taiwan)	The Big Issue (Taiwan) endeavored for the licensing and management system transfer from The Big Issue parent firm. The magazine operates independently in editing and publishing, training the homeless people in sales skills and to work for self-independence.	The material gathering, manuscript writing, editing, publishing, and distribution of a leisure magazine monthly.	Assist the homeless in magazine sales for earned-income to social reintegration.
9. PWR Foundation	A senior manager at Johnson & Johnson, Taiwan now consults PWR Foundation in building home care business; the services provided include: housekeeping, house cleaning, etc.	Home cleaning and housekeeping services.	Assist the Foundation in establishing home care business, exploring the market, and assisting the abused women with employment.

(3) On-site observation

To experience beforehand the meaningfulness of the firms' social service and social value, the authors also visited the facilities of these ventures to observe and experience the social service contents claimed. In addition, documents such as brochures or annual reports were collected.

4. Findings

Operating within an established business environment, social enterprises face challenges of the business resource infrastructure distinct from regular businesses. Not only do social entrepreneurs need to explore, with a different concept of market, the untapped needs, but also to acquire social and business resources from various sources to support the operating capacity of a social enterprise. This study addresses some behavioral patterns in venture resource acquisition, social market development, and changing venture process. Through case analysis, this study compares the social venture process and business models developed by the nine cases.

4.1. *Social market development strategies*

Social enterprises focus on the unmet social needs. This study identified two kinds of social needs: One is the needs of certain products by the disadvantaged population, such as the meals-on-wheel service in case 4, or the community childcare in case 5. The other type of the social needs is the needs of employment by the disadvantaged. All cases in the study are, to various extent, providing employment for the disadvantaged groups. Therefore, social enterprises may consider two kinds of social markets: The market to deliver, and the market to employ. The two kinds of social markets are not mutually exclusive; social enterprises can address the two markets simultaneously by employing the disadvantaged to deliver a service for the disadvantaged.

Social entrepreneurs may adopt different strategies to develop a market and to enter the market. An analysis of the nine social enterprises suggest that three types of market entry strategies can be considered: Embedding social enterprises into existing markets, exploring new markets, and deriving market entry strategies from their social missions. The first market entry strategy is to embed the social enterprises into existing markets. This strategy assumes that the markets are, for various reasons, exclusively ready for specific social enterprises to enter. Cases 2, 3, and 6 belong to this category.

In case 2, the religious NPO already has a membership base large enough to sustain the social enterprise during its initial stage. In case 3, the gas station operated by the social enterprise is an outsourcing contract from the state-owned petroleum corporation. In case 6, the social enterprise was exclusively selected by a big business corporation to provide bakery products for its employees.

The second market entry strategy is to exploring new markets by creating products or services that are highly differentiated or competitive in the mainstream market. Contrasting to the market embeddedness strategy that assumes social enterprises enjoy an exclusive access to markets, the market exploration strategy assumes that social enterprises are facing sheer market competition. Cases 1, 7, and 9 adopt this strategy. In case 1, the social enterprise operating bakery stores and cafeterias competing head to head with commercial ones. In case 7, the small social enterprise making wheat products is competing with other gigantic food companies. In case 9, the social enterprise is operating in the highly competitive home cleaning services industry.

Taking the first two strategies as two extremes with reference to the degree of exclusive access to markets, the third market entry strategy — to develop products or services with strong social mission appealing and sufficient market competitiveness — is in between. Cases 4, 5, and 8 illustrate how this strategy works. In case 4, the social enterprise operating the vegetarian cafeteria is able to provide superb food at a relatively inexpensive price. In case 5, the social enterprise produces hand-made cookies with high quality. In case 8, the social enterprise produces a quality magazine sold exclusively by the homeless people.

Column 4 in Table 2 indicates the strategies adopted by the nine social enterprises. Proposition 1 summarizes the analysis of market types and market entry strategies discussed above.

Proposition 1A: Social enterprises in the stage of opportunity identification may consider the markets from two different but not mutually exclusive aspects: market to deliver and market to employ.

Proposition 1B: Social enterprises may consider three different market entry strategies: Embedding social enterprises into existing markets, exploring new markets, and deriving strategies from their social mission.

Table 2.   Social entrepreneurship models and business behavioral analysis

Entrepreneurship model	Entrepreneur background	Start-up resources	Market entry strategies	Resource acquisition strategies	"Social/business" resources integration
1. Social business chain (Children-Are-Us)	Social service institution member with business operation background.	The business experience and networking; the social image of the social service institution.	(Derived markets). After the initial bakery, stores were expanded to 23 bakeries; apply business concepts-related products.	(External transfer). Production skills, sales skills, and store operation.	Invite external experts for technique instruction and transfer; co-production with volunteers. (Adaptation).
2. Social business diversification (Li-Ren)	Social institution members with business experience.	Religious group advocating organic living to promote "love life" philosophy; staff with management expertise of various backgrounds.	(Market embeddedness). The internal learning and dissemination of life philosophy of the religious organization formed a vast market for organic products, supporting the establishment of organic chain stores and organic vegetarian restaurants.	(Internal formation). Organization members established organic certification system; encouraged suppliers to produce organic products; brought-in members of various managerial expertise and capital.	Integrate members' religious service beliefs with modern business technology and knowledge to form innovative concepts; reach social ideal through the promoting business and social activities. (Integration).

(Continued)

Table 2. (*Continued*)

Entrepreneurship model	Entrepreneur background	Start-up resources	Market entry strategies	Resource acquisition strategies	"Social/business" resources integration
3. Collaborative entrepreneur with commercial business (Victory Gas Station)	The managing director of the social service institution himself is physically challenged.	Design equipment adapted to the capacity of the physically impaired; earn the employment through competitiveness.	(Market embeddedness). The business license and market of the existing gas station.	(External transfer). Strive for the transfer of business technology and management skills to empower the physically impaired with employment.	Accept business technology training and knowledge transfer; through internal learning, transform them into more competitive technology adapted to the physically impaired. (Integration).
4. Business technology transfer (Sunny Kitchen)	Restaurant operation; long-term community service.	Restaurant operation and F&B production techniques; F&B product planning and cost control.	(Self-developed). Strengthening restaurant operation capacity; develop the market; provide the disadvantaged with job training and restaurant management consulting.	(Contract). Accept invitations from NPOs and communities in advising on restaurant operation and food preparation techniques.	Provide skill training and employment; adjust operation procedures and management system to employees' conditions to facilitate job placements for the disadvantaged. (Adaptation).

(*Continued*)

Table 2. (*Continued*)

Entrepreneurship model	Entrepreneur background	Start-up resources	Market entry strategies	Resource acquisition strategies	"Social/business" resources integration
5. Social mission transformation of business (Geng Xin Lian Yuan)	Partnership with business operation and teaching philosophy.	Existing professional skills (elementary education, business management knowledge) pre-school.	(Self-developed). In-depth understanding of the conditions of the families in the community, design product concepts to fit family needs and develop business items.	(Internal formation). Design own community elementary after-school. Care system; acquire support from the community and social institutions.	In the process of after-school care, through continuous learning and service experience accumulation, inspired autonomous operation design. (Integration).
6. Internal market outsourcing (ASUS & Children-Are-Us Bakery)	Social service institution managing director.	High-tech corporation image and inner market, corporate social responsibility and corporate resources.	(Market embeddedness). Factory inner F&B consuming is commissioned to Children-Are-Us Bakery, providing the guaranteed inner market and a portion of the equipment.	(Contract). Through the business organization and policy of the supporting institution, help the business activities of the disadvantaged organization.	The supporting business provides the inner market opportunity and facilities/ equipment; the service institution provides service man power and work guidance. (Complementary).

(*Continued*)

Table 2. (*Continued*)

Entrepreneurship model	Entrepreneur background	Start-up resources	Market entry strategies	Resource acquisition strategies	"Social/business" resources integration
7. Integration of diverse, small suppliers (Rejoice Community Supported Agriculture Group)	Corporate (F&B) experience.	Pastry production and store operation.	(Derived markets). Hire mentally impaired in the production and sales of pastry; engage farmers in growing wheat at lower costs; sell pastry to community at margin.	(Internal formation). Engage farmers in providing land for growing wheat.	Convince farmers in wheat growing and guarantee farmers income with contract; build wheat co-op. (Adaptation).
8. Localizing international social business (The Big Issue)	Business manager.	Experience in print media publishing; traditional physical media is fading out.	(Self-developed). Self-developed domestic market brand and dissemination system.	(External transfer). Acquire from overseas parent company a logo license, business skills transfer, and train sales agents (homeless) training.	External technology transfer and business brand authorization; internal learning and skill accumulation. (Complementary).

(*Continued*)

Table 2.　(*Continued*)

Entrepreneurship model	Entrepreneur background	Start-up resources	Market entry strategies	Resource acquisition strategies	"Social/business" resources integration
9. Employment empowerment platform (PWR Foundation)	Business manager.	The NGO was founded to care for the vulnerable women; initiated the concept of empowering women with employment, but lacked the know-how.	(Derived markets). The NGO invited a business manager to design diversified service products and market channel to provide women with job.	(Contract). Invite a business senior manager to plan the service products and operation system.	The business manager contributes to the business know-how; based on the employment conditions of the disadvantaged women, designs service products and operating system. (Complementary).

4.2. *Resource acquisition strategies*

The resources needed to be invested into a new venture are not always necessarily obvious nor immediately ready for entrepreneurs, not to mention that social entrepreneurs are usually mission-driven and lack of entrepreneurial resources. It is thus necessary for social entrepreneurs to examine their production factors mix and to strengthen their resource portfolio. The study suggests that resources can be considered from two different aspects: social resources and business resources.

Social resources refer to the social capital that the entrepreneurs can mobilize and contribute to their entrepreneurial ventures. NPOs usually have strong social trust, community relations, and supporter bases that may be mobilized for their entrepreneurial initiatives, as witnessed in all cases in the study. Ventures aiming to enhance employment for minorities may attract social support (cases 1 and 3–9). Religion may serve as a source of social resources (cases 2, 5, and 7).

Business resources refer to tangible economic or physical capital as well as intangible knowledge or skills that may contribute to businesses. In case 6, the new social venture depends heavily on the physical space provided by the partnership company. In case 7, the social entrepreneur possesses expertise in industrial engineering, which is a precious resource for the new venture. Skills in business planning are crucial for the success of new ventures, and social entrepreneurs may acquire such skills from their prior business experiences (cases 2–5, 8, and 9).

Social resources and business resources are different but not mutually exclusive. Scholars emphasize a systemic view in assessing resources and their distinctive contributions in business value creation (Foss *et al.*, 1995; Sirmon & Hitt, 2003; Sirmon *et al.*, 2007). Social resources are employed in strengthening organizations' social support, while business resources may contribute to organizations' operational efficiency. In fact, social entrepreneurs need to cultivate both the social capital and economic capital, and the two types of capital need to be integrated (Austin *et al.*, 2006; Stryjan, 2006). Therefore, social entrepreneurs need to pay close attention to their resources portfolio, acquire and deploy resources to build capabilities, and leverage those capabilities for sustainability and greater social impact.

To secure critical resources, social entrepreneurs may consider three strategies: cultivating internal resources, transferring external resources to become internal resources, and contracting with external resources. The first resource acquisition strategy is to cultivate internal resources. In case 2, the NPO has a large base of membership with the same Buddhist religion which is a critical resource that has been successfully converted by the social enterprise to become its customer base. Similarly, in case 5, the social entrepreneurs leverage their Buddhist faith to form the core values for the social business. In case 7, the entrepreneur used his strong experiences in manufacturing to create the social enterprise.

Another resource acquisition strategy is to transfer external resources to become internal resources. In cases 1 and 3, the NPOs identified the business opportunity in bakery. Without possessing the bakery expertise, the NPOs adopted the technology transfer strategy to acquire the knowledge in bakery production and management. In case 8, the social entrepreneur successfully transferred the brand and knowledge of an international magazine to become a local magazine.

The third strategy is to make contract with external resources. This strategy is especially useful when the transfer strategy is too costly or risky. In case 4, the social entrepreneur chose not to become a chain store; rather, it develops informal contracts with other NPOs with similar mission and to assist them for new ventures. In case 6, the renewable facility contract between the ASUS company and the social enterprise allows both parties to flexibly collaborate together. In case 9, the social enterprise developed contractual relationships, rather than formal employer–employee relationships, between the organization and the individuals (mostly females) who receive the training of home cleaning and job match provided by the organization.

Column 5 in Table 2 summarizes the strategies adopted by the nine social enterprises. Proposition 2 highlights the analysis regarding resource acquisition by social entrepreneurs.

Proposition 2A: Social enterprises in the initial stage of entrepreneurship may consider resources from two different but not mutually exclusive aspects: social resources and business resources.

Proposition 2B: Social enterprises may consider three different resource acquisition strategies: cultivating internal resources, transferring external resources to become internal resources, and contracting with external resources.

4.3. *Resource integration*

Social and business resources are different and may result in conflicting value judgment or managerial policies if the social entrepreneurs fail to effectively integrate the resources into the social ventures. The study highlights three strategies to achieve resource integration: resource complementation strategy, resource integration strategy, and resource adaption strategy. The first strategy is resource complementation, which assumes that the social and business resources in concern are complementary and the potential conflicts are minimum. If this is the case, the entrepreneurs simply add the newly acquired resources into their resource portfolio. Case 6 illustrates this strategy. The ASUS Company offers the Children-Are-Us Bakery facilities to sell bakery products and beverages to its employees. For the Children-Are-Us Bakery, this exclusive access to ASUS internal market is considered as a resource complementary to its existing operations as a bakery chain store, for what need to be done is basically to open another new store in the ASUS site. This partnership is relatively straightforward, with minimum efforts in coordination, adjustment, or structuring.

The second strategy is resource integration, which assumes that the social and business resources are not merely complementary but can be integrated to achieve better entrepreneurial results. This often happens when social entrepreneurs possess some unique resources and, based on the uniqueness of those resources, develop resource acquisition strategy to extend their resources portfolio. Case 2, the Li-Ren Organic Food Chain Store, illustrates how this strategy works. The Buddhist association has a large membership base, and the members regularly go to local centers for lessons and meditation. The daily life needs of those members can become opportunities for social businesses. Members are encouraged to be vegetarians, for religious reasons. Hence, the NPO intentionally chose organic food as a priority business target because of a high degree of integration between the religious resources (as critical social resources) and the market demand for vegetarian foods by the members (as critical business resources).

The third strategy is resource adaption, which highlights that new resources for acquisition need to be adapted to fit the entrepreneurial context. The resource integration and the resource adaption strategy are similar but the latter assumes a lower degree of entrepreneurial resource autonomy than the former. In the former, social entrepreneurs may have relatively more choices in resource acquisition in the entrepreneurial process.

In the case of Li-Ren Organic Food Chain Store, the religious NPO with strong resource base, purposefully chose organic food, literally among all markets, for entrepreneurship. If social entrepreneurs have few choices in business resource acquisition, they might have to cope with it and adapt new resources to fit into the entrepreneurial context. Case 7, the Rejoice Community Supported Agriculture Group, illustrates the need of resource adaption. The social entrepreneur operates the Rejoice Bakery, a small bakery and sheltered workshop for people with disabilities. The global food crisis and food price surge in 2008 hit the bakery severely. To turn crisis into opportunity, the entrepreneur decided to create a social enterprise that would organize small farmers in Taiwan to grow wheat when the supply of wheat in Taiwan relied 99% on imports at that time. The Rejoice Community Supported Agriculture Group chose wheat as the initial business target partially because of resource integration (i.e., the Rejoice Bakery needs wheat). But the demand from the small bakery was far less enough to support the new venture. To invite, to train, and to organize the small farmers in diverse areas, the social entrepreneur partners with an information technology company to develop user-friendly mobile application suitable for the farmers, most of them are aged and computer illiterate.

Column 6 in Table 2 highlights the resource integration strategies used by the nine social enterprises, and Proposition 3 summarizes the analysis.

Proposition 3: Based on the various degree of resource autonomy and the specific entrepreneurial context, social enterprises may consider three different resource integration strategies: resource complementation, resource integration, and resource adaption.

4.4. *Social entrepreneurship models*

The act of social entrepreneurship itself is a management innovation with high risk. It faces simultaneously the challenges of identifying the untapped market needs and technical challenges in designing new products. Operating in a social market, entrepreneurs' business objectives are more complicated than regular for-profit businesses. Under inadequate business resources, entrepreneurs must respond to their own resource conditions and adopt different market entry modes to access the market and mitigate the operational risks.

Mair and Marti (2006) considered social entrepreneurship as a process which includes innovative resources acquisition and resource portfolio management to seek social needs and trigger social change. The social enterprise sector has neither a capital market nor economic incentives; it has its intrinsic limitations in attracting financial resources and management talents. Subsequently, the entrepreneur's reputation and degree of recognition on his management capacity play an important role in resource acquisition. The process of how an entrepreneur identifies opportunity, integrates resources, and exploits opportunity to create value are the keys to success.

Through an analysis of the firms' market entry, resource acquisition, and resource integration strategies, nine models are identified as follows (see column 1, Table 2).

(1) Social business chain development

Children-Are-Us Foundation began as an NPO servicing children with Down Syndrome (DS) and their families. Parents are often unwilling to bring their DS children to public areas, and this would have serious negative impact on the cognitive development and quality of life of the DS children. The Foundation founders thus pondered how to, through business activity creation, allow the DS children to become self-reliant while changing societal prejudices. The Foundation finally selected bakery, which required patience and standard procedures, as the start-up venture. The founder of the Foundation was a corporate manager who realized that products and technology are two important market competition factors; therefore, he proactively invited bakers to coach the DS children the necessary baking skills and the products were sold in a bakery managed by volunteers. With the help and assistance of the Foundation's staff, the first bakery actualized the founding goal, leading to the replication of the business model in several major cities. Local experts were invited to engage in local operations, expanding the opportunities for the DS children to engage with the society. This formed a transfer approach to adjusting business technology for social resource applicability to reach social objectives effectively and swiftly (by changing the stereotypes on the mentally challenged).

(2) Social business diversification

Li-Ren Organic Chain Store is a venture by a major religious organization. Through the religious activities, the members learn and spread the concepts of protecting lives and have thus formed a substantial consumer demands for organic products and ecological agriculture. The establishment gathered members of various technological and managerial backgrounds and started organic product chain stores to service its members. In the meantime, to expand the sourcing and suppliers base for organic products, they established an independent company for organic certification to encourage the production and procurement of organic produce. They built chain stores in several cities and even started organic vegetarian restaurants. They have also began extending their business into mainland China.

The profound thinking nurtured by the organization's internal learning activities integrated the members' religious service belief, modern technology (organic agriculture), and business knowledge to form innovative business concepts to promote the execution of the organization's social plan through propelling business to reach its social objectives.

(3) Collaboration between social entrepreneur and commercial business

Victory Gas Station is a joint venture of Victory Potential Development Center for the Disabled and China Petroleum Corp., Taiwan (CPC) to empower the physically challenged through employment and boost the social image of CPC (a state-run commercial corporation). The collaborative mode is that CPC selected gas stations with regular clientele and trained the disabled the skill and knowledge of gas service. With the on-site job coach assigned by Victory and self-designed team workers and operation approach, Victory made the bid for the commissioned operation with a purpose of taking advantage of the stable operation of the existing CPC gas station to enter the market with minimal risk.

The collaborating institutions exchange business knowledge and technology and integrate gas station operating skills into a new system that the organization members can effectively exercise.

(4) Business technology transfer

The manager of Sunny Kitchen, more than a business own, is also a veteran community service participant. One of the services was to promote low-cost (with consistent quality) meal packs delivery to the seniors in the community. With the outstanding meal preparation skills, product planning, and cost control, the founder of the Kitchen is often invited by NPOs and other communities to coach catering and social service skills. To fulfill the community service ideal, the Kitchen manager is not only involved in the restaurant management, she also takes the restaurant as the platform for training the disadvantaged in job skills development. For instance, she mainly employs disadvantaged workers and trains them with food service operating skills. The current project's aim is to integrate the trainee employment with the expansion of the restaurants to actively enhance employment opportunities for the disadvantaged.

The restaurant takes its own business operation resource as the base, and through collaboration via the placements service in the community and NPOs, gives full dimension to the adaptability of its own technology and business model; moreover, this model allows the social service concepts of NPOs to be actualized through the evolution, continued adjustments, and modification of business technology.

(5) Social mission transformation of business

The two partners with business experience and teaching philosophy engaged in after-school teaching. After witnessing how the children from poor families are neglected by their parents, the partnership enhanced after-school care with meal service, which costs are at the parents' discretion. This endeavor earned the supports from local communities, parents, and even the landlords. The partnership then expanded the meal service to a full-fledged restaurant for the convenience of the children and their parents, purchased organic product from NPOs, made processed food for sale, and reinvested the earnings into other philanthropic services.

Through the business activities, the firm transferred the customers' social problems into its own marketing plan, reflecting them through the service products, and endeavored to solve customers' problems in a business-like manner. The social concepts coupled with business skills have set the base for the creation of the enterprise's social values.

(6) Internal market outsourcing to social enterprises

A major (over 5,000 employees) high-tech manufacturer, to comply with the government regulation on hiring a certain quota of disadvantaged employees and to promote the corporate social image, commissioned its in-house food and beverage services and café (created for its staff) to Children-Are-Us Bakery. The firm provided the venue and equipment for the operation to empower the physically challenged and the NPO with a chance for development. The firm commissioned the operation, by providing the market security, to substantially facilitate the entrepreneurship and employment of the disadvantaged. The firm did not get involved with the activity of social value; they only commissioned the internal consumption needs to the social enterprise for independent operation, to lower the venture risks for social enterprise without changing the corporate business concept and to reach the corporate philanthropic goals.

(7) Integration of diverse, small suppliers

The entrepreneur had previous experience in pastry manufacturing and marketing. In view of the fact that the imported flour did not substantially benefit the farmers (the profits went to international suppliers), and that Taiwanese farmers were disfavored by international prices and could not enjoy the benefits of price fluctuations, the entrepreneur encouraged subsistence farmers to contract wheat growing in Taiwan to stabilize the depressing farming economy. The firm also hires vulnerable women in pastry production and sells the products to the local communities with minimum profits. Hence, pulling together a large number of small farmers in diverse areas to change to grow wheat, the social enterprise was able to become supplier of wheat products for the market.

Capitalizing on his own techniques and cost control experience in pastry production, the entrepreneur gained the wheat farmers trust. With a steady material supply guaranteed by farming contracts, the entrepreneur transformed the farmers' social relationship into supply partners of the social enterprise. The firm is constantly adjusting its operation design to meet its own social philanthropic ends.

(8) Localizing international social business

The entrepreneur is experienced in Internet marketing. He was inspired by the Big Issue, a culture and entertainment magazine sold by the homeless people who get empowered with some humble income. The entrepreneur made a trip to the company (The Big Issue) headquarters in the UK, to acquire license of the brand name and to learn how to train the homeless. This enabled the entrepreneur to replicate the magazine business model in Taiwan.

The firm directly transferred an overseas business model, social service concept, and brand licensing; then through internal learning, it created its own localized knowledge and operation skills in training, and sales commission with the homeless.

(9) Employment empowerment platform

The non-governmental organization (NGO) initiated the concept of creating employment opportunities for the vulnerable women; however, they were unfamiliar with the business operation. As a consequence, a senior manager of a commercial corporation was invited to plan an adequate service products, design a business plan, and develop the approaches to develop the market.

By leveraging his past business experience in commercial setting, the manager integrated the employment conditions of the disadvantaged women and the needs of the job market and further utilized a planning to develop skills, train the women, create the market, design products, and the operating system.

According to the characteristics of the firms' venture process, market entry strategy, and resource acquisition strategy, nine models can be identified as shown in Proposition 4 (Fig. 1).

Proposition 4: "Market entry" and "resource acquisition" can serve as two aspects for social entrepreneurs to develop their entrepreneurial models. The nine entrepreneurial models are (1) social business chain development, (2) social business diversification, (3) collaboration between social entrepreneur/commercial business, (4) business technology transfer, (5) social mission transformation of business, (6) internal market outsourcing, (7) integration of diverse, small suppliers, (8) localizing international social business, and (9) employment empowerment platform.

Fig. 1.   The market entry and business resource acquisition aspects

5. Managerial Implications for Social Entrepreneurs

The distinction between social resources and businesses resources is emphasized in the study. Some social enterprises are initiated as commercial ventures by NPOs. These social enterprises might have relatively strong social resources but weak business resources. In contrast, social entrepreneurs who possess strong business skills and capital may be relatively inexperienced in developing social mission, social support, or services for the target disadvantaged social groups. To strengthen entrepreneurial resources, the study suggests that social entrepreneurs need to be aware of their strengths and weaknesses in resources and to act strategically. Social entrepreneurs may evaluate their needs for operational resources, take advantage of the resources at hand, and develop entrepreneurial models that are coherent with strategies in market entry and resource acquisition.

With regard to market entry, strategies with lower risk are to enter the markets with exclusive access by the social enterprises or strong bases of supporters that can be converted into customers. It is also noted that product competitiveness is crucial for entering mainstream markets and to sustain the businesses. The study also indicates the importance of resource acquisition. The resources possessed internally by social entrepreneurs are the primary source for the entrepreneurial endeavor. Nevertheless, transferring technology from or contracting with external sources is often used by social entrepreneurs as strategies for acquiring critical resources. It is emphasized in the study that social resources and business resources may be complementary but resource integration and contextual adaption may be needed so as to create synergy and achieve high social impact.

6. Conclusion

The study selected nine social businesses to analyze their entrepreneurial models from a resource base perspective. Each of the nine cases demonstrated its uniqueness in formulating business models and developing resource bases. The nine cases vividly illustrated from a resource aspect the variety of opportunities and challenges that the creation of social businesses may involve.

The study emphasizes that social resources and businesses resources are different so that social entrepreneurs need to carefully craft strategies to enter the market, to acquire needed resources, and to integrate resources for sustainability and greater social impact. Through an analysis of nine cases, the study highlighted three strategies for market entry: Embedding into existing markets, exploring new markets, and deriving markets from the social missions. In addition, three strategies for resource acquisition in the initial stage of social entrepreneurship were identified: Cultivating internal resources, transferring external resources to become internal resources, and contracting with external resources. Moreover, the study suggested that social entrepreneurs may, based on the characteristics of the entrepreneurial context and resource portfolio, align their resources through resource complementation, integration, and adaption. In sum, the study shed new light to the understanding of the complicated relationships among market entry, resource acquisition, and business model development.

References

Austin, J. E., Stevenson, H. H., & Wei-Skillern, J. (2006). Social and Commercial Entrepreneurship: Same, Different, or Both? *Entrepreneurship Theory and Practice*, 30(1), pp. 1–22.

Blyer, M. & Coff, R. W. (2003). Dynamic Capabilities, Social Capital, and Rent Appropriation: Ties That Split Pies, *Strategic Management Journal*, 24(7), pp. 677–686.

Bornstein, D. (2007). *How to Change the World: Social Entrepreneurs and the Power of New Ideas*. New York: Oxford University Press.

Dees, J. G. (2001). The meaning of "Social Entrepreneurship", *Center for the Advancement of Social Entrepreneurship, Fuqua School of Business, Duke University*. Retrieved from http://faculty.fuqua.duke.edu/ centers/case/files/dees-SE.pdf (search date September 6, 2009).

Dixon, J., Makarov, D., & David, M. (1998). *Poverty*. London & New York: Routledge.

Foss, A. J. E., Alexander, R. A., Jefferies, L. W., & Lightman, S. L. (1995). The Effect of Melanin Bleaching on Immunohistochemical Techniques, *British Journal of Biomed Science*, 52, pp. 22–25.

Guclu, A., Dees, G., & Anderson, B. B. (2002). *The Process of Social Entrepreneurship: Creating Opportunities Worthy of Serious Pursuit.* Article published by the Center for the Advancement of Social Entrepreneurship, Version: (A)10/24/02, pp. 1–15, Duke University.

Hammersley, M. & Gomm, R. (2000). Introduction, in R. Gomm, M. Hammersley, & P. Foster (eds.), *Case Study Method: Key Issues, Key Texts*, Thousand Oaks, CA: Sage, pp. 1–16.

Haugh, H. (2007). Community-Led Social Venture Creation, *Entrepreneurship Theory and Practice*, 31(2), pp. 161–182.

Hu, J. H. & Chen, C. Y. (2009). The Essence, Tasks and Development of Social Enterprise, *Journal of Entrepreneurship Research*, 4(4), pp. 1–28.

Kretzmann, P. & McKnight, J. F. (1993). *Building Communities from the Inside Out: A Path toward Finding and Mobilizing a Community's Assets*. Published by the Center for Urban Affairs and Policy Research, Northwestern University.

Lin, N. (1999). Social Networks and Status Attainment, *Annual Review of Sociology*, 25, pp. 467–487.

Mair, J. & Marti, I. (2006). Social Entrepreneurship Research: A Source of Explanation, Prediction, and Delight, *Journal of World Business*, 41, pp. 36–44.

OECD (1999). *Social Enterprises*. Paris: OECD.

Peredo, A. M. & McLean, M. (2006). Social Entrepreneurship: A Critical Review of the Concept, *Journal of World Business*, 41, pp. 56–65.

Sirmon, D. G. & Hitt, M. A. (2003). Managing Resources: Linking Unique Resources, Management and Wealth Creation in Family Firms, *Entrepreneurship Theory and Practice*, 27, pp. 339–358.

Sirmon, D. G., Hitt, M. A., & Ireland, R. D. (2007). Managing Firm Resources in Dynamic Environments to Create Value: Looking Inside the Black Box, *Academy of Management Review*, 32(1), pp. 273–292.

Stake, R. E. (2000). Chapter 1 The case study method in social inquiry, in R. Gomm, M. Hammersley, & P. Foster (eds.), *Case Study Method: Key Issues, Key Texts*, London: Sage, pp. 19–26.

Stryjan, Y. (2006). The Practice of Social Entrepreneurship: Theory and the Swedish Experience, *Journal of Rural Cooperation*, 34(2), pp. 197–229, in Tirole, J. (1989). *The Theory of Industrial Organization*. Cambridge, MA: The MIT Press.

Westlund, H. (2003). Implications of social capital for business in the knowledge economy: Theoretical considerations. *International Forum on Economic Implication of Social Capital, Economic and Social Research Institute Cabinet Office* (Tokyo), Japan, March 24 and 25, 2003.

Yang, K. (2007). Individual Social Capital and its Measurement in Social Surveys, *Survey Research Methods*, 1(1), pp. 19–27.

Yin, R. K. (2003). *Case Study Research Design and Methods* (3rd edn.). Thousand Oaks, CA: Sage Publications.

Zahra, S. A., Gedajlovic, E., Neubaum, D. O., & Shulman, J. M. (2009). A Typology of Social Entrepreneurs: Motives, Search Process and Ethical Challenges, *Journal of Business Venturing*, 24, pp. 519–532.

2

Social Value Creation through Innovation of Social Technology

Tzu Yang Chang
Fu Jen Catholic University

1. Introduction

The business-centered economy model accumulates and utilizes social resources based on knowledge and globalized market systems. This model has brought collective prosperity to society by creating a global operation system of mass production and supply. However, it has simultaneously intensified developments such as the M-shaped society with a poor distribution of wealth; the cross-border shift or reduction of traditional labor employment; the exploitation and costliness of natural resources; and the living conditions resulting from relative discrepancy in regional infrastructure. This has not only weakened lower income purchasing power but also government social care to disadvantaged groups. What these marginalized sectors need is not "social relief" but a "social economic system" that fits their living conditions. In Taiwan, the society generally emphasizes the development of economy through high technology industries and large-scale companies as the main ways to improve overall social wealth. Consequently, the unequal distribution of social resources and social welfare are more significant.

The capitalist system satisfies people's needs depending on government public resource distribution and the economic usage of business' private property. The market exchange mechanism satisfies the daily needs of the individual. The function of government lies in planning, collecting, and allocating public social resources. However, because of bureaucracy within the government system, diverging opinions in policy formation, and rigidity of government organization, government agencies often refrain from effectively creating, delivering, and adjusting their services to meet individual needs (Davidson & Davidson, 1996).

When government services fail, society turns to business. However, business often concentrates so heavily on generating profit that its policies lack a social philanthropic spirit, causing "market dysfunction" (Hansmann, 2003). As private businesses are reluctant to step in and government fails to perform, society then turns to non-profit organizations (NPOs) as a supporting sector to make up the social needs gap. Although NPOs are equipped with public service ambition, without bureaucracy constraints, this form of organization often lacks public resources and does not engage in profitgenerating activities, but must depend on government subsidies or private fundraising to sustain their services. The state of the economy can easily affect their fundraising goals, gradually leading to the phenomenon of "volunteer dysfunction" (Salamon, 1990). Meanwhile, in the past two decades, some small enterprises with social-oriented goals have been built-up by private efforts. These enterprises have shown some remarkable innovation in product concept, processing design, and organization capability to overcome the obstacles in social institutions and commercial systems. The established infrastructure of Taiwan society is constructed mainly for pure economic purposes; many changes are still needed in developing social enterprise.

Social enterprise in Taiwan is still in its starting stage, but social injustice is growing fast. It is the hope of this chapter that the academic knowledge and practical experiences can be better structured, that more social entrepreneurships could be achieved gradually. This chapter tackles the existing under-satisfied needs of the disadvantaged from the perspectives of market dysfunction and the blindness of business to analyze the characteristic of supply and demand. This chapter hopes to explore the meanings of innovations for social enterprises, particularly in the product development for non-market needs, the marketing for social cognition change, the design of manufacturing process for disable workers, and in the management of a multiple goals organization which are different with pure commercial companies.

This chapter presents these social value inclined business concepts and technology innovations with four cases, explaining four kinds of innovation in social technology. The objective of this study is to contribute to the theories of management in social enterprise and to enhance the social engagement actions in the existing business.

2. The Market Mechanism and Social Needs

2.1. *The social functions of business and market*

Traditional economic theories explore the pricing mechanism based on their arguments of free market transactions, a structural relationship between market supply and demand, and reaching equilibrium. Price fluctuation and supply or demand returns created in this equilibrium process are judgments based on buyer or seller interests, to reach the maximum benefits of resource utilization and demand satisfaction. In this supply–demand structure, consumers are dispersed individuals who have no manipulation ability toward the demand curve. Conversely, suppliers are business entities engaged in mass production who can manipulate the supply market with business decisions that affect the market supply–demand structure and exchange decision (Wilber & Jameson, 1992).

According to the market scale or number of businesses, the market can be divided into four types of market structure: monopoly market, monopolized market, monopolistic competition, and complete competition (Begg *et al.*, 1991). To pursue a favorable position, businesses will try to monopolize the supply market, either through exclusive ownership of market position, production factors, or innovative technology (Von Krogh & Grand, 2002). Firms will manipulate the market mechanism to obtain greater economic rents, putting consumers in a relatively disadvantaged position.

Consumers can only make their purchase policy based on their financial condition, which reflects the purchasing power of the demander. Suppliers, however, decide product supply based on profit margin. Davidson and Davidson (1996) indicated these behaviors, the purchasing power of consumers, and the supply decision of manufacturers, because the voluntary supply decision of manufacturers will tend to neglect low-purchasing power or low-profit markets (Sweberg, 2003).

2.2. *Analysis of market dysfunction and business blindness*

Based on the structure of market supply–demand conditions and the values of manufacturer's business decisions indicated by Hu and Chen (2009), this chapter analyzes the blind spots of services toward societal needs to confirm the eight scenarios of market dysfunction (Figs. 1.1–1.6).

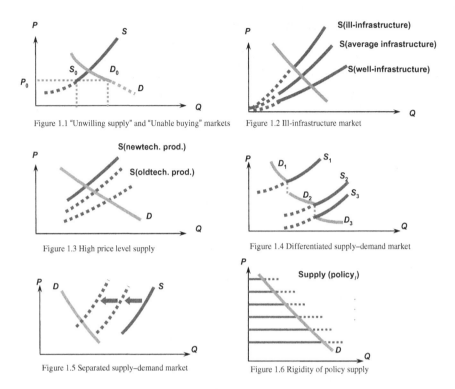

Figure 1.1 "Unwilling supply" and "Unable buying" markets

Figure 1.2 Ill-infrastructure market

Figure 1.3 High price level supply

Figure 1.4 Differentiated supply–demand market

Figure 1.5 Separated supply–demand market

Figure 1.6 Rigidity of policy supply

Fig. 1. Supply–demand molds in market dysfunction
Source: Hu, J. and Chen, C. Y. (2009).

2.2.1. *Blind spots of the market mechanism*

Dysfunction 1: Disabled buying market

Limited to their own income level and living expense budget allocation, consumers have a limited budget for certain commodities and cannot afford certain products (Fig. 1.1, the demand curve below D_0), resulting in an unrealistic market with the inability of buying the supply (Sharp *et al.*, 1996).

Dysfunction 2: Unwilling supply market

When the commodity price is below direct production costs, or when marginal cost exceeds marginal profit, due to profit consideration, manufacturers do not produce products below P_0 price (Fig. 1.1, the supply curve below S_0), which results in an empty market with no supply.

Dysfunction 3: Poor-infrastructure market

The underdevelopment of infrastructure in certain regions, such as geographic remoteness and inconvenient transportation, lack of information and communication facilities, and a meager commercial environment, causes a dramatic increase in supply operation cost, resulting in decreased services provided (Fig. 1.2). Persons living in mountainous areas or remote villages, for example, will generally suffer from higher living costs, education, and other necessities, and receive fewer services from either the social or commercial sector.

Dysfunction 4: High price level supply

To maintain dominance in product technology, enhance market value, and create higher profit, manufacturers tend to move toward more sophisticated, multifunctional, and monopolistic high-end products, which inevitably ignore the demand for established technology or outdated product design from the lower-end market (Fig. 1.3).

Dysfunction 5: Differentiated supply–demand market

Market differences not only exist in consuming power or geographic location. Product design and supply that meet the demand from various markets need to be considered. Many demands stem from differences in physical (physically challenged), family (abused women and children), or even social structures (senior citizens living alone, minorities). However, these marginal markets often receive minimal attention. Market manufacturers do not see or are reluctant to address the special needs for products and services that differ from the mainstream market (Fig. 1.4).

Dysfunction 6: Separated supply–demand market

When the public is willing to pay for certain quality products and consume products designed for the public good (solar battery and other developing "green" products), because of underdeveloped technology or insufficient infrastructure, the quantity and price of these products are clearly separate from the level of consumer capacity (Fig. 1.5). Government subsidies need to compensate for this discrepancy.

2.2.2. *Reflections on business decision making*

In the pursuit of profit maximization and cost minimization, business encourages rational thinking that is economical or technical, even though over emphasizing engineering resource efficiency may tend to neglect the importance of market consumption ability and manufacturer's social responsibility (Govindarajan & Fisher, 1988). The notion that a business's social responsibility is to maximize its operation efficiency has become the popular rule and logic for business decision making. This logic greatly affects total social resource efficiency as follows:

Dysfunction 7: The target blindness of profit maximization

The purpose of business management is to create maximum return on investment, which leads to emphasis of largest scale markets, highest profits or the most advanced product technology, and investment on the best resource efficiency (Friedman, 1963). On the contrary, established business often neglects the need for small scale, low consumption power, and basic functioning products.

The profit-maximization principle encourages business to pursue the lowest production cost. Consequently, the foremost social resources to be sacrificed are pollution, environmental damage, workplace safety, labor welfare, or shortage of nature resources, which place all social living quality at stake (Copeland *et al.*, 1996).

Dysfunction 8: "Resource distortion" caused by competition

To protect its own sustainability, a business has to fight for its market share and constantly compete with the overwhelming production scale, which supplies the market. Exploiting social resources to achieve individual business resource efficiency does not result in social resource efficiency. Given its immense research and development (R&D) capacity, business can efficiently use numerous undeveloped discarded materials or unutilized resources to develop technologies in alternative resources, renewable resources, and recycle resources, rather than exploiting rare resources to compete for and to generate profit.

3.   Mission of Social Enterprise

Businesses often create economic wealth through technology innovation to promote product values and lower operation costs. However, their judgment of social value, particularly regarding social opportunity costs and commodity supply for a low-buying power market, often comes only after the economic value. Social enterprises do not seek high-priced products for high-buying power, or the least cost regardless of the social burden.

Therefore, even though social enterprises utilize resource technology and operation systems as ordinary businesses, in value judgment and logical thinking, they differ in their concept definition and operational technology improvement.

3.1. *Tasks to serve the unsatisfied social needs*

Social enterprise focuses on creating values for unsatisfied needs. Therefore, the management mission lies in bridging the gap between social needs and business outputs. To target the eight unsatisfied social needs, enterprises must guide their technological capacity and business capabilities for involvement in product innovation and management transformation to serve social needs. The term "technology" here is understood as the making, modification, usage, and knowledge of tools, techniques, systems, methods of organization, to solve a problem, advance a preexisting solution, perform a specific function or achieve a goal.

Task 1: Enrich disabled buying individuals

The following approaches can accomplish social enterprise: to provide job opportunities through enterprising to raise buying power, and to lower product price or create substitutable products (Haugh, 2005; Kerlin, 2006).

Task 2: Motivate unwilling supply

Through product development of substitutable materials for natural resource shortage, a frugal product design with simplified functions, reutilization of outdated technology, and development of an efficient supply system, the social enterprise's mission would continue creating business profits that supply low-priced products and encourage more active trading in suppliers (Islam, 2007; Pearce, 2003).

Task 3: Supply in a poor-infrastructure market

Remote communities with low populations often suffer from poor infrastructure, which affect commodity supply efficiency or business interests under normal circumstances. An innovative logistic system is required to strengthen the efficiency of product distribution, such as providing a public trading platform, lowering supplier costs in marketing, logistics, and distribution services; building a self-sufficient production, supply, and consumption network in communities.

Task 4: Supply of comprehensive values mix

Because of the nature of profit, the goal for product R&D naturally aims at high-tech products that enjoy monopoly advantage and excessive profit; hence, the supplier's management trend deviates from the needs of the disadvantaged. The mission of social enterprise therefore lies in adjusting the direction of product development that meets social needs (Emerson, 2003; Hines & Thomas, 2004). The technology challenges faced would include using existing technology to recycle and transfer applications; frugal or green design, simplified functions, and economized material.

Task 5: Supply for differentiated markets demand

Businesses often deliberately forsake a small market or a low-profit market, causing a differentiated market against the disadvantaged. The responsibility of social enterprise then lies in overcoming the barriers in product technology and delivery service, which include the modification of product technology in the market to meet the demands of the physically challenged; the promotion of social entrepreneurship and operation transformation for NPOs, and enterprising of their product/service operations.

Task 6: Match the supply–demand gap

Immature technology leads to limited supply, high costs, and disabled buying demand, causing an ill-structured market. From the perspective of ethical and social benefits and social ownership, Allan (2005) suggested that the mission of social enterprise is to lower the technical barrier of social products and total cost. The challenges in technology R&D would include the striving for government subsidies and encouragement to support continued business R&D; the learning from lifestyle, to develop and improve the skills of specific societies.

Task 7: Enhance the target of non-financial value

Under the motive of profit maximization, the revenue target drives managers to value a high-consumption market, and the cost target causes managers to overlook the invisible cost of waste handling, and the deferred social cost they should share, which causes potential negative effect to society (Allan, 2005). Based on public welfare, social enterprise must have distinct value in its management policy making (Hines, 2005). That includes changing the value of its operation goal that maximizes stakeholders' total profit and optimize distribution; changing the items of operational expenditure, and add the concepts of social cost and invisible cost.

Task 8: Effectiveness of resources utility

Business competes for the market using social resource and overpowers its rivals, leading to the distortion of natural resources for the commercial battle. The main responsibility of social enterprises is to emphasize the suitable and effective use of social resources (Haugh, 2005; Hines, 2005), which includes: valuing in-depth service for its social customers to strengthen its survival with social satisfaction; strengthen the output of creating social value, not seizing and exploiting resources, nor hoarding for profit; emphasizing the maintenance and sustainability of social total ecology, not just the sustainable competitiveness of a single business.

To accomplish these tasks, managers of social enterprise should adopt business technologies as ordinary companies do, but with social values rather than economic values. We will discuss the meanings of technologies with social values, which will be named as "social technology" thereinafter.

4.   Research Method

To render the propositions of the social technologies accurately, this research chose the multiple case comparison as its research method (Yin, 2003). With regards to the four social technologies, this research applied the theoretical sampling method, and chose four social enterprises that contained the proposed theoretical implications as its research objects. All these social enterprises possessed clear social value objectives and were stable and self-contained business entities.

4.1.   *Case selection — Characteristics of social enterprise cases*

Bao Ban Phoung: Due to the changes in the societal environment of Taiwan, there exist a good number of foreign workers or spouses, who have to stay for a long time in Taiwan. These new family members of the Taiwan society, who have contributed to the development of the society, are mostly working at lower level of the society. They often have to endure the loneliness of being away from their own country and living in a foreign culture. In responding to this situation, the founder of Bao Ban Phoung has decided to set up a foreign language newspaper specifically for these people. The paper now includes the Vietnamese, Pilipino, Indonesian, Thai, and Cambodian languages. Through this, the founder Mr. Chang has fulfilled the idea he received from his professor and mass media education. Mr. Chang believes that media not only should voice "for" the marginalized but also allow the marginalized to speak for themselves. Thus, he has come up not only with the newspaper that provides reading material to the new residents and workers but also a social platform where they can write and communicate with each other. Amid the great competition of mainly Chinese newspaper, this newspaper has provided an innovative, non-competitive in terms of business, and new product concept.

Rejoice Cooperation Group: The founder Mr. Shih, who was an IT factory manager with IE professional background, set up the organization with the simple idea of providing jobs for the intellectually challenged youth. Mr. Shih thought of setting up a bakery, where those intellectually challenged youth can work and build their self-confidence. However, he soon came to realize that these intellectually challenged youth were facing the difficulties in learning the existing technology and the operation of the equipment. Mr. Shih did not give-up; instead he pursued his idea. He dropped the conventional practice of purchasing new equipment and training the workers to operate them. Instead, he decided to redesign an easy to learn product operational system, which is in accordance with the learning capacity of the workers. Further, the price competition and mass production of agricultural products from abroad have caused many of the Taiwan local farmers to stop planting and a lot of land has therefore become idle. In responding to this situation, the Rejoice Cooperation Group has encouraged these farmers to utilize their idle land to grow wheat. As the business of the Rejoice Bakery kept growing, the need of raw material increased and more farmers joined the program. This collaboration solves the wheat supply issue and creates income for the farmers. This concept not only facilitates the forming of the community of small wheat plantation farmers but also changes the value chain of the organization.

Antique Assam Tea Farm: The tea farm is originally a large-scale tea plantation and production factory. However, as the price of tea tumbled and the competition from the South-East Asian countries, the business of the factory declined and the plantation became idle. Due to the use of chemical or synthetic fertilizer and insecticide, the ecosystem of these farms was seriously damaged and had very little agricultural value left. However, some senior managers of the factory and some young people who possessed the modern agricultural knowledge decided to implement the agro-ecological farming method to restore the farm and turned the factory into a cultural product. In order to introduce the ecological friendly and leisure concepts into the factory and the farm, they rented the factory and the farm from the owner, and established the ecological promotion and leisure tea culture organization, which has the "agro-ecological farming and life education" as their main objective. The company attracted many visitors and consumers. These visitors would have to attend the life and family educational program offered and experience the agro-ecological farm themselves. This Antique Assam Tea Farm has introduced fresh business perspective and the "social caring" and "life value" transformative strategic forces into their outdated company.

Children-Are-Us-Bakery (CAREUS): The bakery is one of the business arms of the Children-Are-Us (CAREUS) Foundation, an NPO that specifically cares for the intellectually challenged children. The organization is established in the 1990s. They started from a more passive approach of taking care of the intellectually challenged children, and moved on to a more positive approach of building the self-confidence of the children and by helping them to integrate themselves more into the mainstream society. The organization trains the intellectually challenged children how to produce different kinds of bread and pastry. The organization also set up the bakery for the society to understand what these challenged children can do and to enjoy the food they produce, with the hope to remove the stigma the society had on these children through daily contacts. Although the process is a difficult one, the bakery is able to change Taiwan society's perception on the intellectually challenged children. The organization can be considered successful in carrying out the social marketing mission.

Table 1 as Managerial Comparison of these four Social Enterprise as study cases gives an overview of these four cases, their Managerial Emphases, Organizational Characteristics, Objectives, Operational Technologies, and Social Issues Tackled.

4.2. Data collection

The research data consists of the public speeches, interviews of the person in-charge, and site visits, which are data acquiring methods that can reflect the deep experiences of the researchers. We talk with them about the ideas of the buildup of their social entrepreneurship, the social-oriented objectives, the combinations between commercial goods and social needs, the innovative changes in business technologies, etc. We also observe their real operations on site about the platform design which can integrate the resources from social fields and commercial environment. On conditions in necessary to inquire in-depth their adaptive design of business

Table 1.　Managerial comparison of social enterprise cases

Cases Managerial Emphases	Bao Ban Phoung	Rejoice Cooperation Group	Antique Assam Tea Farm	Children-Are-Us-Bakery (CAREUS)
Organizational characteristics	A newspaper for foreigners to make their voice heard, and to communicate with each other.	Designs easy to learn and to operate techniques and facilities, where the marginalized youth can express the capability and develop self-confidence.	By changing the traditional operational concept and technology, the organization transforms from mere profit making into an educational organization that emphasizes life, ecology, family value, and leisure culture.	Changing the misperception of the public on intellectually challenged children and improving their social status by helping the children to produce products that sell through business channel.
Objectives	A media voices for and by the marginalized.	Designing operating system that allows the marginalized youth to show their capability.	Not only profit but also ecosystem and the meaning of life.	We are all different but must be respected just the same.
Operational technologies	Transforming social needs into product concept.	Allow people to show their capability by adjusting the production technology.	The persuasion and transformation of objectives and strategy.	Changing misperception by service interaction in the market.
Social issues tackled	The marginalization of foreigners.	The marginalization of the intellectually challenged marginalized farmers and unproductive land.	The pollution of ecosystem, idle resources, and the health of the operators.	The misperception on the intellectually challenged children.

technologies, the researchers experienced their real operations. These data offer researchers meaningful materials about technological innovations for enterprise's social goals.

5. The Technology Innovation of Social Enterprise

Zhuang and Wheale (2004) posited that the sustainable values of a corporation should consist of four dimensions: (1) cost and risk reduction; (2) enhance legitimacy and reputation; (3) technology development and innovative product; (4) identifying unmet market needs. This is parallel to an understanding of Schumpeterian entrepreneurship, which may involve innovation in product, process, management, and marketing (Dees, 2001). These understandings are a useful framework for innovative managerial design, which must consider the sustainable goals of social benefit and economic rents. Social enterprises must respond to social needs and operational tasks, which differ from the typical market, different philosophies, service systems, design techniques, manufacturing, and delivery, which are required. This study tackles the effect of technology innovation in business value creation, and how innovation in product, process, management, and marketing can transform into social technology, consisting of social values and meanings.

5.1. *Technology innovation and value creation*

Technology is the means by which an organization can utilize, control, and change its production approaches. Rosenberg and Frischtak (1985) believed that technology is knowledge and capacity controlled by its internal specialized groups, accumulated through continued design and production activities. Therefore, technology is not an objective entity, but an action composed of long-term problem solving. Technology can also be seen as function-oriented value creation approaches, which help the producer lower the uncertainty of reaching a specific target (Rogers, 2003).

Normann (2001) classified the output value created by business technology innovation into intrinsic value and positional value. The former stresses that firm production should meet customer demands and emphasizes the adjustments on firm's resource structure and output value. Using technology innovation, it redefines market performance output or creates a new value curve of the firm's output to grab more abundant market value (Kim & Mauborgu, 1999). The latter stresses coordination of the convergence process of value activities between organizations or promoting knowledge exchange for common value, which engages the value output of value coproduction (Ramirez, 1999).

Technology innovation helps business to transform and alter its competitive status. Businesses generally identify Schumpeterian innovation as an important element to gain excessive surplus and build competitive edge (Lieberman & Montgomery, 1988). Branson (1966) advocated that "technology should include product design, production method, and the enterprise system needed for planning, organizing, and executing the production plan."

Typical enterprise will attempt to manipulate the technical technology innovations of its products and process, and management technology innovations in strategy and marketing, to ensure competitive advantages such as market exclusiveness and leadership. This type of managerial philosophy, however, tends to focus on fulfilling the demands of high-profit markets and neglecting low-profit, small, marginal, and poor-infrastructure markets. Because of the risk and expenditure involved in technology innovation, organizations with different resource capabilities should adjust their technology spectrum in response to social needs, from a strategy of knowledge and transformation of social distribution service, to the transformation of product development and the manufacturing process.

5.2. *Innovation of social technology*

Adapting the technology construct of business as the management tool for social enterprise to create values in responding to social needs, this chapter proposes that this so-called "social technology" consists of four corresponding technology elements: product, process, management, and distribution elements (Branson, 1966). In order to emphasize the responsibility of applying "technologies" in relation to social needs, this chapter has renamed them: social product technology, social process technology, socialization strategy, and social marketing technology.

5.2.1. *Social product technology*

Henderson and Clarks (1990) classified product into components and architecture. The degree of innovation that affects the "architecture" or the "components" of a product can be classified into four types: (1) **Modular Innovation** — creating overturned innovation on the components and core design of the existing product, while the link between product architecture and components remains unchanged; (2) **Incremental Innovation** — expanding the design function of existing products and making only slight changes in the components, while the link between product architecture and components remains unchanged; (3) **Radical Innovation** — not only creating a new core design but also changing the components and architecture, this type of innovation creates a design with a new dominant power; and (4) **Architectural Innovation** — product components and core design remain unchanged, except for changes in product structure. To compliment the new product structure, when necessary, it will change the size, function, and style of the existing product.

Against the demand from the disadvantaged market, social enterprise must engage in the development design and production of actual products or services to respond to consumer behaviors. However, the development design of social products not only includes R&D of higher technology, but a simplified redesign of existing technology, and the modification of specific demand situations, to adapt to the needs of specific or disadvantaged groups.

For example, Bao Ban Phuong newspaper, initiated the idea of a newspaper that voicing for and voicing by the foreigners. The effort eases the sense of loneliness for being away from one's own country and simultaneously stands as platform for communication and exchange of experience. The newspaper, which might be seen as a redesigned version of the common newspapers, is a helpful and innovative product to respond to specific social needs. In this way, the organization responses specifically to tasks 2, 3 and 5, that motivates unwilling supply, supplies in a poor-infrastructure market, and supplies for differentiated markets demand.

Therefore, the meaning of social product technology rests in "the developing, simplifying and re-using of design capacity, which positions the concept, function, and style of the product/service to satisfy social needs."

5.2.2. *Social process technology*

Business often concentrates on developing process that meets the needs of its background, management style, internal coordination, and cross-organizational interaction (Garvin, 1995). The operational process is equivalent to designing primary activities in a value chain, taking added business value as its core and integrating up and down-stream operations (Morash & Clinton, 1998). The management process is similar to designing support activities, by promoting cross-organizational operation integration. Through the disaggregation and aggregation of business and industry value activities and the connection of cross-enterprise resource and activities, enterprise value production will hopefully be more flexible and dynamic (Tapscott, 1999). Business integrates operation activities such as manufacturing, marketing, and R&D. Through changing technical skills, value repositioning, and operation coordinating, business creates a process technology with better value output. The market demands that social enterprise faces differ from ordinary business. Based on existing enterprise technology, social enterprise needs to create a social process technology with a value output that can better satisfy specific social needs. Social process technology is thus defined as: business activities designed for fulfilling and delivering social products and services.

The Rejoice Cooperation Group discovered the potential of intellectually challenged youth and the idle farmers. Therefore, the organization designed an operational system based on the human nature and capacity; and the potential of the idle land and farmers. An easy to learn and use procedure is created, that is not centered on the machines, where the potential of the marginalized may be expressed and developed. Further, by changing the supply chain process, the organization solves its own supply issue and creates alternate opportunities for the local small-scale farmers. In this way, the ideas of tasks 4, 6, and 7 that are to supply comprehensive values mix, match the supply–demand gap, and enhance the target of non-financial value, are fully reflected.

5.2.3. *Socialization strategy technology*

The ultimate goal of social enterprise is to actualize the effect of social philanthropy. This is often the core value of its development strategy, demonstrated in its mission and values (Guclu *et al.*, 2002). The important features of social enterprise include innovation and social effect, but not necessarily financial gain (Mair & Marti, 2006). In another words, in its enterprising activities, social enterprise should gradually expand its social effect.

Boschee and McClurg (2003) suggested that social enterprise have apparent commercial activities and maintain continuous financial sources, to sustain its social service. Therefore, the philosophy of social enterprise should include two values: maintaining stable financial revenue or self-sufficiency, to distinguish itself from the pure NPO; and emphasizing the value of social philanthropy as a strategic goal, to distinguish itself from ordinary business.

Perrini and Vurro (2006) considered social enterprise as an entrepreneurial process that extensively applies multiple social resources. These resources include elements such as environment, society, entrepreneur, entrepreneurship (with innovation), organization (social enterprise), social welfare, and social change. Therefore, business plans to adjust its operation value to increase its social contribution involve more than just redefining its strategic goal; its strategy needs socialized innovation to guide the value network of social enterprise, the development of strategic resources, and the integration of the service target and service operation, to effectively achieve its objectives (Mair & Schoen, 2007).

The Antique Assam Tea Farm targeted the issue of pollution, holistic health, and life's meaning, and incorporated them into financing operations by creating a tourism farm. The organization restores and reuses the abandoned farm, introduces the agro-ecological farming methods, and invokes the concepts of holistic health as its strategy. Therefore, not only is the Antique Assam Tea Farm innovated tourism farm with both educational and leisure concept include, but also a comprehensive and innovative selling and marketing strategy. The concepts of 4, 7, and 8 that include the supply of comprehensive values mix, the enhancement of non-financial value, and specifically the effective utility of resources are present.

Given the social needs that social enterprises face, the meaning of "socialization strategy" lies in the operational goals that cover social value and financial performance, the operational system design that integrates social resources, and the creation of social values and sustainability.

5.2.4. *Social marketing technology*

Mair and Marti (2006) believed that the capacity to uncover social needs is a fundamental capacity of a social entrepreneur. Dees (2001) identified that personal experience often drives and inspires creativity. The personal experiences of family or friends who encounter problems that cause societal discontent not only lead to innovative solutions, but often induce the business motive for social entrepreneurs. The Children-Are-Us Bakery has moved from a passive stance of taking care of the mentally disable children to a positive stance by integrating them into the society. The organization has introduced a product that consist both commercial value and social value, where through the work of the children that the society may come to know more about the disable children. In this way, the tasks 1 and 6, which involve the improvement of disabled individuals and the matching of supply–demand gap, are reflected.

The values of a social enterprise, in serving society, stem from the social product concept based on understanding social needs. Contrasted to the pure commercial transaction approach, social enterprise designs a marketing system, such as non-conventional reverse logistics and a self-sufficient community, which attracts social-consciousness identification, gathers social resources, propagates social value, and promotes a non-mainstream market. Social enterprise strives to innovate a social marketing concept and model to meet social satisfaction. The meaning of social marketing can therefore be understood as the identification of social needs and the corresponding market positioning and related selling service and promotion activities in a social market.

6. Conclusion

Social enterprise derives from satisfying the gaps of social supplies and demands. These gaps drive social entrepreneurs to discover, evaluate, and employ opportunities in establishing their organizations. Shane and Venkataraman (2000) indicated the importance of the entrepreneur as (1) a mechanism that transforms social technology information into products and services; (2) a mechanism that discovers inefficiency (temporary and spatial) and alleviates that inefficiency in the economic system; (3) a mechanism that drives product innovation and the production process and is the engine driving the change. The entrepreneur therefore is an important means to balance the market and a process for discovering, evaluating, and utilizing opportunities. However, the entrepreneur does not necessarily have to start a new organization for that purpose. New market opportunities can be sold to other individuals or an existing organization.

"Social Enterprise" is an organizational concept that integrates social benefits with profitability, the fusion of ordinary business and NPOs. However, due to the nature of fusion, it is possible that a new business could diverge into an organizational pattern. Therefore, to investigate social enterprise management, it is necessary to examine the managerial concept, strategy, and system, and the technology capacity of ordinary business, adjusting existing theories to create value outputs that meet social demands.

This chapter adopts the business perspective to fuse the knowledge of business management theories with social service demand, to face the social demand that ordinary business is incapable or reluctant to encounter. This research also introduces social value into business strategy to transform socialized business strategy. Only when businesses realize the existence and characteristics of unsatisfied social needs, can they produce and transmit specific value output to specific social groups, through social innovation and development of product technology, and redesigning the social process technology.

This research consists of two academic contributions. First, by using the traditional market economic analysis, this research has identified the possible under-serviced or under-satisfied market (non-market) and the incomplete market, which provides legitimate academic inference of the existent social enterprises. Second, in accordance with the characteristics of the needs of the non-market and incomplete market, and based on the actual operation observed, this research has pointed out the four critical operational technologies that social enterprises need to develop. These proposed technologies may also be seen as the operational tasks for social enterprises in general. These four technologies include the social product technology, social process technology, socialization strategy technology, and social marketing technology. Through these four technologies, social enterprises can produce social values that ordinary businesses do not wish to emphasize. These technologies may also be seen as supplements to the conventional managerial theories lacking deliberation on social enterprise management.

The findings of this research, especially the four social enterprise management technologies, may be critical guides to social enterprise practitioners in the development of relevant capabilities, and to people specialized in business or NPO management in combining their specialties in developing managerial concepts that are more suited to social enterprises.

References

Allan, B. (2005). Social Enterprise: Through the Eyes of the Consumer, *Social Enterprise Journal*, 1(1), pp. 57–77.

Begg, D., Fischer, S., & Dornbusch, R. (1991). *Economics* (3rd edn.). London: McGraw Hill, pp. 157–170.

Boschee, J. & McClurg, J. (2003). Toward a better understanding of social entrepreneurship: Some important distinction. Retrieved from www.se-alliance.org/better_understanding.pdf (search date March 20, 2008).

Branson, J. (1966). Transfer Technology Knowledge by International Corporation to Developing Countries, *American Economics Review*, May, pp. 259–267.

Copeland, T., Koller, T., & Murrin, J. (1996). *Valuation: Measuring and Managing the Value of Companies.* NY: Wiley.

Davidson, G. & Davidson, P. (1996). *Economics for a Civilized Society* (2nd edn.). London: Macmillan Press, pp. 79–83.

Dees, J. G. (2001). The meaning of social entrepreneurship. Retrieved from http://www.fuqua.duke.edu/centers/case (search date January 15, 2008).

Emerson, J. (2003). The Blended Value Proposition: Integrating Social and Financial Returns, *California Management Review*, 45(4), pp. 35–51.

Friedman, M. (1963). *Capitalism and Freedom.* Chicago: Chicago University Press.

Garvin, D. A. (1995). Leveraging Processes for Strategic Advantage. *Harvard Business Review*, 73(5), September–October, pp. 76–90.

Govindarajan, V. & Fisher, J. (1988). Strategy Control System and Resource Sharing: Effects on Business-unit Performance, *Academy of Management Journal*, 33, pp. 259–285.

Guclu, A., Dees, J. G., & Anderson, B. B. (2002). The process of social entrepreneurship: Creating opportunities worthy of serious pursuit. Retrieved from http://www.fuqua.duke.edu/centers/case/documents/dees_SE.pdf (search date June 15, 2008).

Hansmann, H. B. (2003). The role of trust in nonprofit organization, in H. K. Anheier & A. Ben-Ner (eds.), *The Study of Nonprofit Enterprise: Theories and Approach*, NY: Kluwer Academic/Plenum Publishers, pp. 115–122.

Haugh, H. (2005). A Research Agenda for Social Entrepreneurship, *Social Enterprise Journal*, 1(1), pp. 1–12.

Henderson, R. & Clark, K. (1990). Architecture Innovation: The Reconfiguration of Existing Product Technologies and the Failure of Established Firms, *Administrative Science Quarterly*, 35(1), pp. 9–30.

Hines, F. (2005). Viable Social Enterprise — An Evaluation of Business Support to Social Enterprises, *Social Enterprise Journal*, 1(1), pp. 13–28.

Hines, F. & Thomas, C. (2004). *Turing Big Ideas into Viable Social Enterprise: Investigating the Ways in which the Right Technical Business Support Can Turn Real Social Needs into Viable Social Enterprises: A Report Prepared for Tridos Bank.* Cardiff: BRASS Centre.

Hu, J. & Chen, C. Y. (2009). The Essence, Tasks and Development of Social Enterprise, *Journal of Entrepreneurship Research*, 4(4), pp. 1–28.

Institute for Social Entrepreneurs (2000). Retrieved from http://www.socialent.org/overview.htm (search date August 10, 2009).

Islam, Z. (2007). A New Model for Supporting Social Enterprise through Sustainable Investment, *Social Enterprise Journal*, 3(1), pp. 1–9.

Kerlin, J. A. (2006). Social Enterprise in the United States and Europe: Understanding and Learning from the Differences, *Voluntas*, 17, pp. 247–263.

Kim, W. C. & Mauborgne, R. (1999). Strategy, Value Innovation, and the Knowledge Economy, *Sloan Management Review*, 40(3), pp. 41–54.

Kim, W. C. & Mauborgne, R. (2005). *Blue Ocean Strategy*. Boston: Harvard Business School Press.

Lieberman, M. B. & Montgomery, D. B. (1988). First-Mover Advantages, *Strategic Management Journal*, special issue 9, pp. 41–58.

Mair, J. & Marti, I. (2006). Social Entrepreneurship Research: A Source of Explanation, Prediction and Delight, *Journal of World Business*, 41(1), pp. 36–44.

Mair, J. & Schoen, O. (2007). Successful Social Entrepreneurial Business Models in the Context of Developing Economies, *International Journal of Emerging Markets*, 1(2), pp. 54–68.

Morash, E. A. & Clinton, S. R. (1998). Supply Chain Integration: Customer Value Through Collaborative Versus Operational Excellence, *Journal of Marketing: Theory and Practice*, 16(4), pp. 104–115.

Normann, R. (2001). *Reframing Business: When the Map Changes the Landscape*. West Sussex: Wiley.

Pearce J. (2003). *Social Enterprise in Anytown*. London: Calouste Gulbenkian Foundation.

Perrini, F. & Vurro, C. (2006). Leveraging social change through entrepreneurship, in F. Perrini (ed.), *The New Social Entrepreneurship: What Awaits Social Entrepreneurship Ventures?* MA: Edward Elgar.

Ramirez, R. (1999). Value Co-Production: Intellectual Origins and Implications for Practice and Research, *Strategic Management Journal*, 20(1), pp. 49–65.

Rogers, E. M. (2003). *Diffusion of Innovations*. New York: The Free Press.

Rosenberg, N. & Frischtak, C. (1985). *International Technology Transfer*. New York: Praeger.

Salamon, L. M. (1990). The nonprofit sector and government: The American experience in theory and practice, in H. K. Anheier & W. Seibel (eds.), *The Third Sector: Comparative Studies of Nonprofit Organizations*, New York: Walter de Gruyter, pp. 219–220.

Shane, S. & Venkataraman, S. (2000). The Promise of Entrepreneurship as a Field of Research, *Academy of Management Review*, 25(1), pp. 217–226.

Sharma, A., Krishnan, R., & Grewal, D. (2001). Value Creation in Markets: A Critical Area of Focus for Business-to-Business Markets, *Industrial Marketing Management*, 30, pp. 391–402.

Sharp, A. M., Register, C. A., & Grimes, P. A. (1996). *Economics of Social Issues*. Illinois: Richard Irwin.

Short, J. C., Moss, T. W., & Lumpkin, G. T. (2009). Research in Social Entrepreneurship Past Contributions and Future Opportunities, *Strategic Entrepreneurship Journal*, 3, pp. 161–194.

Sweberg, R. (2003). *Principles of Economic Sociology*. Princeton, NJ: Princeton University Press.

Tapscott, D. (ed.) (1999). *Creating Value in the Network Economy*. Harvard Business Review Book, Boston: Harvard Business School Press.

Von Krogh, G. & Grand, S. (2002). From economic theory toward a knowledge-based theory of the firm, in C. W. Choo & N. Bonits (eds.), *The Strategic Management of Intellectual Capital and Organizational Knowledge*, Oxford: Oxford University Press, pp. 163–184.

Wilbert, C. K. & Jameson, K. P. (1992). *The Political Economy of Development and Underdevelopment*. New York: McGraw-Hill, Inc.

Yin, R. K. (2003). *The Application of Case Study Research*. Thousand Oaks: Sage Publications.

Zhuang, C. & Wheale, P. (2004). Creating Sustainable Corporate Value: A Case Study of Stakeholder Relationship Management in China, *Business and Society Review*, 109(4), pp. 507–547.

3

Creating Social Value through Frugal Innovation

Anthony Kuo

Fu Jen Catholic University

1. Introduction

Innovation has been an important topic in the study of economics and business. It is well accepted that innovation is the catalyst to both economic and business growth. Economist Joseph Schumpeter considered innovation the driving force for economic growth. Entrepreneurs use conceptual breakthroughs to carry out new combinations, he argued, destroying the status quo to create something better. This process of "creative destruction" was what actually drove the economy to grow (Schumpeter, 1934).

Extending from Schumpeter's perspective, business strategy scholars find that innovation enables business firms to create economic value for their customers, and thus enhances these firms' competitiveness (Grant, 1996; Lengnick-Hall, 1992). Researchers in various disciplines such as organization, marketing, engineering, and new product development have conducted numerous studies on the origin, forms, types, and processes of innovation. The resulting literature has provided fruitful insights to advance our knowledge of innovation. However, far more attention on the study of innovation has been paid to economic value creation than to social value creation. How to create social value via innovation has yet to be fully tapped by scholars. This study aims to fill this gap by exploring cases from the emerging or developing economies.

In emerging or developing economies, resources are usually limited due to incomplete economic development. It is impossible for government, non-profit organizations (NPOs), or businesses to invest heavily on new, breakthrough technologies to cater to their local needs. Specifically, the disadvantaged in the developing world suffer the most, since their needs have long been overlooked or underserved. Under such circumstances, frugal innovation, initiated from emerging markets by various organizations to overcome resource constraints and address the needs of the "bottom of the pyramid" (BOP), has come to rescue. The no-frill, cost-cutting, and resource-saving nature of frugal innovation has successfully created significant social value to meet certain basic human needs in emerging and developing economies and attracted broad attentions. Some businesses have also endeavored to remove the non-essential functions of their products, simplify their service offerings, or trim down their processes to cut cost, seeking to offer affordable products or services to fulfill neglected needs and made significant profits. More and more businesses have thus started to redesign their products and rethink their business models toward this direction as well. With an increasing number of organizations involving in this novel approach, frugal innovation will undoubtedly create higher social value and benefit the society as a whole. Hence, we would like to delve into the details of how various organizations create social value through frugal innovation.

In the following sections, we will first introduce the approach of frugal innovation and related literature. Then we will describe our methodology, followed by research findings, discussion, and conclusion.

2. Literature Review and the Frugal Innovation Approach

Innovation scholars usually trace the origin of innovation theory to Joseph Schumpeter (Schumpeter, 1934), who was concerned with answering the question: "What creates economic development?" In the eyes of Schumpeter, the main principle of economic growth was innovation (creative destruction), instead of competition (the invisible hand). This perspective naturally leads to the next logical question — what creates innovation? Schumpeter's answer was "entrepreneurship." Entrepreneurs initiated the creative destruction process, because they use conceptual breakthroughs to carry out new combinations and risks — destroying the status quo to create something better (Birkinshaw, 2001).

Schumpeter's perspective, later echoed by French sociologist Gabriel Tarde, emphasized the originality of innovation derived from the activity of one individual, rather than a collection of individuals or an organization. Sundbo, in his book "The Theory of Innovation," categorized this perspective as "entrepreneurial innovation theories" (Sundbo, 1998). The individual-based innovation theory soon gained popularity, but as "the fourth Kondratiev wave" began (an event that Sundbo dates to the late 1930s), a paradigm shift occurred in economic and sociological studies on innovation. This shift put emphasis largely on technology as the driving force behind economic development. This "technology–economics paradigm," also known as "Schumpeter II" (Freeman, 1982), emphasized technological development as the main innovation factor. Numerous researchers have since dedicated themselves to the study of technological innovation, greatly advancing our understanding of how technologies drive innovation and consequently economic growth (see Mowery & Rosenberg, 1991 for a review).

For most extant studies on innovation, either based on the entrepreneurial innovation theories or the technology–economics paradigm, the objective to create something new is to capture its economic value. The motive of innovation has been implicitly and unanimously set to be profit-seeking — entrepreneurs create new ventures to profit, and new technologies are developed to yield financial returns. Hence, the economic consequence has been the main concern of innovation researchers. How innovation can create social value has far less been explored. However, as emerging markets are reshaping the global economic landscape, innovations from these countries have been attracting unprecedented attentions, and opened a new window of opportunities for scholars to look at innovation from different angles.

To seize business opportunities in the emerging countries, firms need to tackle the challenges such as limited purchasing power and incomplete infrastructure in highly resource-constrained environments. Therefore, products aiming for consumers in the emerging markets need to be remarkably re-designed to cater to unique local needs overlooked before. Specifically, as emerging markets have been going through the process of rapid growth and industrialization, the BOP (Prahalad & Hart, 2002) market appeared to be attractive, driving business firms to develop new business models to target at providing goods and services to the economically disadvantaged people. They have started to take the needs of budget-constrained consumers as a starting point and working backwards (Economist, 2010). Through focusing on the essential needs, simplifying the product or service design, minimizing the use of resources in development, production and delivery, business firms effectively reduce the cost of a product and its production, making it affordable for the majority of people in the emerging markets.

Such "frugal innovations" (Economist, 2010; Zeschky *et al.*, 2011) or "jugaad innovations" (Radjou *et al.*, 2012) have become prevalent in the emerging markets (Bellman, 2009), and gradually diffused to other parts in the world (Agarwal & Brem, 2012; Bellman, 2009; Economist, 2010). Famous examples of frugal innovation are found throughout the emerging and developing countries: from the Nano, the world's cheapest family car launched for 1 lakh (100,000) rupees (US$2000) in 2009 by the Tata Group from India, to M-Pesa, a mobile-phone based money transfer and microfinancing service for Safaricom and Vodacom in Kenya and Tanzania. Different studies or reports have defined frugal innovation differently, but most of them agree on the following characteristics:

(1) Focusing on the fundamental needs or the essence of needs.
(2) Eliminating non-essential functions of products.
(3) Trimming down the processes (e.g., service processes or manufacturing process).
(4) No-frill.
(5) Cost-cutting.
(6) Tough and easy to use. (Frugal products need to adapt to harsh environments in the emerging or developing world.)
(7) Sparing in the use of resources.

Due to the current lack of a general definition of frugal innovation, this study provides a working definition of frugal innovation as the following:

> *New products or services which focus on fundamental needs, spare in the use of resources, or eliminate non-essential functions to simplify the design.*

Frugal innovations do not necessarily aim to create economic value — some of them are carried out to create social value, i.e., "to contribute to the welfare or well-being in a given human community" (Peredo & McLean, 2006). However, studies focusing on social value creation of frugal innovation are relatively scant. We thus conduct the current research to explore how organizations create social value through frugal innovation. Traditional quantitative methodologies are not suitable for such a new phenomenon, so we use qualitative approaches for this study. In the following paragraph, we will illustrate why and how we choose the qualitative approach.

3. Methodology

We adopt the qualitative method to conduct the current study for the following reasons. First, when organizational processes such as innovation processes are involved, quantitative measurements are either inappropriate or less preferred (Strauss & Corbin, 2007; Van Maanen, 1979), as are survey-based methodologies (Yin, 1983). Second, exploratory fieldwork is essential in emerging areas of research that lack an extant body of both theories and data (Glaser & Strauss, 1967; Noda & Bower, 1996). Third, exploring fine-grained processes of how organizations create social value through the process of frugal innovation requires a level of analysis not available through survey-based researches (Yin, 1983). Finally, the use of exploratory case research enables ideas to be developed for further study (Noda & Bower, 1996). Therefore, in this study, we use case study for the purpose of elaborating upon a set of concepts necessary for process theory development.

Three cases were selected for case studies. These cases were chosen through purposeful sampling (Patton, 2001), which is a criterion-based selection method that permits a sample to be constructed fitting a predefined profile. We follow the principle advocated by Patton (2001) to select "information-rich cases — cases in which one can learn a great deal about matters of importance and therefore worthy of in-depth study" (Patton, 2001, p. 242). To be eligible for selection, each case has to be involved in both frugal innovation and social value creation. The data required for the study were collected mainly from publicly available archival sources, including company websites and documents (such as financial reports, annual reports, corporate press releases, public conferences, and magazine or newspaper reports). The data obtained from different sources were triangulated, revealing a high level of consistency (Denzin & Lincoln, 2005; Miles & Huberman, 1984). The analysis of data revealed differences in frugal innovation processes and types of social value created by organizations as discussed in Sec. 4.

4. Case Description

4.1. *mPedigree's drug verification services to fight counterfeit drugs*

The issue of counterfeit drugs has long been a serious problem for the world. Counterfeit drugs or "fake" drugs, also known as "spurious/falsely-labeled/falsified/counterfeit (SFFC) medicines," are medications or pharmaceutical products produced and sold with the intent to deceptively represent its origin, authenticity, or effectiveness. A counterfeit drug can take various forms. It may contain inappropriate quantities of active ingredients, or none. Sometimes, toxic chemicals are even substituted for the real medicine and improperly absorbed by the body. It may also contain ingredients that are not on the label, or may be supplied with inaccurate or deliberately fake packaging and labeling. Other than fraud, some drugs might instead be "substandard," lacking in correct scientific specifications (e.g., dosage, ingredients, etc.) due to negligence or human error (e.g., factory errors, being stored improperly, being out of date, etc.). Substandard drugs may consequently be ineffective, harmful to the patient, or even exploited by criminal counterfeiters to produce fake drugs.

Counterfeit drugs have posed serious problems all over the world. Globally, criminal sales were estimated to total more than US$35 billion annually (Cockburn *et al.*, 2005). Unfortunately, the problem is especially rampant in developing and emerging countries. In some African and Asian countries, more than half of drugs sold are fakes (Cockburn *et al.*, 2005). According to the *Wall Street Journal* (quoting the Center for Medicine in the Public Interest), about 30% of branded drug sales in developing countries are counterfeit (Chu, 2012). India's Business Standard reports that counterfeits in India account for about 20% of the total pharmaceutical market and typically happened in the top 25–30 best-selling brands. Around 8 to 10% of a drug's production cost goes to efforts protecting against counterfeiting, they estimate (Dey, 2012). In contrast, the World Health Organization (WHO) estimates that only about 1% of the medicines marketed in developed countries are counterfeit (WHO, 2012).

mPedigree, an African social enterprise from Accra, Ghana, aims to change that dismal scenario. Co-founded by Bright Simons, mPedigree has developed a service that allows consumers to instantly verify the source of pharmaceuticals free of charge at the point of purchase, using standard 2G mobile phones and text messages. Working with Hewlett-Packard, trials were first launched in Ghana and Nigeria in the summer of 2010. Other countries including Kenya, Uganda, and Tanzania have all expressed interest.

With the new service, patients purchasing a range of drugs manufactured by participating pharmaceutical companies, such as May & Baker Nigeria PLC and the KAMA Group of Ghana, can instantly verify whether the products they intend to buy are genuine. Pharmaceutical companies imprint special codes on the tablets or syrup bottles that are recorded in the database maintained by HP and mPedigree. When consumers purchase a drug, they can scratch off a coating on the drugs' packaging to reveal the unique code. This code can be text messaged by the consumer or medical professional to a free short message service (SMS) number to verify the authenticity of the drug. After sending the code, consumers get an immediate response by a short message as well, showing whether the product is genuine. If the drug packaging contains a fake code, the consumer will receive a message alerting them that the pack may be a counterfeit, along with a phone number to report the incident.

Since the service is free, users do not need to own a phone to use it — they can simply borrow one from somebody nearby. mPedigree persuaded the mobile-phone operators and drug manufacturers to pay for the text messages. With mPedigree's service, mobile operators increase their traffic, and pharmaceuticals can also increase their sales of genuine medicines if sales of counterfeit drugs drop. In addition, drug companies can use data from mPedigree for marketing use, such as tracking sales geographically and analyzing consumer profile of each product to target their advertising. The data also could help law enforcement agencies to fight against counterfeits. And, most important of all, consumers benefit from safeguard against hazardous counterfeit drugs.

mPedigree's solution to protect against pharmaceutical counterfeiting is neither the first nor the only one. Others, for example, have provided anti-counterfeit holograms that can be attached to drug packaging. Yet, mPedigree's services cost less than holograms and radio-frequency identification (RFID) and can thus be affordable for most people in the developing or emerging countries. The company plans to introduce the services across Africa and eventually into other parts of the world where problems of counterfeit drugs are rampant.

4.2. A Liter of Light: My Shelter Foundation's solar bottle bulb

In the Philippines, the rising cost of power leaves many unable to afford electricity, especially people who live in the underprivileged areas. Homes in underprivileged areas are often built so close to each other that they have no windows or are unable to access natural light. Hence, many slum-inhabitants often have to live in near darkness. Founded by Illac Diaz, the Philippines-based, not-for-profit My Shelter Foundation, brought the simple and cheap lighting technology through his project — "A Liter of Light" — to homes that are either without light or are on the verge of having their electricity cut off.

The simple innovation is called the "solar bottle bulb." The "bulb" is basically a recycled plastic bottle filled with bleached water, installed into holes in a corrugated iron roofs. These bottle bulbs then reflect sunlight into a room during the day, creating the equivalent of 55 Watts of light. It only takes five minutes to make, using a hammer, nails, metal sheets, sandpaper, and resin adhesive. Most importantly, it costs only about US$1 per piece to produce and install. The simple technology of the solar bottle bulb was originally developed in Brazil by Alfredo Moser in 2002. With the help of a group of students from the Massachusetts Institute of Technology in the US, the solar bulb used in the Philippines has been modified to meet local needs.

The Philippines is reported to have the most expensive electricity in Asia ("Philippines has most expensive electricity in Asia," 2011). Unable to afford electricity, slum families are forced to use candles or illegal connections as their lighting source. These approaches can be risky, as it is not uncommon to hear of fire accidents caused by candles or faulty wiring, which sometimes destroy whole communities. In addition to providing decent lighting for the slum homes, "A Liter of Light" has also helped alleviate these issues.

The My Shelter Foundation believes in the importance of green technology for everyone. Unfortunately, the state-of-the-art green technologies are only accessible to those who can afford it, mostly from the developed world. In the developing and emerging countries, people cannot afford to buy imported, patented, or manufactured green solutions from the developed world. They cannot afford to wait until these technologies become affordable, either. Under such circumstances, the foundation is "taking sustainable building solutions to the grassroots level — the people who are in most need of low-cost infrastructures" ("A Liter of Light: About My Shelter Foundation," 2012).

Starting from Manila, the capital city of the Philippines, "A Liter of Light" has then donated a number of solar bottle bulbs to other areas across the Philippines to replicate the project. With the support from many local governments, the project of "A Liter of Light" has grown to "brighten up 28,000 homes and the lives of 70,000 people in Metro Manila alone" ("A Liter of Light: About My Shelter Foundation," 2012). The project has then been extended to India, Indonesia, and even Switzerland.

4.3. *ChotuKool: A low cost battery-powered refrigerator*

A refrigerator is a ubiquitous household appliance that keeps low temperature to store food. A lower temperature in a confined space decreases the reproduction rate of bacteria, so the refrigerator reduces the rate of spoilage. In modern times, refrigerators used in households rely on enduring electricity power to transfer heat from the inside of the fridge to its external environment so that the inside compartment is kept cooled to a temperature below the ambient temperature outside the fridge. In developed countries where electricity supply is ubiquitous and stable, refrigerators are widely used. However, in emerging and developing countries such as India, the supply of electricity power is limited and unstable, so the use of typical refrigerators becomes unrealistic for most people.

The Indian refrigerator market is estimated to stand at 8.5 million units a year, with an annual growth rate of 18% ("Godrej to take ChotuKool fridge to more markets this year," 2011). However, the adoption rate of refrigerator is still low — less than 18% of households in India own a refrigerator (London & Hart, 2010). Some studies suggested even a much lower rate at 8% (Singh *et al.*, 2011). On the other hand, lack of necessity is never the reason of low adoption rate of refrigerators in India. According to India's Consumer Electronics and Appliances Manufacturers Association, "more than 8 months of the year, 90% India faces hot humid weather," so "refrigerators in India are an inevitability" (CEAMA, 2012). Heat and high humidity are detrimental to food preservation, and the situation is further worsened with frequent power cuts. It is estimated that a combination of frequent power cuts, heat, and high humidity is responsible for one-third of India's food loss and spoilage (Chakravarthy & Coughlan, 2011). In rural areas where electricity power is supplied intermittently, traditional refrigerators appear to be inadequate. Even in regions with stable access to electricity, the price of a regular bottom-of-the-line fridge, around US$200, is still much too high for most of the villagers. Hence, the adoption of refrigerators is particularly low in rural areas.

Aiming to provide the cooling solution for the underserved, Godrej, established in 1897 as one of India's oldest business groups, which is involved in everything from fast-moving consumer goods to furniture, figured it could meet the needs of a huge new group of consumers if it could design the product right. It sent surveyors into rural areas to discover the needs of farm families. Their research indicated that the targeted customers did not need full-scale refrigerators; they required only limited storage, which would save milk, vegetables, and leftovers from spoilage for a day or two (Innosight, 2012). In addition, portability is important since many of the potential customers live in small one-room homes, where household items have to be relocated every evening to make sleeping space, and these customers-to-be migrate frequently, due to financial constraints and/or job-hunting activities. The company finally in 2011 introduced a top-loading, compact, and portable refrigerator called "ChotuKool," a name combining cute-sounding variations of the Hindi word "Chotu" (affectionately used for referring to a little boy) and the English word "cool" ("Godrej to take ChotuKool fridge to more markets this year," 2011).

The product looks more like an icebox or a cooler for fishing. It comes with a tiny size (about 1.5 feet tall by 2 feet wide), a light weight (7.2 kg), and two handles on the sides, intending to tackle constraints of small living spaces and to ensure portability for the migrant workers who move a lot. To cope with the issue of unstable power supply, such as power surges and outages, it provides the option to run on batteries. To cut down costs, Godrej reduced the number of product parts from 200 in regular refrigerators to 20 and replaced compressors, the regular cooling method for refrigerators, with thermoelectric cooling mechanism, which runs on a cooling chip along with a fan similar to those used to cool computers (Chakravarthy & Coughlan, 2011). In fact, thermoelectric cooling has been widely used in developed countries for high-end CPUs in computers or coolers to keep beer and wine cold, but was never employed to replace compressors to serve as a low-cost cooling engine. With those efforts of cost reductions, Godrej has been able to sell the product for only US$70, which is affordable for most of households in rural villages.

The operational cost of ChotuKool is also kept low as it consumes only half the power required by regular refrigerators, so the electricity bills remain at a level most people can afford. The fridge opens from the top, instead of the front, to ensure cold air to stay down in the compartment when the door is opened. ChotuKool consumes between 55 and 62 Watt power and runs on dual power supply (230 V AC and 12 V DC). With the low price and low operational cost, many people in India can now afford to buy a refrigerator to keep their food from spoilage. Godrej expects to sell 100,000 ChotuKools in only the product's second full year on the market (Innosight, 2012).

5.   Research Findings and Discussion

The above cases have showed various frugal innovations employed by a range of organizations, including business firms and NPOs, in different countries, to create social value. A summary of the cases and how these

Table 1. How case organizations create social value through frugal innovation

	mPedigree's drug verification services	My Shelter Foundation's A Liter of Light	Godrej ChotuKool
Social needs	Safeguarding against counterfeit drugs.	Lighting in the underprivileged areas.	Low-temperature food storage for the BOP.
Local challenges and constraints	Unable to afford costly technologies such as hologram and RFID. The general public's limited affordability.	No access to electicity power. Underprivileged families' limited affordability to electricity.	Lack of stable electricity power. BOP's limited affordability. Small living spaces. Portability needs for the migrant workers.
The disadvantaged who benefit from the innovation	The sick people.	The underprivileged families.	The BOP population.
Social value created	The decrease of threats posed by counterfeit drugs. Peace of mind when buying drugs.	Basic lighting for the underprivileged families. The reduction of potential fire accidents.	Basic food storage for the BOP. Better energy efficiency.

organizations create social value through frugal innovation is provided in Table 1.

The analysis of case data and an iterative process of data comparison enabled us to understand how social value is created through frugal innovation. We found that, first, in the cases selected, organizations which initiated frugal innovation could all effectively discover the basic needs which had never been well addressed by government organizations, businesses, or NPOs before. These underserved needs invoked the case organizations to take certain actions to solve these problems. Hence, the first step to create social value through frugal innovations is to effectively identify the underserved population and understand their unfulfilled needs.

Second, simplicity and resource conservation are the key for frugal innovation to create social value. None of the solutions provided by the case organizations apply complicated, state-of-the-art technologies. Nor do they require the heavy use of resources. mPedigree's drug verification services make use of 2G mobile technologies, which may appear to be out-of-date in certain developed countries. My Shelter Foundation's "solar bottle bulb" is no complicated technology but just a recycled plastic bottle filled with bleached water. Godrej's ChotuKool simplifies the architecture of the regular refrigerator, reducing the number of parts from 200 to 20 and replaces compressors with cooling chips to reduce costs and energy consumption. With simple and resource-saving designs, these solutions become affordable to most of the disadvantaged people from the emerging countries. If businesses or NPOs from the developed world can also infuse the spirit of simplicity and resource conservation into their products or services, more social value will be created to benefit the people as well.

Third, in these cases, organizations who undertake frugal innovations can all, based on specific local conditions and constraints, design feasible products or services to solve the problems the disadvantaged encountered. In particular, affordability is a common issue for most of the disadvantaged population. Merely providing existing products or services with the lowest price will not succeed, because in the disadvantaged environments, the challenge of affordability is frequently intertwined with other environmental constraints. To meet the requirement of affordability and environmental constraints simultaneously, it calls for extra efforts to design brand new products or services which are fundamentally different from the low-cost solutions available in the developed world.

For example, costly technologies such as hologram and RFID are the typical solution to cope with counterfeit drugs. However, such technologies appear to be much too expensive for the emerging countries. mPedigree's drug verification services tackle the affordability issue by utilizing locally available technologies with reasonable cost, and cleverly worked with related organizations — HP, pharmaceutical companies, and telecommunication companies — to come up with a feasible solution. Godrej totally re-designed the architecture of the refrigerator and came up with the brand new product, ChotuKool, which employed cooling chips to replace compressors for the purpose of downsizing and better energy efficiency, and equipped the new fridge with battery power to deal with the power cuts issue. Without the total redesign and the new product architecture, it is impossible for the new product to be useful and practical for the low-income families in India. Therefore, it is important for organizations to re-evaluate the feasibility of products or services, and then they can create real social value.

On the other hand, affordability does not mean low-tech frugal innovation can use cutting-edge technologies. Godrej adopted the technology of thermoelectric cooling, which has been commonly used in high-end computers' CPUs, finding an unprecedented use of this sophisticated technology, with a simple design, in a low-cost product for the BOP population. Sometimes, a mix of high technologies and a simplified architecture can bring about remarkable results. Organizations which intend to create social value through frugal innovation should, thus, not limit themselves with primitive technologies when designing frugal solutions.

Fourth, in these cases, in addition to social value creation, some organizations also create economic value at the same time. For example, ChotuKool has brought significant incomes for Godrej. This finding indicates that social value creation may not need to be undertaken at the price of economic value — they can be fulfilled concurrently. Of course, simultaneous creation of social and economic value may not always be achievable, but cases in this study shed some light on the possibility. For social enterprises which apply business strategies to improve human and social well-being while at the same time bring profits for shareholders, frugal innovation may help balance their social objectives with economic objectives. If organizations can come up with more creative practices like frugal innovation, they will be able to alleviate the challenges of achieving both social and economic goals. We believe that this topic is of great interest to both business and social studies and would like to call for more researches in this direction.

Fifth, frugal innovations which create social value successfully may involve the participation of either NPOs or businesses, or both. My Shelter Foundation's "A Liter of Light" project was mainly undertaken by the NPO. However, in the case of mPedigree's drug verification services, the initiating NPO — mPedigree — worked with business firms — HP, pharmaceutical companies, and cell phone operators — to provide the services, while in the case of Godrej's ChotuKool, the new product was primarily designed and produced by the for-profit organization, Godrej. Both NPOs and businesses play important roles in the process of social value creation, but it calls for more researches in this direction for us to fully understand how NPOs can work with business firms to create social value. Apparently,

NPOs and businesses have distinctive objectives and organization culture. Nonetheless, our case study shows that they can work together to create social value. Hence, how to encourage them to collaborate toward social value creation will be a noteworthy research topic. Governments from all over the world can also proceed to formulate adequate policies to enable more collaboration between NPOs and businesses to benefit the society as a whole.

6. Conclusion

Through exploratory case studies, this research explores the details of how various organizations create social value through frugal innovation. The research found that a range of organizations, including businesses and NPOs, collaborate to undertake frugal innovations, successfully helping various groups of the disadvantaged, and the research also provided practical experiences to be shared with various organizations.

As emerging countries are gaining more ground on the global economy, frugal innovation has attracted increasing attentions. An increasing number of frugal products and services have been launched by different organizations and gained popularity in the emerging countries. The central characteristics of frugal innovation, such as focusing on the fundamental needs, sparing in the use of resources, and eliminating non-essential functions to make products or services affordable for consumers at the BOP, have enabled many organizations to re-think and re-design their products or services to address unsatisfied essential needs, and thus create enough value.

The philosophy of frugal innovation has not only been found in social value creation in emerging regions, where resources are relatively scarce, but also flourished in business community and in more developed countries with abundant resources. For example, in the software industry, the conventional business model of persuading customers to "upgrade" to a new version by offering additional features and functions in software appears to be seriously challenged. Most of the software package products are now experiencing the "overshooting effect" — the performance of the product exceeds the needs of most of its users (Carr, 2004; Christensen, 1997). Just imagine how many functions in a software product we have never used, and it will be easy to understand how prevalent the overshooting phenomenon takes place. The phenomenon partly, if not all, explains why low-price, straightforward "apps" are gaining wide popularity today.

In addition to software, overshooting "is a common, perhaps even universal, phenomenon in the computer industry" (Carr, 2004). Complicated personal computers which emphasize on computer power and functionalities give way to simple, lightweight mobile devices such as tablets and smartphones. When designing iPhone, rather than adding more features and functions, Steve Jobs removed the keyboard from the smartphone and replaced buttons with a giant screen (Gallo, 2011). The design of iPad also illuminated needless functions and accessories from a personal computer — the mobile device simplified the architecture to focus only on the fundamental tasks most frequently performed on the go, making the use of the product unprecedentedly smooth and easy. "Simplicity is the ultimate sophistication," as Leonardo Da Vinci put it. Broadly speaking, the design of iPhone and iPad also fits the philosophy of frugal innovation.

In more developed countries where economic development has reached a self-sufficient level, the issue of sustainability has started to attract significant attentions. Economic growth at the price of natural environment or quality of life has no longer been acceptable for most of the countries, and a growing number of people have started to voluntarily reduce their consumptions and possessions toward a higher degree of frugality. Affordable, good-enough products become increasingly popular or even trendy. The rise of low-cost airlines, such as Southwest Airlines, Ryanair, and Airasia, and apparel brands, such as Zara, H&M, and Uniqlo tells the story. If people keep emphasizing sustainability and environmental issues, the lifestyle of simple living will likely to become more prevalent, making frugal innovation even more widely accepted and praised.

All in all, we believe that frugal innovation is a clever and promising way to overcome challenges in resource-constraint environments to create social value. Nonetheless, research on the phenomenon of frugal innovation and its social impacts is still in its infancy. The exploratory nature of the present study undoubtedly limits the insights uncovered. Even so, the author humbly expects it to invoke more studies in this field.

References

Agarwal, N. & Brem, A. (2012). Frugal and reverse innovation — Literature overview and case study insights from a German MNC in India and China. *IEEE Xplore Proceedings of the 2012 18th International Conference on Engineering, Technology and Innovation.*

Bellman, E. (2009). Indian Firms Shift Focus to the Poor, *The Wall Street Journal*, October 20. http://online.wsj.com/news/articles/SB1255989 88906795035 (search date October 8, 2012).

Birkinshaw, J. (2001). *Entrepreneurship in the Global Firm*. London, UK: Sage Publications.

Carr, N. G. (2004). *Does IT Matter?: Information Technology and the Corrosion of Competitive Advantage*. Boston, MA: Harvard Business Press.

CEAMA (2012). Refrigerators in India. Retrieved from http://www.ceama. in/refrigerator.html (search date February 10, 2013).

Chakravarthy, B. & Coughlan, S. (2011). Emerging Market Strategy: Innovating Both Products and Delivery Systems, *Strategy & Leadership*, 40(1), pp. 27–32.

Christensen, C. (1997). *The Innovator's Dilemma: When New Technologies Cause Great Firms to Fail*. Boston, MA: Harvard Business School Press.

Chu, K. (2012). Fake-Drug Raids Are Uphill Battle, *The Wall Street Journal*, July 26. Retrieved from http://online.wsj.com/article/SB1000 142405270230364400457752056315007820.html (search date February 10, 2013).

Cockburn, R., Newton, P. N., Agyarko, E. K., Akunyili, D., & White, N. J. (2005). The Global Threat of Counterfeit Drugs: Why Industry and Governments Must Communicate the Dangers, *PLoS Medicine*, 2(4), e100.

Denzin, N. K. & Lincoln, Y. S. (2005). *The Sage Handbook of Qualitative Research* (3rd edn.). London, UK: Sage Publications, Incorporated.

Dey, S. (2012). Pharma firms spend 10% of production cost on tech tie-ups, *Business Standard*, August 20. Retrieved from http://www. business-standard.com/india/news/pharma-firms-spend-10production-costtech-tie-ups/483777/ (search date February 10, 2013).

Economist (2010). First Break All the Rules: The Charms of Frugal Innovation. *The Economist*, April 15.

Freeman, C. (1982). *The Economics of Industrial Innovation* (2nd edn.). Cambridge: MIT Press.

Gallo, C. (2011). *The Innovation Secrets of Steve Jobs: Insanely Different: Principles for Breakthrough Success*. New York: McGraw-Hill.

Glaser, B. G. & Strauss, A. L. (1967). *The Discovery of Grounded Theory: Strategies for Qualitative Research*. Rutgers, NJ: Aldine de Gruyter.

Godrej to take ChotuKool fridge to more markets this year (2011). *Economic Times*, May 22.

Grant, R. M. (1996). Toward a Knowledge-Based Theory of the Firm, *Strategic Management Journal*, 17, pp. 109–122.

Innosight (2012). How can you enter an emerging market — and improve the lives of millions? Retrieved from http://www.innosight.com/impact-stories/chotokool-case-study.cfm.

Lengnick-Hall, C. A. (1992). Innovation and Competitive Advantage: What We Know and What We Need to Learn, *Journal of Management*, 18(2), pp. 399–429.

A Liter of Light: About My Shelter Foundation (2012). Retrieved from http://aliteroflight.org/about-us/.

London, T. & Hart, S. L. (2010). *Next Generation Business Strategies for the Base of the Pyramid: New Approaches for Building Mutual Value*. Upper Saddle River, NJ: Ft Press.

Miles, M. B. & Huberman, A. M. (1984). *Qualitative Data Analysis, A Sourcebook of New Methods*. Beverly Hills, CA: Sage Publications.

Mowery, D. C. & Rosenberg, N. (1991). *Technology and the Pursuit of Economic Growth*: Cambridge: Cambridge University Press.

Noda, T. & Bower, J. L. (1996). Strategy Making As Iterated Processes of Resource Allocation, *Strategic Management Journal*, 17(S1), pp. 159–192.

Patton, M. Q. (2001). *Qualitative Research & Evaluation Methods* (3rd edn.). Thousand Oaks, CA: Sage Publications, Incorporated.

Peredo, A. M. & McLean, M. (2006). Social Entrepreneurship: A Critical Review of the Concept, *Journal of World Business*, 41(1), pp. 56–65. Doi: http://dx.doi.org/10.1016/j.jwb.2005.10.007.

Philippines has most expensive electricity in Asia (2011). *The Manila Bulletin*, February 23. Retrieved from http://www.mb.com.ph/articles/305841/philippines-has-most-expensive-electricity-asia (search date October 10, 2012).

Prahalad, C. K. & Hart, S. L. (2002). The Fortune at the Bottom of the Pyramid, *Strategy and Business*, pp. 54–67.

Radjou, N., Prabhu, J., & Ahuja, S. (2012). *Jugaad Innovation: Think Frugal, Be Flexible, Generate Breakthrough Growth*. San Francisco: Jossey-Bass.

Schumpeter, J. A. (1934). *The Theory of Economic Development*. Cambridge: Harvard University Press.

Singh, M. G., Gambhir, A., & Dasgupta, J. (2011). Innovation in India: Affordable innovations, in S. Dutta (ed.), *The Global Innovation Index 2011: Accelerating Growth and Development,* France, Fontainebleau: INSEAD, pp. 77–86.

Strauss, A. & Corbin, J. (2007). *Basics of Qualitative Research: Techniques and Procedures for Developing Grounded Theory*. Newbury: Sage Publications.

Sundbo, J. (1998). *The Theory of Innovation: Enterpreneurs, Technology and Strategy.* Cheltenham, UK: Edward Elgar Publishers.

Van Maanen, J. (1979). Reclaiming Qualitative Methods for Organizational Research: A Preface, *Administrative Science Quarterly*, 24(4), pp. 520–526.

WHO (2012). *Medicines: Spurious/Falsely-Labelled/Falsified/Counterfeit (SFFC) Medicines (M. centre, Trans.).* Geneva, Switzerland: World Health Organization.

Yin, R. K. (1983). *Case Study Research: Design and Method.* Newbury Park: Sage.

Zeschky, M., Widenmayer, B., & Gassmann, O. (2011). Frugal Innovation in Emerging Markets, *Research-Technology Management*, 54(4), pp. 38–45.

4

Social Impact Measurement for Social Enterprise

Tzu Yang Chang
Fu Jen Catholic University

Gautam Kamath
Fu Jen Catholic University

Chien Hsien Lee
Fu Jen Catholic University

1. Introduction

1.1. *Breaking the walls between non-profit sector and commercial businesses*

Measuring social impact is not a new necessity, and it has been a problem in the non-profit sector for as long as the non-profit sector has existed in an organized form. One of the most famous examples of this happening is Florence Nightingale's efforts in the Crimean War of 1853. She used pioneering statistical techniques (known as polar area charts) to demonstrate the dire need for better healthcare on battlefields. Every non-governmental organization (NGO) regardless of scale has to worry about how to draft their annual reports in a manner that helps put their performance in perspective, both for their current (and future) donors and for internal management purposes. Understanding social impact measurement therefore requires a holistic understanding of the purposes of measurement, the nature of the NGO under scrutiny, the type of inputs and outcomes that occur and the performance metrics of both the NGO and the donor.

Some of the problems that NGOs face with regards to impact measurement have been solved to some degree by big donors (international organizations like the World Bank, or institutions like the Bill and Melinda Gates Foundation) and their well-intentioned efforts to universalize impact measurements (using set frameworks, methods and clearly defining rules and principles). Understanding the purpose of impact measurement is therefore the first logical step toward examining the tools used by any stakeholder to conduct impact assessments. The World Bank, for one, uses a myriad of impact assessment tools and frameworks to support its projects. Many influential academics, politicians, economists and other intellectuals have long decried these methods for their many limitations, with accusations ranging from disproportionate allocation of resources for measurement, to perpetuating the dependence of NGOs in the developing world on development consultants to help with impact measurement.[1] These accusations are interesting in that they set the stage for perhaps the most important challenge of impact measurement (whether conducted by NGOs, international organizations or big donors): that "one-size can never fit all."

Brunner (2004) points out that these contradictions arose when in late 2002, the World Bank introduced a program on New Bank Practices in Civic Engagement, Empowerment, and Respect for Diversity (CEERD) to help coordinate and integrate the work of existing technical units and bring "human factors" in impact assessment to the foreground of the Bank's M&E techniques. This policy shift has brought "conceptual models" that claim to include the significant ambiguities of human factors (trust between local communities, trust between communities and development practitioners, corruption of local institutions, etc.) through participatory methods, surveys and consultations (the result of which was the formal adoption of the Poverty and Social Impact Analysis — the PSIA). What these conceptual models do not define is the relativity of context, and is therefore useful only as frameworks for guidance, rather than to make a concrete comparison between assessments.

To illustrate this point, say the World Bank wanted to see whether two similar projects (for the sake of argument, waste-management programs in Mazar e-Sharif and Tbilisi) were successfully implemented, they will have two different sets of metrics to measure and evaluate the impact these

---

[1] Perhaps, the most scathing critique of the World Bank's policies came from Nobel Laureate Muhammad Yunus, who argued in his book "Banker to the Poor" that among other things, the World Bank should move its headquarters to Dhaka to get in touch with "real poverty".

projects had. This is fine, because the criticism that development is not merely a technical field is valid, and in much of the World Bank's work, context is of the essence. However, there is also reason to believe why such a shift might prove to be slightly problematic, not for the recipients of aid, but internally for the Bank — for the purposes of making comparisons and learning from past mistakes.

Social impact measurement, by definition, cannot be universal, because we live in societies that are very different from one another. The impact from monetary aid itself cannot be accurately measured in universal terms due to currency and purchasing power (US$1 in Europe is a very different amount from US$1 in Sub-Saharan Africa). Furthermore, social impact by nature is very ambiguous and almost always eludes quantitative measurement, even when the change witnessed is concrete. To illustrate this point, let us take an example — how do you measure the social impact of providing jobs to an ex-convict? We could start by looking at the money that the State would save in welfare spending, but it is doubtful that we could accurately measure the happiness of the ex-con's family, or the increase in economic opportunity of the ex-con's offspring. The question to ask is, is there a need to even try and measure social impact in a "one-size-fits-all" manner from the perspective of non-profits?

The answer, based on the criticism leveled against international donors like the World Bank, was a resounding no. Local problems are different in different countries, and it makes no sense to create the same criteria for reporting social impact, especially when there are no monetary pressures to do so. Donor–NGO relationships are built in good faith, and it is not uncommon for big donors to fly in consultants armed with extensive tools and methodologies to conduct impact assessments based on a common set of guiding principles in line with the donor's objectives. Based on this dynamic, even the smallest NGO attempts to create some sort of performance measurement within their means to be included in reports to donors — using interviews, surveys, photo-essays and statistics, each of which are unique in their approach and which thrive on their ability to persuade. However, the very fact that the non-profit sector has exploded in the past few years makes the need for measuring social impact in an objective and comparative fashion all the more relevant.

The explosion of non-profits has also seen a consequent rush in the field of "strategic philanthropy," with private individuals, institutions, foundations and networks of philanthropists increasingly becoming more selective with their "impact-driven investments." Impact investment can be defined as *private equity, debt and/or real estate investments that generate financial returns as well as measurable social and/or environmental returns beyond comparable industry standard investments* (Olsen & Galimadi, 2008, p. 10). This rather rigid definition aptly captures the spirit of competition that has gripped the world of non-profits in recent times. While this activity is good, the infusion of private wealth has also brought with it a corporate drive for results — the ability to compare and validate anecdotal claims has become thorough and mandatory, rather than merely perfunctory window-dressing.

This shift between traditional donor–NGO contexts has also meant a surge in popularity in social enterprises. The influx of capital has brought radical changes in the organizational structures of non-profits, to the point of transformation into social enterprises. Allen Grossman, a Harvard Business School professor predicted this paradigm shift 10 years ago, when he observed that "the absolute amount of capital, the stages at which it is available during organizational development, and the conditions of its acquisition that all work together to create a powerful influence on management behavior and organizational culture. It is imperative that the world of non-profit philanthropy undergoes systemic changes."[2]

Finally, this chapter will also attempt to make a clear distinction between the types of tools available to social enterprises to measure social impact, especially those that prefer to assign "economic values" to social impact ("quantitative tools") with those that merely try to capture the social impact as accurately as possible ("qualitative tools"). This distinction is important, because in order to lay the foundation for a universal framework of analyzing social impact, these two types of methodologies must be reconciled and act complementarily to one another, rather than the current trend of negating each other's value.

1.2. *What is social impact measurement?*

Social impact measurement has its roots in a concept called Social Impact Assessment (SIA) devised in the 1970s by international organizations (like the UN and World Bank) to the end of "analyzing, monitoring and managing the intended and unintended social consequences, both positive and negative, of planned interventions (policies, programs, plans, projects) and

---

[2]Grossman, A. (2000). Getting it done: Improving non-profit performance. *Working Knowledge: A Report on Research at Harvard Business School*, Vol. IV, No. II. URL: http://hbswk.hbs.edu/item/1692.html.

any social change processes invoked by those interventions. Its primary purpose is to bring about a more sustainable and equitable biophysical and human environment."[3] The key idea behind SIA is to measure, both qualitatively and quantitatively, the impact that socially beneficial interventions have on the communities that are affected by such change.

Today, the activity of measuring social impact lies in the ambit of four different types of stakeholders: (1) governments, (2) international organizations, (3) philanthropists and (4) social enterprises. Understandably, the methods used by these different stakeholders are also very different from another in both their forms and objectives. For example, governments disbursing development aid to NGOs have fewer incentives to measure social impact in monetary terms, as compared to a philanthropist with the title of a "strategic social investor." Furthermore, international organizations will be much more concerned with the "Monitoring and Evaluation" aspect, rather than trying to measure whether a certain model of operation is disruptive and can be replicated. Therefore, the definition of social impact will vary based on the stakeholders' requirements and resources.

For the purposes of this chapter, we will focus on two out of the four different perspectives and use the definition favored by "strategic social investors" and social enterprises alike. Social impact is essentially a cost-benefit formulation rooted in traditional cost-benefit analyses, with a slight twist, namely that the benefits accrued are measured, not always in monetary terms, but in the benefits to the communities affected and society as a whole. However, the main obstacle facing practitioners today is the question "how," rather than the question "what." Everybody agrees on a social cost-benefit analogy; however, the question (that this research attempts to answer) is "how can we measure something as abstract as social impact."

2. Literature Review

2.1. *Defining social impact*

The first step toward understanding the tools available for social impact measurement is to provide a definition of social impact that works. Surprisingly, this is one of the biggest challenges of social impact measurement due to the ambiguities surrounding social impact. Let us

---

[3]Becker, H. & Vanclay, F. (eds.) (2003). *The International Handbook of Social Impact Assessment: Conceptual and Methodological Advances*, Cheltenham, UK: Edward Elgar, p. 29.

return to the ex-convict example, organization X helps provides jobs to ex-convicts by lobbying with employers and providing counseling services to the recipients of their services. Now when we speak of social impact of the organization, there are essentially three different dimensions to what we mean: (1) the business model of the organization itself — whether it is innovative enough, whether it is sustainable and whether it can be replicated by other organizations in other parts of the country; (2) the monetary impact of the organization — whether it has contributed by raising incomes for ex-convicts, whether it has contributed to the GDP growth of the country by reducing unemployment; and (3) the social welfare impacts of the organization — whether the ex-convicts themselves are happier, whether their families are better looked after, and whether their children have brighter futures as a result of their work.

In other words, social impact itself is tricky because these three dimensions are often mixed up and not properly understood. Essentially, there are three different levels where impacts occur, the individual, the community and on a universal scale when the business model has been successfully replicated elsewhere.

Measuring each of these different levels of impact creates several ambiguities and challenges on an organizational level. To be clear, this research uses a very specific definition of impact — "the total portion of the outcome that happened as a result of the activities conducted by the enterprise, above and beyond what would have happened anyway." In social science, this can be proven through a counterfactual (a control experiment, designed to remove the variables). The problem is with social impact, this can prove to be costly, and can never be proven with certainty (as in psychology, for example), which is what causes most of the confusion — the epistemological fallacy. Measuring social impact is therefore wrecked with philosophical traps, alongside the practical nuisance of conducting accurate impact assessments.

2.2. *General problems when defining social impact*

The first major problem of ambiguity arises when one tries to differentiate and compare the three levels of impact described above. Using our ex-convict analogy to illustrate this problem, we want to know the individual impact of hiring an ex-convict. This might seem straightforward, but measurement might not take into account many different factors that are essential to get an accurate assessment of impact. From the above model, for example, hiring ex-convicts with families would have a greater social impact on an individual level than ex-convicts who are single, and prone to relapsing into criminal activities. However, on the community level, the impact of hiring a "single ex-convict who is prone to relapse" (assuming that single convicts are more prone to relapse) is higher; as his rehabilitation is beneficial to the community he lives in.

This brings us to the next problem of comparison — how do we judge whether one form of social impact is of greater significance than the other? This is an essentially philosophical question, with arguments that will come from the Novak's individual liberty, Mills' individualism to the Utilitarian approach favored by Bentham. Without embarking on a philosophical tangent, the key point here to make is the difficulty in quantifying social impact. Measuring social impact is difficult because what we are trying to *measure* is beyond the scope of *quantitative* and *objective measurement*.

This brings us to the third big problem of defining social impact — the lack of universality and the use of different forms of "proxies" or shadow values. One example illustrating this is how the Dutch government measures "poverty" within its borders. The poverty threshold is defined as 60% of the median, standardized income by the Central Bureau of Statistics (CBS). This means that people below the per capita annual income of US\$24,577 are considered in "poverty" (as the median income is US\$40,961 in 2008). Essentially, the problem here is in using benchmarks — only 30 countries pass the Dutch poverty mark in terms of their median incomes. This benchmark is very different from the UN Benchmark of US\$1 a day (or US\$365 a year), which would put no poor people at all in most of the Northern Hemisphere (hence, the concept of "relative poverty"). Using the correct benchmarks to define social impact is therefore one of the biggest hurdles of establishing common proxies applicable in different geographies and across different program areas. However, there have been encouraging steps being taken to overcome this last hurdle, in terms of creating databases of proxies that could be used to quantify social impact in a variety of different situations, as well as re-evaluating the role that SIA can play in making investment decisions. We will examine these steps in Sec. 3.3.

The last problem with impact measurement has to do with defining social impact itself. Traditional NGO–donor contexts allowed for impact measurement to take place on a limited scale, with the *results* of many activities being published in annual reports. However, the overall methodology used to conduct these activities, or the "innovativeness" of the operating model was never taken into account. This was fine, because traditionally impact measurement was reserved for the purpose of measuring results — how much of the aid donated has gone toward helping those people that the aid was meant for. However, the rise of social enterprises has put an additional dimension to impact measurement that has not only changed the way we look at social impact but also increased the scope of the potential impact that an organization could have. The key difference between an NGO and a social enterprise lies in the operational model — in an NGO, the aid donated would only benefit the entitled recipients, with sustainability and innovation always remaining an afterthought, an additional bonus if achieved. On the other hand, social enterprises have brought innovativeness and sustainability to the core of their activities. The success of a social enterprise is measured, not only in the limited short-term impacts its activities are having but also on its ability to cause disruptive change in their areas, and their ability to replicate their successes elsewhere.

This broadening of scope of what social impact can mean has also brought additional challenges to the measurement of social impact. Some organizations like Ashoka put these additional dimensions at the core of their social impact measurement methodology by conducting both self-assessment surveys and objectively measuring these dimensions through their own consultants periodically. Ashoka focuses its "Design" element in measuring social impact through asking a series of questions to try and determine whether the idea is sustainable, replicable, and has caused disruptive policy change on the government level.

2.3. *Defining the methodology for measurement*

Measuring qualitatively requires a clear methodology, and as with most social measurement techniques, the logical structure of measurement forms the backbone of any tool. One thing that each of the examined social impact measurement tools had in common was this methodology of measurement — each and every tool focused on sorting out what we are trying to measure, and laying out the logical structure of measurement, before going about the task of measurement itself.

2.4. *Choosing the right tools for measurement*

The next question that any social enterprise looking to conduct thorough impact assessments must ask deals with the tools that could be used to aid their assessment. Many factors would contribute to making such a decision, especially, the amount of resources required to utilize a certain tool, the effectiveness of the tool itself in generating the outcomes desired, and the key objectives of donors, investors and other stakeholders behind conducting the assessment. To illustrate these factors, let us come back to the earlier example of the social enterprise that aids ex-convicts find jobs: the first question to ask would then be — how big is this social enterprise? Are there enough consultants on payroll to be able to conduct an exhaustive assessment? The second question to ask would be "which assessment tool would be most appropriate to illustrate the impact that this social enterprise is aiming to achieve?" and lastly, "what kinds of effects are expected from conducting such an assessment?"

These questions are important, because, if the organization is trying to attract funding from, say, a network of wealthy business-minded philanthropists, the tools that would be most appropriate would involve quantitative measures, and extensive demonstrations of impact (for example, like Social Return on Investment (SROI)). However, if a more qualitative assessment is desired (for example, for mass-fundraising purposes), another simpler tool (e.g., the "Quality First" tool) could be utilized using a lot fewer resources. In Sec. 3, most of the tools selected have been analyzed against such a list of criteria that will help organizations looking to answer the critical question — "which tool should I use?"

This question has become even more difficult to answer given the proliferation of different tools in recent years that serve very specialized types of social enterprises, but could be misused by other types of social enterprises that it has not been designed for. Of course, the opposite has also happened on occasion, most famously, when REDF (formerly, The Robert Enterprise Development Fund) devised the SROI model to aid precisely the same type of organization that I have used above as an example. However, the vast repository of tools available to social enterprises today has (aside from their obvious benefits) served to confuse potential investors and the enterprise practitioners themselves. During the course of my research, I examined no fewer than 27 different types of tools, illustrating the demand, as well as enthusiasm for the development of such frameworks.

The problem also lies in the trade-off between focusing on quantitative metrics while leaving out the big-picture narrative and making decisions based on numbers that do not adequately reflect the totality of impact, given the pressure on social enterprises to attract investment from donors and foundation. As Susan Stout, recently retired Manager of the World Bank's Results Secretariat cautioned: — "There is incredible 'silver bulletism' around in the donor (and perhaps foundation) worlds — seeking that 'one special number' that will tell us if we are succeeding or failing. This is driven by bureaucratic fantasy, not reality. The chances that we could come up with a metric that avoids an inevitably subjective process of judgment and choice are infinitely small (else, politics would be a much simpler and boring topic). It's usually driven by a desire to define a bottom line that will do for philanthropy and public sector management what profit/loss statements do for the private sector. It's just not going to happen that way."[4]

3. Research Method

3.1. *Analyzing different tools of measurement*

Throughout this research, we have emphasized the need to separate the different types of tools used for social impact measurement. In this research, we use four different criteria to make this distinction — tools that are fundamentally different in the following four ways:

(1) *Qualitative tools*: These tools express social impact as qualitative data, often through models tracking their social value creation expressed as narrative. These tools serve the purpose of trying to comprehensively *describe* social impact, without falling in the trap of relying solely on numbers — and in doing so are able to appeal to a much larger audience. However, the drawbacks lie in the qualitative nature of assessment, often done within the organization, and do not reflect the needs of strategic investors looking for some quantitative basis of comparison. Examples of this can range from simple narratives in annual reports to more concrete frameworks like the Big Picture.

(2) *Quantitative tools*: These tools express social impact using numbers — shadow values of the level of impact created expressed solely in terms of monetary or economic impact. The purpose here is to provide a basis of comparison (either *within* project areas or *across* project areas, depending on the tool) and give the strategic investor a monetary

---

[4]Stout, Susan. Re: Perspectives on Cost-Benefit Analysis and Cost-Effectiveness Analysis in Global Health, e-mail communication to Philip Setel, April 2008. Quoted in Tuan, M. (2009). *Measuring and/or Estimating Social Value Creation: Insights Into Eight Integrated Cost Approaches*, Bill and Melinda Gates Foundation.

sense of the impact being created. The drawback here is over-reliance on these numbers in the decision-making process (much like a traditional cost-benefit analysis), as well as not being able to accurately capture the nature of impact by excluding more abstract elements from the analysis. One last consideration is the amount of data required to conduct any one of the quantitative analyses mentioned in this research — most methods require the collection of extensive data, as well as the training and capability to analyze this data, something smaller social enterprises might not be able to provide. Examples of this method include the SROI and the LM3 (Local Multiplier).

(3) **Design**: The third category refers to social impact measurement tools that focus on the business model of the social enterprise — the "design," including factors such as whether a business model is innovative, replicable, scalable and sustainable in the long-run. These factors are important, yet largely excluded from most of the tools examined in this analysis. One of the most notable practitioners in the field — Ashoka has pioneered the use of these tools as a central element to both their selection and monitoring process. Another local organization that uses these tools is Flow, Inc.

(4) **Internal tools**: The final category of social impact measurement tools belongs to those tools that exclusively focus on the internal dynamics of the business in order to achieve social impact. This category includes a wide range of organizations, from for-profit business that use "green" technologies and conduct corporate social responsibility (CSR) activities, to social enterprises measuring their carbon footprint. These tools look at the "design" of the operational model from an internal perspective (rather than an external one) and try to measure how a company's activities within the organization contribute to social impact, just as a performance measurement tool would do for a traditional business. While no tools have been found that focus exclusively on internal process (that would be myopic and useless, considering social impact is an external outcome), some tools seem to focus on this aspect more than others, including the Social Balanced Scorecard approach and the Third Sector Performance Dashboard.

3.2. *Qualitative tools*

Several qualitative tools were examined for this analysis, including the World Bank's PSIA, the Big Picture developed by the Scottish Council for

Volunteers, the EFQM Excellence model,[5] the Global Reporting Initiative Guidelines,[6] Prove It! developed by the New Economics Foundation (nef) and the Social Impact Measurement for Local Economies (SIMPLE). According to the criteria discussed above, two different qualitative tools will be examined in greater depth in this research — the Big Picture and the World Bank's PSIA.

3.3. *Quantitative tools*

Several quantitative tools were examined during this research, including the Social Accounting Framework, the RobinHood Foundation's Cost-Benefit Ratio, Center for High Impact Philanthropy's (CHIP) Cost per Impact ratio and the SROI framework. In essence, all the methods examined had a simple concept at the core — trying to measure the expected social return on any investment/project based on the impact and outcomes. Paul Brest, President of the William and Flora Hewlett Foundation puts a simple equation at the heart of all quantitative methodologies, namely[7]:

$$\text{Expected Return} = \frac{(\text{Outcome or Benefit} \times \text{Probability of Success})}{\text{Cost}}.$$

As a simple rule of thumb, the above simplification of all the integrated cost methodologies is helpful, as they were drawn from traditional cost-benefit methods. However, the differences exist when each of these methods try to answer more complex questions, such as how the benefits are quantified (e.g., randomized control experiments, outputs used as proxies for outcomes, timeframes, etc.), how costs are calculated (e.g., cost of grants and administration, cost of total program, etc.), how uncertainties and partial attribution of results accounted for? (e.g., probability of success, philanthropic contribution, interdependencies, etc.), and how the outcomes are translated into units (or monetized, either using proxy values, discount rates, etc.).

---

[5]Developed by the European Foundation for Quality Management. For more information, please refer http://www.efqm.org/en/Home/aboutEFQM/Ourmodels/TheEFQMExcellenceModel/tabid/170/Default.aspx.

[6]For more information, please refer http://www.globalreporting.org/Home.

[7]Tuan, M. (2009). *Measuring and/or Estimating Social Value Creation: Insights Into Eight Integrated Cost Approaches*, Bill and Melinda Gates Foundation, p. 13.

3.4. *Internal tools — measuring process*

Many impact measurement tools focus on the organizational processes in a social enterprise to investigate whether resources are being allocated efficiently, and to aid in making both strategic and management decisions. Often, activities of a social enterprise are so intertwined with the processes of the organization, that such impact measurement is necessary to get an accurate picture of social impact. Take the case of a social enterprise employing disabled people (say the "Children-Are-Us" foundation in Taipei[8]) — in order for them to have the biggest impact, processes within the firm must be placed under firm scrutiny, given that the employees are also beneficiaries of the impact. Given that such organizations are not uncommon, choosing the right internal tools might be critical to impact measurement success.

3.5. *Design tools*

Looking for social impact tools that included measuring the effectiveness of the business model in play remained the biggest challenge of this research. While social enterprises have long been distinguished from non-profits due to their ingenious business models, no tools have been developed to empirically measure the impact of their innovation. This is not surprising, given that innovation itself is always difficult to measure. However, this researcher believes that certain critical elements of a business model can be deconstructed and qualitatively assessed — this already happens implicitly and regularly with regards to socially responsible venture capital.

4. Conclusion

In this research, we have investigated four different types of social impact measurement tools — qualitative (causality), quantitative (proxies), internal (performance measurement), and design (business-model). These different tools reflect the different objectives of social impact measurement, and must be selected according to organizational needs where appropriate. However, to gain a holistic perspective, elements of all four types must be present in any analysis, and reaching such a conclusion should be the goal

---

[8]For more information on Children-Are-Us, please visit http://www.c-are-us.org.tw/style/front001/bexfront.php?sid=1409832325.

of efforts to harmonize social impact measurement. The approach should be of consensus building among the different types of stakeholders (social enterprises and non-profits, international organizations, funders, foundations, and strategic philanthropy investors) to decide which elements of the "holistic approach" should be used, including as many different types of social enterprises and NGOs as possible. Social impact measurement is a continuously evolving field, and a principles-based approach that accommodates all four elements described above should be the vision, rather than selecting one tool over others. Doing this is extremely necessary if social accounting and audit is to become a mainstream profession, and if social enterprises are to attract private capital markets.

References

Brunner, R. D. (2004). Context-Sensitive Monitoring and Evaluation for the World Bank, *Policy Sciences*, 37(2), pp. 103–136.

Grossman, A. (2000). Getting it done: Improving non-profit performance, *Working Knowledge: A Report on Research at Harvard Business School* 4-2. Retrieved from http://hbswk.hbs.edu/item/1692.html.

Olsen, S. & Galimidi, B. (2008). *Catalog of Approaches to Impact Measurement — Assessing Social Impact in Private Ventures*. San Francisco: Social Venture Technology Group, May.

Tuan, M. (2009). Measuring and/or estimating social value creation: Insights into eight integrated cost approaches, *Bill and Melinda Gates Foundation*. Retrieved from http://cmapspublic.ihmc.us/rid=1LHK87JH8-F72NL0-2R6P/WWL-report-measuring-estimating-social-value-creation%5B1%5D.pdf.

5

Reliability Bookkeeping
for Non-Financial Transactions
of the Social Network Organization

Yasuhiro Monden

University of Tsukuba

1. Purpose of This Chapter

There are many "non-financial" or non-monetary transactions, negotiations, and activities in the business as well as in the general personal relationships. Within the inter-personal and inter-firm's relations, there are quite a few commitments or promises between the consigner and the consignee on non-monetary matters. The consigner and the consignee are similar to the creditor and the debtor for the financial matters, respectively. If fulfillment of the commitment is facilitated and emphasized, then it follows that the long-term reliability relationship between persons will be built and the unity (or ties) between persons could be strengthened. The default-free commitment of non-monetary matters between persons will be the absolute premises for fulfillment of "monetary" debt and credit, too.

The author developed such system of assuring the human commitment and coined it as the "Reliability bookkeeping" of "Non-monetary bookkeeping," which will also be called "R-bookkeeping" as an abbreviated term, whereas the traditional bookkeeping is called "monetary bookkeeping and abbreviated as "M-bookkeeping" in this chapter.

The novelties of the reliability bookkeeping can be seen in its extension of the traditional concepts of "debtor" (or Dr.) and "creditor" (or Cr.) and the traditional mechanism of double-entry bookkeeping to the non-monetary commitment between persons.

The reliability bookkeeping will use the e-mailing system for the inter-personal or inter-firm's non-monetary transactions, by classifying the

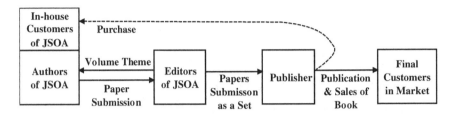

Fig. 1.   Fabless and store-less network of JSOA

recorded data into debtor and creditor and further rearrange them for preparing the useful reports.

In this chapter, the author will explain the system of the R-bookkeeping by using the case of a network organization or supply-chain related to the publication business of the not-for-profit academic society called Japan Society of Organization & Accounting (JSOA),[1] as illustrated in Fig. 1. Such R-bookkeeping could also be applied to the profit-making corporations.

The meaning of the social network in the title of this chapter will first be explained in Fig. 1. It consists of both of the reliability relation between authors and editor and the same relation between academic organization (JSOA) and publisher. The former is inter-personal relation and the latter is inter-firm relation. The latter relation will be formed through the legal contract on the publication business to be signed by two parties. This is a legal alliance relation. The R-bookkeeping could reinforce each of the reliability relations.

Actually, there exist many companies that are the "fabless" or "store-less" network organizations. For example, Apple who produces and sells the smartphone and tablet is specialized in only the product development and

---

[1]The name of the non-profit organization (NPO), we deal with in this chapter is the JSOA, which annually publishes the book series whose series title is the *Japanese Management and International Studies* (JMIS). Focusing on Japan and Japan-related issues, the series is designed to inform the world about research outcomes of the new "Japanese-style management system" developed in Japan. However, as the series title suggests, it also promotes *"International Studies"* on the interface of managerial competencies between Japan and other countries that include Asian countries as well as Western countries under the globalized business activities of Japanese companies. For details of JSOA and JMIS, please see the home page: http://jsoa.sakura.ne.jp/english/index.html.

design functions and consigns the manufacturing function to the consignee called EMS, which is Taiwanese company called Hon-Hi (having its plant in China). Sony and Sharp also use the similar business model nowadays. Store-less business model is widely used by the automobile companies, for example, who use the sales dealership companies as the individual auto-maker's franchise chain stores.

Therefore, the R-bookkeeping that assumes the case of Fig. 1 in this chapter could be applied in many other profit-oriented companies.

2. Mechanical Similarity between Double-Entry Bookkeeping and E-Mailing System

R-bookkeeping has a similar mechanism as the traditional double-entry bookkeeping as follows (see Fig. 2):

(1) The e-mailing system has the double entries of each transaction into the receiving tray or the sending tray as the journal entries of the traditional bookkeeping.

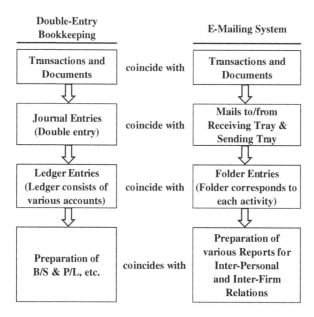

Fig. 2. Corresponding relationship between the double-entry bookkeeping and the mail systems

Behind each transaction of traditional bookkeeping, there exist the personal names of the debtor and creditor as well as item name (called the account title) as will be shown in detail in Sec. 3. On the other hand, behind each mails of e-mailing system, there are the personal names of debtor and creditor and the item title. In other words, in the e-mail system, when some sender (somebody other than me) of the mail asked a request to the recipient (me), I will reply if the request can be accepted (approved) or not. Conversely, when I asked a request to somebody else, the recipient will respond me if my request is acceptable or not. In this way, the e-mail correspondence accompanies the double entry of pair of mails.

(2) The data put into both the traditional bookkeeping and the e-mail systems are coming in according to the chronological order just as we put records on the personal diary on a daily basis.

(3) Each "account" in the ledger book of double-entry bookkeeping is corresponding to each "folder" of the item title of the activity item in the e-mail system. Both of them are items re-filed or classified according to the item name recorded in step (1).

(4) By using various accounts of the double-entry bookkeeping, the financial statements can be prepared. Correspondingly, by using various item folders of e-mail system, the various reports of human contracting relations could be prepared.[2]

3. Concepts of Debtor and Creditor in the Traditional Double-Entry Bookkeeping

According to the history of the traditional double-entry bookkeeping, the debt and credit relations between people have been identified and recorded by the personal names of debtor and creditor, respectively, as the memorandum notes of their commercial transactions. That was at the beginning of bookkeeping.[3]

It began with the "**personal name account**" that records the personal names of debtors (i.e., customers) for the amount of the merchandize sold on

---

[2]Other than the reports of R-bookkeeping for reliability accounting, the e-mail system using its folders can prepare the reports for environmental affairs and the reports of corporate social responsibility (CSR) affairs, etc.

[3]For the historical understanding of Dr. and Cr. of various accounts, the writer is indebted to Kojima (1964) and (1977).

Accounts Receivable a/c	Accounts Payable a/c
List of Debtors **(List of Customers)**	**List of Creditors (List of** **Merchandize Suppliers)**
Mr. ABC $ xxx	Supplier A (Mr. A) $ yyy
Mr. BCD $ xx	Supplier B (Mr. B) $ yy
Ms. CDF $ xxxx	Supplier C (Mr. C) $ yyy
Ms. EFG $ x	

Fig. 3. Accounts receivable a/c showing list of the customers' names, and accounts payable a/c showing list of the suppliers' names

Cash a/c controlled by Cash Custodian (Cashier) X	Short-term Debt a/c lent by Mr. Y
(Debtor **is the cashier X)**	**(Creditor is** **the money-lender Y)**
Cashier X received **Money ($10,000)**	**Short-term Debt** **$10,000 lent by** **the money-lender Y**

Fig. 4. Cash a/c controlled by the cashier X, and short-term debt a/c lent by creditor Mr. Y

credit, or the personal names of the creditors (i.e., suppliers of merchandize) for the amount of the merchandize purchased on credit. This was the origin of the account receivable or the account payable, and also the origin of the debtor (Dr.) and creditor (Cr.) of the double-entry bookkeeping (see Fig. 3).

Such concepts of debtor and creditor have also been applied to the **"matter and material" accounts** such as cash account and merchandize account, by assuming the custodian of cash (cashier) or the store-keeper of merchandize who were assigned by the manager (in charge of the book-keeping) of the business separated from the investors (see Fig. 4).

The debtor and creditor concepts were also expanded and applied to the **"nominal accounts"** such as the expense and revenue accounts, regarding them as additions to the debt (i.e., expense) or to the credit (i.e., revenue) of the investor (proprietor) in question. These records were done on the investor account.

Until 15th century, the forms of commerce and trade have been the so-called "Adventure" one or "Temporary" one finished for each journey or trade. They collected funds from many investors before the trade and allocated the earnings and repaid the principal amount of investment to each investor after the trade. Such accounting method is called "Partierechnung" (income calculation for each trade). The gross margin on sales was calculated after selling all of the merchandize inventories on each merchandize account, and considered as the debt of merchandize account (i.e., merchandize store-keeper) and thus transferred to the creditor side (revenue) of the investor account (see Fig. 5).

The above concepts of debtor and creditor can also be applied in the reliability bookkeeping. How the traditional debtor and creditor concepts could be used in the reliability bookkeeping will be explained in Sec. 4.[4]

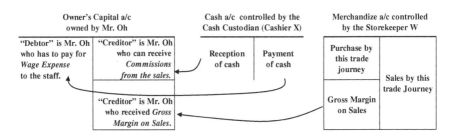

Fig. 5.   Owner's capital a/c of the investor for revenue and expenses

---

[4]The concepts of non-financial debt and credit were first found by Asanuma (1984) in the network of assembly maker and parts supplier of the Japanese automobile industry, and then such debt and credit relations of auto industry were elaborately studied by Kimura (2008), though they did not develop the system of the R-bookkeeping.

According to Asanuma, the amounts of cost reduction (called "surplus") achieved by the parts makers through their continuous improvements in the manufacturing phase and their value-engineering activities in the product development phase are recognized between the assembler and the parts supplier as the "*long-term relations of debt and credit*" between them from the incentive viewpoint to the parts suppliers. Asanuma says as follows: "The surplus created by the above

4. Debt and Credit (or Debtor and Creditor) in E-Mail System

4.1. *Building the reliability relationship based on the information communication*

Reliability among people in the organization will stand for mutual well-understanding. For attaining the ultimate goal or mission of the organization, such reliability among people could be gained if each member of the network is familiar with the contents of the task, its goal level, and the limit-time to achieve the task. Because, when such task requirements are clearly grasped among people, all of them can have "predictability" of the resulting outcomes of their colleagues or comrades. If the "predicted" contents of the task are assured by the commitment recognized by e-mail system, they will be able to rely on the future behaviors of the colleagues.

When this reliability principle is applied to the mutual relationships between the editor and the individual authors of a certain volume of the book series to be published by JSOA, (1) the editor can be responsible for collecting all of the paper manuscripts from the authors with satisfying the requirements in terms of its quality and limit-date (deadline). At the same time, (2) each author also can be responsible for submitting his or her paper manuscript that fulfills the requirements given by the editor in terms of its quality and limit-date. In other words, both editor and authors can take their mutual responsibility (or promise or commitment).

In short, thanks to e-mail system, both editor and authors can obtain mutual recognition of their own responsibility or commitment for their tasks in regard to the targets. At the same time, they can control their proceeding grade periodically by using the e-mail system.

---

improvements may be (1) partly kept by the parts-maker, (2) totally retained by the parts-maker for six months or one year, or (3) totally absorbed by the automobile maker for the time being but evaluated in the sequence of regular price revisions, with high priority being subsequently given to the parts-maker in question over similar, competing, parts-makers." The readers can understand that the assembler keeps in mind the "*long-term relations of debt and credit*" with the parts-maker in the above third option.

4.2. *Debit and credit relationship between the consigner and the consignee under e-mail system*

The persons will begin their action based on the contact between the related persons about the specific activity. In the contract, there is an agreement on a certain matter between the consigner (i.e., client) and the consignee (i.e., trustee). The e-mail is also a kind of information exchange between the consigner and the consignee.

When a consignee was entrusted a certain activity matter and has promised to do this activity, then he or she who is a consignee will be obliged to achieve the activity in question (i.e., execution of the commitment). The e-mail in question will be evidence that he or she has the obligation or a kind of "debt." In other words, he or she will be a "debtor" on that matter. However, when the debtor achieved his or her obligation, then the debt will disappear just as the real monetary debt was paid back and written off.

On the other hand, if the consigner has trusted a certain activity matter, this consigner in question will be a kind of "creditor," who can claim the debtor to pay back the liability. However, when the debtor has achieved their obligation, the consigner's claim or credit will disappear just as his or her lending loan was paid back.

As these debt and credit relations will be evidences, the e-mails of either the accepted mail or the sent mail have the "name" and address of the receiver (consignee) and the sender (consigner) and the item title (i.e., activity matter).

5. Design of the Hierarchical Structure of "Item-Folders" in E-Mail System

For the purpose of building the R-bookkeeping system, most of the item folders in the e-mail system should be classified according to the various organizations, in which the mailing system owner is involved. Such various kinds of organizations correspond to various kinds of *activities* in which the e-mail system owner is involved. Therefore, we can prepare various kinds of reports on the current position and performance for each involved activity.

Thus in order to treat the activities of the network organization depicted in Fig. 1 for example, you had better make the folders of the participating members of your direct belonging organization (JSOA, for instance) and the allied organization (publisher, for instance) outside your own organization.

In case of JSOA, for example, in order to clarify the relations among editor, author, and publisher, it would be good to introduce the **big folder** called "*English book series*," the **middle folders** called "*Vol. #*" for each volume, and the **small folders** called "*Desk editor of Vol. #*" of the publisher and "*Author of Vol. #*" containing all the mails of each author in a hierarchical manner as shown in Fig. 6.

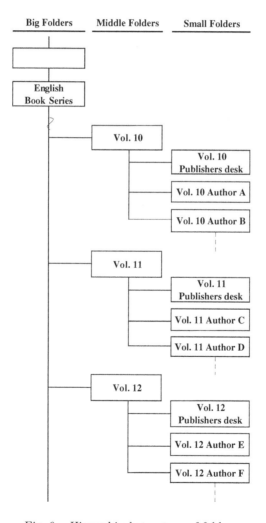

Fig. 6.   Hierarchical structure of folders

Then in each **folder of** *"Author of Vol. 12"* for example, there must be mails that imply:

(debtor : author) vs. (creditor : volume editor).

Also in each **folder of** *"Desk editor of Vol. 12"* **of the publisher,** there must be mails that imply:

(debtor : volume editor) vs.

(creditor : desk editor of the publisher).

6. Management of Three Processes for Building the Reliability Relations Among the Volume Editor, the Authors, and the Publisher for Each Volume

Although each one volume of our book series is published annually, it takes a lead-time of about two years and a half for each publication. During such long period of time, all of the authors, the volume editors, and the desk editor of the publisher must achieve each of their commitments so that the book could be published timely on the predetermined date each year.

Although there is no "financial" transaction (i.e., monetary receipt and disbursement based on the financial debt and credit) during this long period of time, there are important "non-financial" transactions that create the mental debt and credit (or mental commitment), and thus we have to assure such various commitments of each production process during the whole lead-time.

Such assurance will be enabled by the reliability bookkeeping that uses e-mail data. Let us take a look at how the whole process can be effectively treated. We will divide the whole process into three separate processes: namely, the up-stream process, the middle process, and the down-stream process.[5]

---

[5] Although it takes two years and a half as a total production lead-time for each volume, actually, the new volume will be published to the market every year one by one. Therefore, the series editor is always involved in three volumes that are in the up-stream, middle-stream, and down-stream processes at the same time. On the other hand, since the volume editor is in principle in charge of editing the specific volume only, this person will not have the jobs of three volumes at the same time.

6.1. *The R-bookkeeping and preparation of its reports in the up-stream process*

As in the case of manufacturing process of industrial goods, the up-stream process usually takes longer lead-time since its operations will not flow like water in the river since it hardly makes one-piece by one-piece production, but it is rather a kind of big lot-size or big-batch job. However, the series editor and the volume editors can complete their job in this phase as quickly as possible by using the e-mail system applied to the series and volume editors, the authors, and the publisher.

Although the ultimate goal in the up-stream process is to prepare the PROPOSAL to the publisher on the contents of upcoming volume to be published next, there are two steps here. The first step is for the series editor and the volume editor to decide the whole theme of the volume in question, and the second step is to collect the possible candidate authors.

Step (1) The first criteria that should be considered for establishing the theme of the book is that the book must pay in the market. In other words, the book should compensate for the costs and the fair profit of the publisher, because only the publisher has the final responsibility of taking the risk of such coverage. However, the book that should appeal to the market itself is not the only factor that the series and volume editors should consider. Because, even though the target market-oriented theme is good, it would be "a pie in the sky," unless there is enough number of authors who can write such topics. Thus, the editors should think of both "resources" (capability of the authors' candidates) and "attractiveness of the target market." The book theme must be determined by the end of March, each year.

Since preparation of the whole theme of the next volume is the core point of the PROPOSAL, it is similar to the preparation of the "product concept" in the development and design phases of industrial product. It must be the most important phase that requires market sense and innovative ideas.

Step (2) Just after the book theme was determined, the volume editor will send all members and related researchers the "Call for Paper" using the mailing list of JSOA and others to ask them submit the papers for the book theme.

Through this process, the volume editor must ask the candidates of contributors to submit the editorial committee of JSOA (1) author's name, (2) topic of the paper, and (3) abstract or outline of the paper by the end of May.

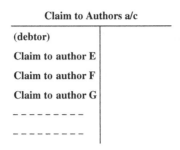

Fig. 7.   Summary of "Claim for Author" a/c

Then various replying mails come to the volume editors and the correspondence mails will be repeated between the editor and the possible authors. Such correspondences mails will be transferred to the small folders of the e-mail system depicted in Fig. 7. For example, confer the small folder "Vol. 12 author E" in the right side of Fig. 7.

Thus, finally the promise of paper submission and reception (but not yet "acceptance") will be made between the editor and the candidate contributors, and then the relationship of obligation and claim (or debt and credit) will be built between two parties. This is the similar relation as the *"personal name account"* in the traditional monetary bookkeeping, as explained in Sec. 3.

Thus, from each **folder of** *"Author of Vol. 12"* for example, the following summary of "ledger entry" will be made at this point in time:

The above ledger entries are done by the editor of JSOA who is in charge of publishing the book series. The editor is a creditor to the author and at the same time a debtor to the publisher.

Based on the above summary of the ledger entries, the PROPOSAL to the publisher will be prepared. The most important reports as an output of R-bookkeeping in this up-stream process would be the PROPOSAL document to be submitted to the publisher, which will be sent by the end of July (see Fig. 8). Actually, the PROPOSAL document usually has nearly 10 pages since the collected abstracts of all papers take bigger space. The contents of PROPOSAL will be gradually prepared by introducing the contents (author name, title, and abstract) of each e-mail folder of the author, into the folder of editor's personal computer.

This PROPOSAL will be transmitted via e-mail, which is also a kind of another "journal entry," and will be immediately transferred to the small

Japanese Management & International Studies Vol. 12

PROPOSAL (Summary)

Vol. 12: Book Title ------------------------------------

Volume Editors: Names, Titles & Affiliations

Obligation of Editors & Authors

    Due Date of Manuscripts Submission:

        September 30, 2014

Obligation of Publisher

    Due Date of Vol. 12 Publication:

        August 31, 2015

Research Theme of Vol. 12

Table of Contents of Vol. 12

Contributors obliged to write papers;

    Chapter 1: Author's name E,
    Paper title & Abstract
    Chapter 2: Author's name F,
    Paper title & Abstract
    Chapter 3: Author's name G,
    Paper title & Abstract

Fig. 8. Sample of the PROPOSAL to publisher (summary)

folder called "**Vol. 12, Publisher's desk**," for instance. This folder entry implies the following "ledger entry" of Fig. 9.

When the PROPOSAL was approved by the management of the publisher in the middle of July, then the publication agreement "contract" between the volume editors and the publisher's management will be immediately signed. At this time, the obligation of the editor to submit the whole manuscript as a set to the publisher will be formally determined, and the obligation of the authors to submit each paper manuscript to the editor will also be formally determined.

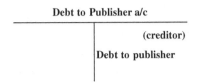

Fig. 9.   Debt to the publisher a/c

Reliability Balance Sheet
(at the end of the up-stream process)

(debtor)	(creditor)
Claim to author E	Debt to publisher
Claim to author F	(Obligation of submitting all manuscripts)
Claim to author G	
(*"Accounts payable"* in	
M-bookkeeping)	
- - - - - - - - - - - - -	
- - - - - - - - - - - - ·	
(Claim for each manuscript)	
(*"Accounts receivable"*	
In M-Bookkeeping)	

Fig. 10.   Reliability balance sheet in the up-stream process

Based on the ledger entries of Figs. 7 and 9 and the contract, the following "**Reliability Balance Sheet**" of R-bookkeeping will be prepared at the end of the up-stream process (see Fig. 10).

The detailed contents of the "Claim to each author" and the "Obligation of submitting all manuscripts" in the Reliability Balance Sheet are well written in the PROPOSAL. They consist of the author's name, the title of paper, and the abstract of paper, etc. Therefore, the PROPOSAL is essentially the final report to be prepared in the up-stream process.

Some readers may think that the claim to the author a/c is identical to the contents of the "Customers' Ledger" in the traditional bookkeeping that shows all customers names, to whom the merchandizes were sold on credit. However, the main difference between them lies in its timing. The "Customers' Ledger" of M-bookkeeping is prepared when the actual transfer of merchandizes happened through sales activities and the monetary amounts are already determined. But in the R-bookkeeping, the transfer of merchandize (paper manuscript) is not yet done and also the monetary amount is not yet determined and booked.[6]

---

[6]The R-bookkeeping, when viewed only from its utilization of the non-monetary measure, might be considered as a kind of the "multi-dimensional accounting"

6.2. *Reports of R-bookkeeping in the middle process*

After the contract is agreed and signed by both the volume editors and the publisher, the implementation of the commitments among the editor, the authors, and the publisher will be vitally important because fulfilling the promise (or commitment) is the core of keeping the reliability relationship. This process is the middle process of our publication business of JSOA.

The R-bookkeeping in this process consists of the following steps.

(1) From the volume editor to the authors: Urge the authors to prepare the manuscripts

The volume editor must urge the contributors to write the papers by the limit date. This urge process will be made three times during the coming year according to the writing schedule, which will be used as a guideline for the author to produce the paper in a smoothed or leveled manner during a year. It is composed of (a) the deadline of submitting the *draft paper* that will be followed by the first review and comments by the editors and reviewers, (b) the deadline of submitting the *revised paper* that will be followed by the second review and comments, and then (c) English translation of the final manuscript and its editing by the native professionals and the submission of final paper.

Further, during one year of this schedule, the author should present his or her paper in the academic workshops and conferences where they should take into account of the various comments and questions to revise the paper. This is another means of assuring the quality of papers.

(2) Final manuscript submission to the volume editor

When the authors provided the final English-written and edited manuscript to the volume editor, their obligation or debt in the debtor side of Figs. 7 and 10 will disappear. At the same time, the debt of the volume editor to the publisher in the creditor side of Figs. 9 and 10 will disappear when such final papers are submitted to the publisher.

The actual job of the volume editor at the time of author's submission is to save the files of completed full manuscript in the folder of the "*Vol. 12 Final manuscripts*" of the personal computer.

---

advocated by Ijiri (1966). However, the R-bookkeeping is not equivalent to his "triple-entry bookkeeping" proposed by Ijiri (1982), of which "triple-entry" is against the term of "double-entry" in the traditional double-entry bookkeeping.

(3) Mail communications from the publisher to the volume editor

(a) The publisher also presses the volume editor to steadily proceed with the production of manuscripts. For this request, the editor must submit the *report of proceeding rate.* (b) The publisher sends the *sales promotion questionnaire* to the editor about how the book in question could be sold, and the editor must send the reply.

6.3. *Reports of R-bookkeeping in the down-stream process*

The down-stream process in the publication business stands for the activities after the book was actually published by the publisher, and various monetary affairs will be communicated between the accountant of JSOA, the volume editor, and the authors. Thus, actually various monetary transactions and their recordings of M-bookkeeping must be done.

Although this chapter has been emphasizing the non-monetary aspects up to this point, the publication of the book series cannot continue unless the publication costs in the side of publisher are monetary covered in each volume. Thus, in this down-stream process, the R-bookkeeping will be connected to the conventional M-bookkeeping.

Now let us consider both the economic aspects that entail monetary transactions in the economic society and at the same time, the non-monetary aspects of the JSOA as NPO.

The author will release the paper by the annual book series of JSOA that has an aspect for the JSOA to sell the "service" of giving the authors the opportunity of publishing their research results. Authors are buying this service by paying the rate or price. This point is essentially identical to the trade of general merchandize in the market. Because, the authors are qualified to write paper to the book series so long as they are the formal members of JSOA by paying the "membership fee." In addition, they have to pay a kind of the paper "submission fee," just as like as the first class academic journals such as AAA (*American Accounting Association*) for example. (However, even though the author is not a formal member, they can submit paper if they pay the total amount of membership fee plus the submission fee at a time. Such procedure is also taken by AAA.)

From the above viewpoint, the authors are essentially the *customers* for the JSOA. The "service" provided by JSOA to the authors is not confined to providing the paper publication chance, but it entails the benefits of their promotion and job hunting. More essentially, the service will give the opportunity for the authors to contribute to the people in the real world, which is also the *raison d'etre* or mission of JSOA. Such mission or purpose is also the same one that any goods and services of the businesses in the world have.

On the other hand, the author is a *provider* of the contents of paper contained in the volume of the book series, and thus they are performing the function of a supplier of labor service. Therefore, they are the "volunteers" who receive no salary or wage. Likewise, all directors and the president and vice presidents are also "volunteers" who receive no monetary reward for their service given to JSOA, which is NPO.

However, the publisher as a core-allied firm of JSOA is a profit-oriented enterprise, which cannot survive unless it can earn profit in the market competition. Since the employees of the publisher are all salaried people, their labor costs must be paid. Further, even though the printing job is ordered to the subsidiary printing firm, its costs of the printing machine and workers must be compensated by the charge on the publisher. In addition to these costs, the publisher has to get some fair profit. This does not mean that the corporate-wide expenses and corporate profit must be covered by the book series of JSOA, but only the direct costs, the allocated indirect costs, and the fair profit attributable to the book series project of JSOA should be partially covered.[7] The efforts that the publisher will make to compensate for their costs, etc. may be regarded as a kind of venture capital injection to the JSOA, but this is the most critical point that JSOA should develop their own business model.

6.4. *Risk sharing in the world of R-bookkeeping*

Since JSOA is mostly formed by the academicians, the true values of their papers may not be easily recognized by the market in a short period of time, though they may contribute to the world in the long-run. Therefore, the ultimate assurance of salability of the book series in the market should be at least partially assumed by making the attractive and useful contents

---

[7]This point is the most different point of JSOA when compared with the publication activities of many other academic organizations, which publish their routine journals totally by their own fund so that the publisher need not take the risk of sales in the market at all.

of the book through the efforts, ideas, and insights of JSOA. In other words, since any merchandize will be demanded by the consumers, thanks to its usefulness and attractiveness in the market, such factors should be imbedded in the contents of the book provided by the JSOA rather than the publisher.

Therefore, although it is not written in the publication contract, JSOA decided to have a "**risk sharing**" scheme between JSOA and the publisher for covering the costs of production and sales of the publisher (see two arrow lines of sales in Fig. 1). Thus, JSOA will try to continue purchasing a certain number of copies of each volume when published. This scheme is to enhance the *long-term reliability* for making the cooperative joint efforts between two parties.[8]

This action is a (*implicit*) commitment[9] of JSOA to the publisher, and this aspect is a world of R-bookkeeping for assuring the reliability as shown in Fig. 11. However, because this action eventually accompanies the monetary transactions, the R-bookkeeping will support the M-bookkeeping and connected with each other at this stage.

The reliability on the publisher, authors, and readers (in the debtor side) is the "*intangible assets*" or the expectation that JSOA has thanks to the JSOA's stakeholders, where the publisher, authors, and readers are customers or debtors to JSOA in one aspect. Such intangible assets may

---

[8]The *risk sharing* system is often used for the purpose of the *Joint profit allocation* between the core firm and the member firms of their network for motivating the members to participate in the grand coalition of the total network. For this purpose, the joint profit is allocated by using the *incentive price* or the *lump-sum subsidy* for the inter-firm transfer of goods or services. (For details of this topic, see Monden and Nagao (1987/1988) and Monden (2012)).

The inter-firm systems of cooperation between auto-maker and parts-maker in their network organization are also extensively shown by Monden (1983) and (2012).

[9]Since such system is the "informal" one that is not written in the formal contract, it is the "implicit incentive" so-called in the theory of contracts of the institutional economics (Ishiguro, 2012). The relative importance of the role of such implicit incentive to the publisher may vary depending on the different stages of economic conditions in the sales of the market. The amount of subsidy (i.e., amount of purchased copies of the published book) offered by JSOA may be relatively bigger in the early stage of this book series because the sales of this series in the market might be smaller due to lack in popularity, while the amount of subsidy could be smaller in the growing stage of the book series in the market.

Balance Sheet of
R-Bookkeeping of JSOA

(Intangible Assets owned by JSOA)	(Social Capital given to JSOA)
Reliability on the publisher, authors & readers (debtors)	Social support rendered by the publisher, authors & readers (creditors)

Fig. 11.   Balance sheet composed of the intangible assets and the social capital of JSOA

correspond to the *accounts receivables* of M-bookkeeping. On the other hand, the financial and non-financial supports rendered by the publisher, authors, and readers (in the creditor side) are the *"social capital"* given to JSOA. The concept of social capital, as I see it, refers to the reliability capital based on the inter-human or inter-firm networks (Sawada, 2012). The publisher, authors, and readers are the creditors of JSOA in this aspect, where JSOA is the debtor. Such social capital may correspond to the *accounts payables* and stockholders' equity of M-bookkeeping.

6.5.   *Linking the R-bookkeeping to the M-bookkeeping in the down-stream process*

Journal entries of M-bookkeeping
Journal entries in the down-stream process will be as follows:

(1) Journal entry when the authors paid their amount of purchasing copies to the JSOA:
Cash xxx/deposit from the formal members and authors xxx
(Liability of JSOA for the members and authors)

(2) Journal entry when the publisher paid the amount of royalty to the JSOA:
Cash xxx/revenue of royalty from the publisher xxx

(3) Journal entry when the accountant of JSOA transferred the amount of purchasing copies to the bank account of the publisher:
Merchandize to arrive xxx/cash xxx
    (Claim of JSOA for the publisher)

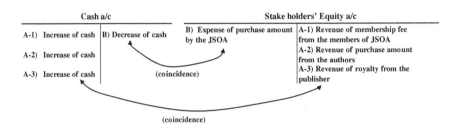

Fig. 12.   Ledger entries of M-bookkeeping

(4) Journal entry when the books were sent to the authors and members, and when the books were received:

Deposit from the formal members and authors xxx/merchandize to arrive xxx

Ledger entries of M-bookkeeping

Following the journal entries shown above, the ledger entries will be as shown in Fig. 12.

The "Social Capital" shown in the creditor side of the balance sheet of R-bookkeeping (Fig. 11) will be linked to the monetary figures of the creditor side of the stakeholders' equity a/c of Fig. 12.

Numerical figures in both sides of the stakeholders' equity a/c will show the target (or estimated) figures of R-bookkeeping or managerial accounting before the traditional bookkeeping is applied. When the gap between the target figures and the actual (or estimated) figures is found, then some remedial actions must be devised and applied.

As a result of M-bookkeeping of Fig. 12, it follows that the monetary relations of debt and credit between the JSOA, members, authors, and the publisher were written off and the reliability relations among them would be assured. Also, the future cooperative joint-efforts for their continuous publication will be assured.

At the end of the above monetary transactions, the ending cash balance of the cash a/c will coincide with the ending retained earnings of the stakeholders' equity a/c, as shown in Fig. 13.

It is important that the ending balance figure of the stakeholders' equity a/c should be *positive* each year end, and would be accumulated year by year, so that the organization could grow year by year.

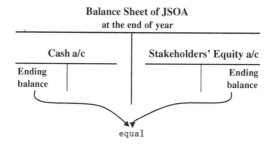

Fig. 13.   Ending balances on the balance sheet of M-bookkeeping

7.   Conclusion

As we have shown by Fig. 1, the social networks in this reliability account-ing consist of (1) reliability relation between the authors and editor and (2) reliability relation between JSOA and the publisher. The former is the inter-personal relationship and the latter is the inter-firm relation.

These two relations are connected with each other and their ultimate objectives are common, which is to contribute the people in the world through continuous publication of the book series: *Japanese Management and International Studies.*

Let us consider how this common objective will be achieved from each of the reliability relationships.

(1) The good relationship between the editor and author will enhance the motivation of authors to write their paper on the book series and even-tually assure the loyalty of the members for their participation in JSOA publication activities.
(2) The good relationship between JSOA and the publisher will enable the risk sharing of publishing the book series.

Assuming the above propositions that "the stronger reliability relation-ship based on stronger ties can bring the better performance," we have developed the R-bookkeeping system up to this point. The above is the summary of intention that I emphasis in this chapter.

However, there are two different propositions in the empirical researches in the field of sociology and management. One is that the "stronger ties" will bring the better performance (Coleman, 1988), and the other is that the "weaker ties" will result in the better performance (Granovetter, 1973).

These two conflicting propositions could be selectively applicable contingent on the environmental conditions (Rowley *et al.*, 2000) and also on its seeking purposes (Iriyama, 2012).

As for the ties between the publisher and JSOA, let us consider the market condition of the publication business, where the sales of a book are dependent on the attractiveness of its contents and so the sales are not so stable. Therefore, the risk sharing between two parties is necessary for assuring the stable sales. Thus, under such economic condition, the stronger ties will assure the *"continuous publication"* of rather academic book series. Also, the stronger ties in the relations between the authors and editor can better motivate the authors to achieve the *"timely production"* of the book according to the schedule, which is the performance measure for the purpose of *operations management* that requires the steady discipline in the daily efforts of authors.

On the other hand for the individual volume editor and the individual author, the "weaker but wider ties" with their colleagues throughout the world would help them to find and develop the better theme or topics of the book and papers, since these activities are for the purpose of a kind of *innovations.*

In this chapter, the writer developed the system of the reliability book-keeping by using only e-mail system. However, there are many other systems of social networking in the information technology such as Twitter, Facebook, and mixi. How to utilize these systems of the Social Network Services (SNS) for enhancing the inter-personal and inter-firm reliabilities may also be explored as extensions of the reliability accounting.

References

Asanuma, B. (1984). Structure of Parts Transactions in the Automobile Industry, *Contemporary Economics*, 58(Summer), pp. 38–48.

Coleman, J. S. (1988). Social Capital in the Creation of Human Capital, *American Journal of Sociology*, 94, pp. 95–120.

Granovetter, M. (1973). The Strength of Weak Ties, *American Journal of Sociology*, 78(6), pp. 1360–1380.

Ijiri, Y. (1966). Physical measures and multi-dimensional accounting, in R. K. Jaedicke, Y. Yuji, & O. Nielsen (eds.), *Research in Accounting Measurement*, American Accounting Association, Menasha, Wisconsin: George Banta Company, pp. 150–164.

Ijiri, Y. (1982). *Triple-Entry Bookkeeping and Income Momentum.* Sarasota, FL: American Accounting Association, Studies in Accounting Research Series No. 18.

Iriyama, A. (2012). *What are the Professors of Management in the World Thinking of?* Tokyo: Eiji Press (in Japanese).

Ishiguro, S. (2012). The Theory of Contracts, An Introduction, *The Nikkei*, August, 6–15 (in Japanese).

Kimura, S. (2008). Roles of "Debt & Credit" in the Inter-Firm Managerial Accounting, *Research in Cost Accounting*, 32(1), pp. 33–41 (in Japanese).

Kojima, O. (1964). *A Study on History of Bookkeeping.* Tokyo: Moriyama Shoten (in Japanese).

Kojima, O. (1977). *Introduction to Bookkeeping.* Tokyo: Moriyama Shoten (in Japanese).

Monden, Y. (1983). *Toyota Production System* (1st edn.). Norcross, JA. Industrial Engineering and Management Press, IIE.

Monden, Y. *Toyota Production System* (4th edn.). New York, NY: CRC Press, Taylor & Francis Group.

Monden, Y. (ed.) (2012). *Management of an Inter-Firm Network.* Singapore: World Scientific Publishing Company.

Monden, Y. & Nagao, T. (1987/1988). Full Cost-Based Transfer Pricing in the Japanese Auto Industry: Risk Sharing and Risk-Spreading Behavior, *Journal of Business Administration*, 17(1 and 2), pp. 117–136.

Rowley, T., Behrens, D., & Krackhardt, D. (2000). Redundant Governance Structures: An Analysis of Structural and Relational Embeddedness in the Steel and Semiconductor Industries, *Strategic Management Journal*, 21(3), pp. 369–386.

Sawada, Y. (2012). Exploring the "Ties As Capital: As a Driving Force of Restoration for the Disasters", *The Nikkei*, December 18. "Economic Seminar" (in Japanese).

6

A Horizontal Inter-firm Network of Small- and Medium-sized Enterprises Specializing in Prototype Solutions: Business Model, Management Control, and External Effects

Naoya Yamaguchi
Aoyama Gakuin University

1. Introduction

In recent years, deindustrialization caused by the reduction of domestic demand and expansion of overseas production has resulted in many Japanese industrial agglomerations facing continuation crises. Therefore, both the agglomerations themselves and the companies within them have made efforts for revitalization, such as establishing local brands and constructing clusters aimed at taking on growth industries and creating new industries.

This chapter deals with the case of a horizontal inter-firm network of small- and medium-sized enterprises (SMEs) specializing in prototype solutions: Kyoto Shisaku Net ("Shisaku" means *prototyping* in Japanese) in Kyoto, Japan. Kyoto is well known globally as an area symbolizing Japanese culture. Moreover, in recent years, as some companies in Kyoto have taken original approaches to management, some researchers have analyzed them specifically as Kyoto companies and Kyoto-type businesses (Suematsu, 2002; Murayama, 2008; Kita & Nishiguchi, 2009; Horiba, 2011). Most of these previous studies analyze individual large companies with good performance.

On the other hand, Kyoto Shisaku Net is original because of its establishment of an innovative business model involving SMEs. It is a horizontal inter-firm network specializing in prototype solutions utilizing industrial connections effectively for the survival and growth of SMEs in Kyoto. In recent years, many local governments and SMEs faced with decline in their local industries have taken a keen interest in the network and have established their own original networks based on their industrial connections. The Polishers' Syndicate, a network of small buffing companies Yamaguchi (2011a, 2011b) examined, is one of them.

Previous studies on Kyoto Shisaku Net include those by Suematsu (2002), Fujisawa (2003), Morioka (2005), Ogushi (2010), and Onishi (2010). Suematsu (2002) analyzed Kyoto Shisaku Net as an example of business deployment through a module and interface system utilizing a network of SMEs. Fujisawa (2003) analyzed it as an example of a network functioning as the basis of utilization and development of *social capital* as conceptualized by Putnam (1993). Morioka (2005) analyzed the network by using Porter's (1998) *cluster* concept as an example of small-sized clusters in narrow geographical areas (mini-clusters) independent of economics of scale. Onishi (2010) also used Porter's (1998) cluster concept to analyze the network as an example of a cluster core of a new industrial cluster. Ogushi (2010) analyzed the network's order process management.

These studies all take the perspective that Kyoto Shisaku Net functions as a basis for utilizing the local business resources of SMEs effectively through cooperation among them. Premised on this perspective and using Gulati *et al.*'s (2012) concept of *meta-organization*, this chapter clarifies the business model and management control of the network itself as a single meta-organization and the external effect for members.

This chapter is based on an interview held in March 2013 with the present representative director of Kyoto Shisaku Net, Mr. Masatoshi Takeda (president of Cross Effect Incorporated).

2. Kyoto Shisaku Net

2.1. *Background of Kyoto Shisaku Net*

Kyoto Shisaku Net was founded in July 2001 by 10 machinery and metal SMEs located in the southern Kyoto area. This network offers prototype solution services from part processing to equipment development.

The network was born through a study exchange session involving members of the Kyoto Machinery and Metal SMEs Youth Liaison Association. This association, which was founded in 1982, is the exchange organization for executives of machinery and metal SMEs located in Kyoto Prefecture. Faced with the collapse of the 1990s bubble economy in Japan, and supported by the association's alumni, some members discussed how the future should be managed. Then, the members who were serious about the matter gathered and started the study exchange session based on Drucker's (1954) works.

Through the study exchange session, the members came to share the recognition that the foundations of corporate management are *marketing* and *innovation*, and that *the creation of customers* is most important (Drucker, 1954). Then, they engaged in much discussion about the practical methods of customer creation, redefined the obsolete business, and searched for a new management style to effectively utilize their strengths and resources. As a result, they decided to establish a new structure of customer creation by utilizing the Internet.

Moreover, they shared the recognition that the mass production system does not function effectively in Japan, making it necessary to focus on the upstream of the value chain and to develop intellectual businesses to maintain manufacturing in Kyoto. As a result, they decided to develop the business specializing in prototype solutions.

With support from the Kyoto Prefecture Government and Kyoto Industrial Support Organization 21, a public interest incorporated foundation aimed at supporting SMEs in Kyoto, 10 strong-willed companies established Kyoto Shisaku Net as a network specializing in prototype solutions.

In response to the success of this network, some prototyping groups were successively founded in Kyoto. Kyoto Shisaku Center Incorporated was founded in Kyoto City in July 2006 to support these groups with contributions by 27 companies in Kyoto. The Center supports them by taking orders for prototyping and related businesses, allocating orders among the groups, facilitating mail order businesses via the Internet, and so on. In other words, it allocates among multiple groups orders that cannot be dealt with by a single group because of lack of scale or expertise, and plays the part of the contracting entity on behalf of the groups for orders for which customers demand a non-disclosure agreement (NDA) (prototyping groups that are not legal entities cannot be parties to a contract).

The foundation of 10 prototyping groups has made it difficult for customers to decide which group they should order from, and their search cost burden has become heavy. Since this also affected the prototyping groups negatively, by taking into account the requests from customers, Kyoto Shisaku Net united all the other groups and became a single prototype group in October 2012. At present, there are 96 member companies:

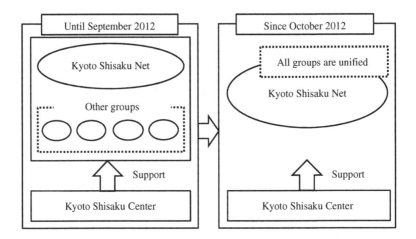

Fig. 1.   Development of Kyoto Shisaku Net

26 core companies and 70 non-core companies. The development of Kyoto
Shisaku Net and the relationship between the network and Kyoto Shisaku
Center Incorporated are presented in Fig. 1.

Around the same time, the first representative director of Kyoto Shisaku
Net, Mr. Saburo Suzuki, became the president of Kyoto Shisaku Center
Incorporated. Until then, although presidents were dispatched from the
shareholder companies, they could not support the prototyping groups effectively. However, since Suzuki became president, cooperation with Kyoto
Shisaku Net has been enhanced. For the purpose of unifying the contact
point for customers, Kyoto Shisaku Net and Kyoto Shisaku Center Incorporated are considering future integration.

2.2.   *Missions and philosophies of Kyoto Shisaku Net*

Kyoto Shisaku Net defined its missions and philosophies as follows. Furthermore, at present, its vision is *to make Kyoto the largest cluster area of
prototyping business.*

Missions:

(1) To create prototypes that exceed customer expectations faster than
    does anyone else.
(2) To make the process of prototyping as easy as possible.

Philosophies:

(1) Improving development efficiency by working with you from the initial stage of product development and providing proposals from processing companies.
(2) Applying our shared knowledge to the creation of your prototype to provide solutions with added value.
(3) Providing our people with an opportunity to grow as professionals through the advanced manufacturing involved in making prototypes.

Kyoto Shisaku Net aims to offer business and study opportunities to its members as a platform for achieving SME independence. It was originally founded with the aim of expanding business opportunities through the prototyping business. However, as defined in the third philosophy, the network now emphasizes that members grow through various *learnings* about the prototyping business and communications among the members rather than through the income of the members. Therefore, the network does not admit companies wishing only for the income.

2.3. *Operation of Kyoto Shisaku Net*

Kyoto Shisaku Net is a horizontal inter-firm network of manufacturing SMEs in Kyoto specializing in prototype solutions.

The network prioritizes speed, which is more important in product development than cost. It offers a firm promise of a response within 2 hours for consultation and inquiries from domestic costumers. It offers a firm promise of a response within 24 hours for foreign customers.

When the head office receives a request via its website, e-mail, or fax, it sends the request to all members via e-mail immediately. Then, according to the contents of the request, one or more optimal member(s) reply to the customer with an estimate via the head office (Fig. 2) and negotiate with the customer. If the business arrangement is completed, the member(s) receive the order. In order to guarantee the 2-hour response, core companies are on duty in turns every week, process the orders together with the head office, and determine which member(s) will take the order.

Although requests decreased temporarily after the Lehman shock in September 2008, they have held steady at around 400 requests every year except for that period (2006: 423 requests, 2007: 409, 2008: 273, 2009: 282, 2010: 425). After unifying all prototyping groups in October 2012, requests have increased to 600–700 per year. At present, the network aims

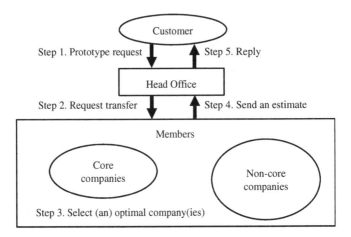

Fig. 2.   Order handling process of Kyoto Shisaku Net

to process 100 requests per month. The portion of sales via the network to all sales varies by member. The highest portion is around 20% and the lowest is 0%.

Formerly, most orders were *prototype processing* for parts. However, with the integration of prototyping groups, the network extended its business domain. At present, it is also engaged in *prototype development*. For *prototype processing*, it engages only in the prototyping of products or parts that customers developed. For *prototype development*, it supports its customers' product development processes completely according to their requests, offering product planning, conceptual design, basic design, detailed design, and production process engineering. Table 1 shows the network's major fields of *prototype development*.

For *prototype processing*, in the case of a single process, a single member generally engages in the work independently; in the case of two or more processes (e.g., metal working and surface treatment), several members jointly engage in the work. On the other hand, for *prototype development*, there are much more compound orders that require the engagement of two or more members.

Although order allocation depends on the case, when an existing customer places an order, if it is similar to a past order (repeat order), the customer generally does not order via the network, instead ordering from the member engaged for the past order. On the other hand, if it is a different order, the customer could (1) order from Kyoto Shisaku Net directly

Table 1.   Kyoto Shisaku Net's major prototype development fields

System and equipment	Parts processing
— Lump-sum contract for machine, circuit board, and software. — Automatic assembly and inspection equipment. — Inspection system for solar cell output characteristics. — Web measurement control system. — Circuit and circuit board pattern design. — Cable checker and control panel wiring. — Sales and production management system. — Hydro-honing. — Chemical equipment (plating, plasma display panel (PDP) film, etc.). — CAD/CAE/PDM system. — High-voltage and high-frequency special electric power unit. — Digital/analog circuit and field-programmable gate array (FPGA) design. — Electronic equipment production.	— Compound canning (processing of sheet metal and precision sheet metal). — Machining/cutting (2D/3D CAD/CAM). — Machine tool and industrial machinery. — Press sheet metal (thin board metalworking and precision processing parts). — Resin treatment and shaping. — Compound lathe, thin lathe processing, and machining center (MC) processing. — Medical (heart simulator, micro forceps, etc.). — Iron, stainless, aluminum, and copper processing. — Industrial equipment parts (aircraft, automobile, etc.). — Laser lithography and casting under vacuum. — Minute and microscopic processing. — 3D razor, wire, thin hole electric discharge, and grinding processing. — Surface treatments (plating, coating, etc.). — Rubber processing.

or (2) rely on the member engaged in the past to search for a company suitable for the order.

Moreover, in the case of (2), the member that receives the request could either (A) search for a suitable company directly or (B) rely on the network to search for a suitable company. The network calls (2)(B) a *substitute contribution*. Although *substitute contributions* are counted as requests to

Kyoto Shisaku Net, (2)(A) scenarios are not counted. However, this is also an economic effect (ripple effect) brought about by Kyoto Shisaku Net.

Since Kyoto Shisaku Net is a matching site for customers rather than a legal entity, it does not have a guarantee-of-quality function. However, to prevent the brand of the network from injury, the core companies have to give top priority to work via the network and to guarantee the quality their customers demand.

In terms of sales and marketing activities, the network emphasizes that it uses both *virtual* and *real* techniques properly. It emphasizes not only advertisements and ordering processing via the Internet (*virtual*) but also face-to-face activities (*real*) such as visits and exhibitions for customer acquisition.

2.4. *Management of Kyoto Shisaku Net*

Kyoto Shisaku Net has a representative director, managing executive board, executive board, operating activity meeting group, selected company on duty each week, and head office.

The representative director is the chief executive and has changed every five years so far. The present representative director, Mr. Masatoshi Takeda, is the third. The head office is located at the company to which the representative director belongs.

The executive board, which is the highest decision-making body, convenes once per month to decide on the strategies for Kyoto Shisaku Net. The board consists of directors selected only from the core companies. Although one person is selected as a director from each core company, he or she must have the right to make final decisions at his or her own company.

Several persons respectively from the Kyoto Prefecture Government and Kyoto Industrial Support Organization 21 attend the executive board meetings as observers. In addition, the Kyoto Prefecture Government specified the five new fields including the prototyping business as the New Kyoto Brand, and it is supporting advances by the SMEs and developing venture companies in the five new fields in Kyoto.

The managing executive board convenes three times per month and deliberates on the bills referred to the executive board, and so on. The board consists of five managing directors selected from among the directors. The present managing directors are the representative director, two vice presidents, the planning manager, and the international sales and marketing manager.

The operating activity meeting group, a council of the sales representatives, convenes once per month. At least one or more persons are introduced as the sales representatives from each core company. At present, there are about 40 representatives. At the meeting, each sales representative reports on the orders received and sales conducted via the network of his or her own company, and the group decides on tactics to respond to the strategies selected by the executive board. Every core company takes a turn on duty processing orders with the head office and determining which member(s) will take orders. This duty rotates weekly.

As mentioned above, the network emphasizes that it uses both *virtual* and *real* techniques properly. However, in order to offer opportunities to learn through communications among members, the network believes that *real* meetings are important for management. Therefore, in addition to formal organizations and councils such as the managing executive board, executive board, and operating activity meeting group, informal private meetings and communications among the core companies are also frequent.

2.5.   *Strategies of Kyoto Shisaku Net*

At present, Kyoto Shisaku Net has positioned the following two strategies as important.

(1) ***Expansion of the business domain***: From *prototype processing* to *prototype development*.
(2) ***Expansion of the geographic domain***: From Japan to Western countries.

For expansion of the business domain, as mentioned above, with the integration of prototyping groups in October 2012, the network extended its business domain to include *prototype development* in addition to *prototype processing*.

For expansion of the geographic domain, the network established an international division in April 2012, held its first foreign exhibition in Chicago in the autumn of 2012, and created an English homepage to raise the degree of recognition in foreign countries, especially in European and North-American areas. Further, it hopes to invite the research and development bases of European and North-American companies into Kyoto to expand its business with them.

3. Business Model and Management Control of Kyoto Shisaku Net

Gulati *et al.* (2012) introduced the concept of a *meta-organization*, defined as an organization whose agents are themselves legally autonomous and not linked through employment relationships. Meta-organizations comprise networks of firms or individuals not bound by authority based on employment relationships but characterized by a system-level goal.

Kyoto Shisaku Net is a network organized around legally independent core companies, and the members share its missions, philosophies, and visions. The network can be regarded as a *second foundation* for SMEs through the meta-organization. The features of the network as a meta-organization are the *business model specializing in prototype solutions*, and the *management control based on belief systems*.

3.1. *Business model specializing in prototype solutions*

Manufacturing SMEs with different specialties in Kyoto constructed a network and systematized and visualized it as an original brand, which has given Kyoto Shisaku Net a competitive advantage. Since prototyping is a means to verify the appropriateness of product design and process engineering, prototype products are generally produced as a single article or as a small lot. Although prototyping companies do not require mass production capabilities, in order to satisfy various prototyping needs, it is necessary for them to acquire capabilities to respond flexibly according to the material, form, processing method, and so on, as well as advanced technical capabilities.

Therefore, capabilities are much more important than capacities for prototyping companies. Because many companies with different capabilities participate in Kyoto Shisaku Net, the network has realized *technical diversity* and *complementarity*. While the network can satisfy various prototyping needs by combining the members' capabilities and taking advantage of their technical diversity and complementarity, each member can specialize in its self-capability and pursue its original capability.

Itami (1998) lists three basic requirements for a division-of-work association to maintain flexibility, that is, the requirements for flexibility: *deep technical knowledge, low division-of-work adjustment cost,* and *ease of establishment.* Since the network members have different capabilities, the network can take advantage of the deep technical knowledge and the low division-of-work adjustment cost to satisfy the various prototyping needs. Here, the division-of-work adjustment cost means the adjustment cost of the dealings among the companies taking charge of the division of work. It is the entire cost required to execute the complicated division of work consistently, such as the cost of finding division-of-work partners, arranging with them to execute the divided processes exactly, changing the design after the division of work has begun, and collecting payment.

Moreover, Suematsu (2002) lists three elements for a network to pursue: *resource sharing, function distribution*, and *load distribution*. Since the members share diversified capabilities (*resource sharing*), the network can realize technical diversity. Each member can strive to pursue an original capability while specializing in its self-capability (*function distribution*). Furthermore, the members can reduce their risks and costs by performing high-cost work or work that would be impossible for any single company, such as sales promotion, exhibition, and foreign deployment (*load distribution*) together.

Kyoto Shisaku Net classifies prototyping into *prototype processing* and *prototype development*. For *prototype processing*, since most orders received are parts units, even when two or more processes are required, it is possible to move work from the former process to the latter like a baton pass in relay. For instance, after a certain member finishes the metalworking, another one could start the surface treatment. Therefore, the adjustment cost for division of work is relatively low.

On the other hand, for *prototype development*, most orders received are compound orders, for which two or more members have to adjust the work mutually. In the case of compound orders, the adjustment cost is generally high and the cooperation among members is indispensable. In Kyoto Shisaku Net, the high-quality communication among the members based on the belief system mentioned later supports this cooperation.

Since prototyping involves making something new for the first time, the solution is not known in advance. Under severe time and budgetary constraints, members have to tackle work with which they have little or no experience and arrive at their own solutions. Therefore, although based on existing core capabilities, in order to strengthen the power to respond to customer needs, every member has to acquire an original capability and continue extending its self-capability through practice.

In order to acquire an original capability, the will to take on the challenge of new types of work is critical — and even more so for prototype development. To develop this will, Kyoto Shisaku Net shares the importance of innovation for acquiring customers among the core companies using Drucker's (1954) management theories and philosophies.

In terms of foreign deployment, the network has carried out various activities to raise its recognition level in the European and North-American areas to acquire difficult orders from these areas and search for opportunities to innovate.

Moreover, Kyoto Shisaku Net has strengthened the sales and marketing process by devoting talented people to customer acquisition and increasing the efficiency of order processing by utilizing the Internet. For customer acquisition, the executives of the core companies themselves visit the customers, participate in exhibitions, and conduct presentations to raise the recognition level of the network and increase the number of orders received. Furthermore, the operating activity meeting group periodically checks the orders received and sales, draws up tactics to increase orders, and implements these tactics promptly.

3.2. *Management control based on the principle system*

Simons (1995, 2000) lists the four *levers of control* as the means by which managers control an organization: *belief systems, boundary systems, diagnostic control systems,* and *interactive control systems.*

In a meta-organization, the agents are legally autonomous and not linked through employment relationships; thus, each agent can decide at its discretion how much it takes part in the activities of the meta-organization. Since the network cannot control its agents directly, it has limited ability to control them through diagnostic control systems. Therefore, it seems that both the sharing of values and action principles through *belief systems* and *boundary systems* and dealing with strategic uncertainties and promoting the emergence of a new strategy through *interactive control systems* are important management control functions to improve the performance of a meta-organization.

Kyoto Shisaku Net emphasizes belief systems as its management control systems. Simons (1995, 2000) defines a *belief system* as an explicit set of organizational definitions that senior managers communicate formally and reinforce systematically to provide the basic values, purpose, and direction they want subordinates to adopt. The primary purpose is to inspire and guide organizational search and discovery. Furthermore, Simons (1995) points out that many of the benefits of creating formal belief systems flow

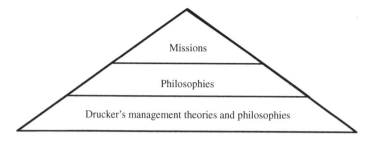

Fig. 3.   Core values of Kyoto Shisaku Net

from the discussion necessary to communicate and understand these beliefs rather than from the credos and statements themselves.

Within Kyoto Shisaku Net, the core companies share and reinforce the belief systems shown in Fig. 3 through the admission procedure and the formal and informal communications after admission.

The qualification requirements for joining Kyoto Shisaku Net are as follows. After the integration of prototyping groups in October 2012, these became the qualification requirements to be a core company.

(1) The company is located in Kyoto Prefecture.
(2) It is a manufacturing company.
(3) It sympathizes with the missions and philosophies of the network.
(4) The company's executives themselves participate positively in various activities of the network and do not leave them to their employees.
(5) The company pays the annual fee of 600,000 yen.

A company wishing to be a core company has to pass through the following steps.

Step 1: The executive must have a first interview with two persons, the representative director and an advisor (the second representative director, Mr. Shosaku Yamamoto), after receiving a recommendation from one of the core companies.

Step 2: If he or she passes the interview, the company will become an associate member for at least six months. An associate member can participate in the executive board councils and operating activity meetings as an observer. Furthermore, the executive must take the network-sponsored Drucker lecture course (six sessions).

Step 3: After finishing the Drucker course, the executive must have a final interview with two persons, the representative director and an advisor (the first representative director, Mr. Saburo Suzuki). If he or she passes, the company will become a core company.

Thus, an executive of a company wishing to be a core company is clearly asked whether he or she recognizes (3) and (4) through two interviews with network executives. Furthermore, after becoming an associate member, the executive is required to change his or her mindset based on a deep understanding of both the missions and philosophies of the network and Drucker's management theories and philosophies through the participation in the councils and meetings as an observer and attendance of the Drucker lectures.

Then, even after being accepted as a core company, the executive is called to understand the missions and philosophies of the network deeply and develop his sense of responsibility to the activities of the network through informal and private meetings and communications as well as participation in the formal councils and meetings.

Sharing core values among the core companies through these communicative interactions supports the *alignment of operations* and the *empowerment of innovation*. The communicative interactions have also achieved the function of an *interactive control system* through which the managers deal with strategic uncertainties and promote the emergence of a new strategy.

4.   External Effects for Members

A meta-organization like Kyoto Shisaku Net is a network whose agents are themselves legally autonomous and not linked through employment relationships. Each agent has more or less its own customers and businesses. Therefore, every agent participates in a meta-organization just because it thinks that it is beneficial.

In analyzing a meta-organization, it is thus necessary to give attention not only to the meta-organization itself but also to the external effects it brings to the agents. Figure 4 shows the external effects for members, especially for the core companies that Kyoto Shisaku Net offers using the framework of Kaplan and Norton's (2001, 2004) *Strategy Maps*.

The external effects can be classified roughly into the *earnings growth effects* and the *organizational capability enhancement effects*. The former

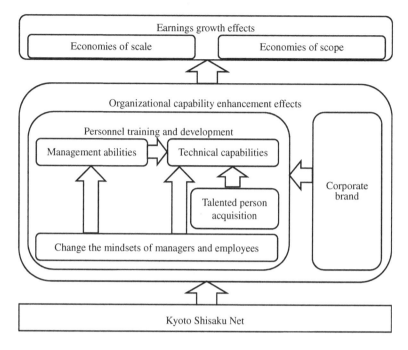

Fig. 4.   External effects for the members of Kyoto Shisaku Net

can be gained from the following two sources: economies of scale (total amount of the orders increases through contracting both orders that the members receive directly and orders via the network) and economies of scope (total amount of orders increases through expansion of the business domain). It is indispensable for each company to extend its own capabilities through the acquisition of an original capability in order to realize economies of scope; therefore, economies of scope can be obtained through organizational capability enhancement effects.

On the other hand, the latter can be classified roughly into personnel training and development and the establishment of a corporate brand. Personnel training and development involves (1) the reform of managers' and employees' mindsets by facing new businesses challenges via the network and through high-quality communication among the members, (2) improving managers' management abilities, and (3) improving technical capabilities at the organization and individual levels.

The establishment of a corporate brand involves increasing the members' popularity through the network's activities. Furthermore, since the establishment of a corporate brand encourages the company to bring out its employees' sense of loyalty and employ talented people with potential abilities, it contributes positively to the improvement of technical capabilities at the organization and individual levels.

Tackling new business by combining managers' management abilities, such as the will to take on new challenges, personnel training and management, and project management, with technical capabilities, each member can extend and reinforce its original capability as an organization at the individual level and acquire earnings growth effects through the economies of scope.

5. Conclusion

Porter (1998) defines a *cluster* as a geographic concentration of interconnected companies, specialized suppliers, service providers, firms in related industries, and associated institutions (for example, universities, standards agencies, and trade associations) in a particular field that not only compete but also cooperate.

The foundation of Kyoto Shisaku Net triggered the successive foundation of several prototyping groups in Kyoto and the expansion of public and private supports by the Kyoto Prefecture Government, Kyoto Industrial Support Organization 21, and Kyoto Shisaku Center Incorporated. As Onishi (2010) points out, the network formed and developed the prototype cluster in the Kyoto area as a cluster core. It unified all prototyping groups and has since played a central role in the prototype cluster as a core organization.

Recently, although *clusters* are attracting attention as a means of revitalizing local industries by exploiting industrial agglomerations in Japan, many of these attempts do not achieve sufficient success. One of the reasons is that it is generally a local government that forms a cluster, and the companies actually doing business in the cluster lack positive and long-term commitment. Furthermore, since revitalization programs of local industries by local governments tend to incline toward financial support to protect uncompetitive companies rather than strengthen competitiveness, they can actually obstruct SME independence.

Kyoto Shisaku Net was not necessarily intended to become the foundation of a cluster. In the process of establishing an original business model for the survival of members and growing as a network, it acquired ripple effects, such as the successive foundation of several prototyping groups and

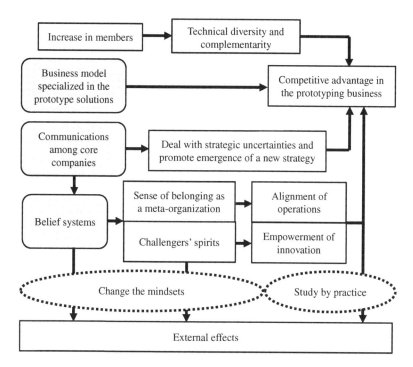

Fig. 5. Business model, management controls, and external effects of Kyoto Shisaku Net

the expansion of public and private support. As a result, it formed the prototyping cluster in Kyoto.

Figure 5 shows the business model, management control, and external effects for the members of Kyoto Shisaku Net. The success factors of the network are a business model that utilizes technical diversity and complementarity effectively, and independent management control based on belief systems that are meta-organization wide.

In order to extend the scale of the prototyping businesses, it is indispensable to develop advanced and diversified capabilities. Because it is a network constructed of SMEs with different capabilities, Kyoto Shisaku Net has realized technical diversity and complementarity, satisfied various prototyping needs, and promoted the pursuit of original capabilities by each member.

For the network, belief systems are the most important. By sharing the network's core values as a meta-organization, it has increased members' understanding of the network and willingness to participate.

The formal and informal frequent and high-quality communications among the core companies promote the sharing of core values and create the sense of belonging to a meta-organization and encourage the will to take on new challenges. This supports the alignment of operations and the empowerment of innovation in the network. The communicative interactions have also achieved the function of an *interactive control system* through which the managers deal with strategic uncertainties and promote the emergence of a new strategy.

Furthermore, because the network promotes both income and learning as important, it prompts the growth of members and attracts companies with high willingness to grow. A virtuous circle means that the expected external effects raise the willingness to participate in the network and the realized external effects revitalize the members.

With the integration of prototyping groups in October 2012, the number of members increased sharply. Since the scale of the network was expanded, it could take on even more diversified capabilities, and the technical diversity and complementarity were improved further.

However, since most members who have joined recently are non-core companies, they cannot necessarily share fully in the core values of the network. In order to fully utilize the scale, technical diversity, and technical complementarity of the network and accomplish the development of the prototyping business, it is important for positive participation by the non-core companies to be encouraged by sharing the core values.

Acknowledgment

I gained a considerable amount of valuable knowledge by conversing with the present representative director of Kyoto Shisaku Net, Mr. Masatoshi Takeda (the president of Cross Effect Incorporated). I immensely appreciate his kindness. Naturally, I am solely responsible for any errors or misstatements in this chapter.

References

Drucker, P. F. (1954). *The Practice of Management*. New York: Harper & Brothers.
Fujisawa, K. (2003). *How does Social Capital Expand a Business Opportunity?* Retrieved from http://www.esri.go.jp/jp/workshop/030325/030325paper5.pdf#search='%E8%97%A4%E6%B2%A2%E4%B9%85%

E7%BE%8E+%E3%82%BD%E3%83%BC%E3%82%B7%E3%83%A3%
E3%83%AB%E3%82%AD%E3%83%A3%E3%83%94%E3%82%BF%E3
%83%AB' (in Japanese).

Gulati, R., Puranam, P., & Tushman, M. (2012). Meta-Organization
Design: Rethinking Design in Interorganizational and Community Contexts, *Strategic Management Journal*, 33, pp. 571–586.

Horiba, A. (2011). *Why are Kyoto Companies Ingenious and Do They
Achieve High Performance?* Tokyo: Kodansya (in Japanese).

Itami, H. (1998). Meaning and logic of industrial accumulation, in H. Itami,
S. Matsushima, S., & T. Kikkawa (eds.), *Nature of Industrial Accumula-
tion:Condition of Flexible Division of Work and Accumulation*, Tokyo,
Yuhikaku, pp. 1–23 (in Japanese).

Kaplan, R. S. & Norton, D. P. (2001). *The Strategy-Focused Organization.*
Boston, MA: Harvard Business School Press.

Kaplan, R. S. & Norton, D. P. (2004). *Strategy Maps.* Boston, MA, Harvard
Business School Press.

Kita, T. & Nishiguchi, Y. (eds.) (2009). *Casebook of the Kyoto Model.*
Tokyo: Hakuto-Shobo (in Japanese).

Morioka, T. (2005). Investigation of Mini-Cluster Formation: Theory and
Proposal for Mini-Cluster Formation, *The Regional Vitalization Journal (Niigata University of Management)*, 11, pp. 37–47 (in Japanese).

Murayama, Y. (2008). *Kyoto-Type Business: Management for Originality
and Continuation.* Tokyo: NHK Publishing (in Japanese).

Ogushi, Y. (2010). Business Process Management for Inter-Organizational
Networks in Small and Medium-sized Enterprises, *The Society of Economics at Niigata University*, 88, pp. 67–78 (in Japanese).

Onishi, T. (2010). A Study of the Relationship Between the Growth Process
of an Industrial Cluster and a Small and Medium Business Enterprise
Network, *Journal of the Faculty of Economics (Kyoto Gakuen University)*, 20(1), pp. 1–23 (in Japanese).

Porter, M. E. (1998). *On Competition.* Boston, MA, Harvard Business
School Press.

Putnam, R. D. (1993). *Making Democracy Work: Civic Traditions in Modern Italy.* Princeton, NJ: Princeton University Press.

Simons, R. (1995). *Levers of Control.* Boston, MA: Harvard Business School
Press.

Simons, R. (2000). *Performance Measurement & Control Systems for Implementing Strategy.* Upper Saddle River, NJ: Prentice Hall.

Suematsu, C. (2002). *Kyoto-Style Management: Strategy of Modularity.*
Tokyo: Nihon Keizai Shimbun (in Japanese).

Yamaguchi, N. (2011a). Business Process Management of Horizontal
Division Networks Created by Companies Specializing in Element

Technology: Based on an Analysis of the "Polishers" Syndicate in Tsubame, *The Journal of Cost Accounting Research*, 35(1), pp. 96–106 (in Japanese).

Yamaguchi, N. (2011b). Inter-firm business process management of companies specializing in element technology: Analysis of a horizontal division network created by a cluster of small enterprises in Japan, in Y. Monden (ed.), *Management of an Inter-firm Network*, Singapore: World Scientific Publishing Co Pte. Ltd., pp. 171–183.

7

A Discussion of Community of Practice and the Construction of Organization Core Competence — A Case Study of BS Supplementary Education Group

Stephen Dun-Hou Tsai
National Sun Yat-sen University

Chih-Yu Lee
National Sun Yat-sen University

1. Introduction

Organization core competence is essential for the initiation of organization renewal and strategic reform (Ljungquist, 2007). When Prahalad and Hamel (1990) proposed core competence early on, they emphasized that organization core competence is the process of the organizations' internal collective learning and knowledge. In particular, core competence can be coordinated and integrated with various technology and abilities within the organization. Commonly, it is not possessed by particular members, but spread among them (Yang *et al.*, 2010; Hamel & Heene, 1994). Implicit in the development of organization core competence learning is that changes and growth in organization members occur in work activities and their context, and this creates experiential learning; it is possible to improve core competence through experiential learning.

According to the perspective of traditional cognitive learning, so-called learning is that in knowledge acquisition, the learner goes through the process of gaining, remembering, and utilizing knowledge to alter his or her psychology and actions. Under this, tenet knowledge is rigid; it is an object which cannot be altered by any person, place, or time. However, this notion of learning is excessively linear in reference and ignores dynamics and emergence in the learning process.

This chapter proposes the perspective of social learning, and emphasizes that learning is not merely an individual cognitive process, but rather is concerned with the process of social context and development.

Through empirical case studies, this chapter focuses on the BS Supplementary Education Group's members learning (branch managers and tutors), and investigates how organization member social learning influences the advancement of core competence. A cram school[1] is a knowledge-based organization and, in its operations, it is critical to have managers with both abundant educational and managerial experience (Aurini, 2006). The relationship of reciprocal reinforcement between these two elements may become a competitive advantage for the cram school in the market. In general, these tutors (tutors) and managers often continuously accumulate educational and managerial experience through a number of study courses, in addition to gradually developing a great deal of implicit personal educational and managerial knowledge. We can assume that a new tutor or manager would find it difficult to accumulate this type of teaching or managerial skill in a short period of time. One point of interest is BS's educational training makes up for the difference in the experience of junior and senior members.

In departing from the definition of a cram school as a place for "remedial" learning allowing students to move on to the next level of education, BS advertises itself as "supplementary" education. They do not utilize well-known tutors, but rather have self-trained tutors lecture. This definition can attract a number of potential customers interested in supplementary education. This know-how is the "teaching logic" and "management strategy" which BS created. When members with greater seniority teach juniors about their work experiences, they discard the traditional top–down education training. Rather, they use the methods of teacher training (for education) and dividing into assignment groups. This allows senior members to lead junior members and for them to learn together. With seniors leading the juniors in interactive discussions, the teaching and managerial logic of

---

[1]In Asia's tutor education culture, cram schools are often created for "augmenting" students' school grades. Many cram schools utilize "celebrity tutors" (famous tutor) in order to attract students. What is more, students may choose a cram school because of these tutors (Kwok, 2004).

the members is slowly triggered, deepened, and created. This interesting phenomenon and, within the community of practice's (COP) point of view, can open a space for explanation concerning core competence.

COP in social constructivism emphasizes social interaction and group cognition. It believes the creative products of work are co-constructed through meaning shared by members (Heo & Breuleux, 2008). The organization can be seen as becoming a community through members' common context and history. Wenger (1998) proposes that community members construct the historical context for their actualized community through negotiation of meaning on the dual elements of participation and reification. Meaning is created through individual participation and sharing artifacts, thoughts, and subjective interaction. As such, interactive discussion between organization members can bring about context learning.

If we reexamine core competence's nature from the perspective of social learning, would it be possible to say this is a product which will allow organization members to create continuously? If so, what ultimately is social learning with respect to organization member work? How does this learning build competence? These questions will be answered in order in the following pages.

2. Learning Comes from Negotiations on Meaning in the Community of Practice

Fenwick (2008) broadly divides literature on vocational learning into three perspectives. First, there is realism, which believes individual learning involves the individual taking part in learning about objective knowledge. This perspective supposes the individual can obtain insights which are the same as objective knowledge. The second perspective is the constructionist one, which emphasizes that an individual can obtain necessary vocational knowledge through entering and being assisted by a network. The two aforementioned perspectives argue for the acquisition of knowledge, and these arguments certainly can help us understand how the learner "obtains" as yet unknown knowledge. However, if we trace this knowledge back to its origins, we find these arguments neglect the connection of the knowledge construction process with the many social contexts behind the individual's knowledge acquisition. Even if every individual can objectively view the same matter, they will form different ideas about the object because of different historical backgrounds. That is, implicit in knowledge itself are many concepts connected by socially constructed contexts. If we only examine this from one perspective of knowledge acquisition, this could easily be construed as a type of decontextualization which solely discusses the argument of individual learning. As such, it is necessary to reconsider the problem of "what learning is."

This study accepts three different arguments. The learning perspective of social constructionism focuses on the notion that exploration and learning are not just a matter of the individual striving to obtain knowledge. Rather, they relate to the learner's involvement in social contexts and a community, and different social contexts and situations bring about the emergence of new experiences, perspectives, notions, and ways of thinking.

Lave and Wenger (1991) were the first to propose the concept of a COP based on social learning theory. COP is defined as "groups of people who share a concern or a passion for something they do and learn how to do it better as they interact regularly." Through regular practice and interactive learning, they refine their concerns and goals. COP is a social relationship system between the people, activities, and the overall world involved in it. Based on these conditions, the COP, which is the social learning network the individual belongs to, comes into existence. Furthermore, newcomers from outside the community can gradually become members of the community through legitimate participation, group practice, and interaction with members in the community (Kimble & Hildreth, 2005)

Furthering this idea, Wenger (1998) proposes, through interactive communal practice within the community, members create the concept of meaning for the actions of themselves and others. The creation of a notion of meaning is connected with interactive participation and reification in communal practice. Through the interaction of these two processes, it is possible to construct an exclusive historical context within the COP. An example of this is teacher training in BS. At the beginning, this only involved Chairman W lecturing on his teaching experience during meetings. This gradually led to the creation of the teacher training system of today in which, through engagement, the individual shares objects, ways of thinking, concepts, and interactive experience, to create significance.

Participation refers to the process by which the individual creates the interactive knowledge of social relationships within the social context he or she is located in (Kimble & Hildreth, 2005). In addition, the uniqueness of the social experiences created by connections and interactions of community members are part of both individual and social participation. With respect to BS, this covers many organizational routines, discussions between members, vocational considerations for the community and individual, the sentiments of the individual toward the group's entrepreneurial endeavors, and individual identity with the group (Wenger, 1998). Reification is beneficial in describing our engagement in the community; it is the concrete actualization of individual meaning. An example of this "speaking" about problem solving results for BS tutors during discussion meetings, as well as "writing these solutions on the blackboard or 'recording' them." These methods provide us with a form of externalization for our experiences and allow us to transform individual experiences into objective reality.

Through the interaction of participation and reification, the individual becomes involved in a negotiation of meaning which allows for an exchange concerning the embedded experiences of the community members. While meaning can be created through contemplation by the individual, this contemplation is conditional upon the individual being situated in the relationships and context of society. It is only through interaction with the community that this negotiation of meaning can possibly exist. It is diverse, complicated, and is not pre-existent but, rather, requires others (community members) for reification; these members must participate and join the negotiation for it to come into existence. Different negotiations of meaning are created based on unique community histories, situations, contexts, and individual traits (Wenger, 1998).

For this reason, contextual factors such as person, place, time, and space come into contact with one another and bring about transformation through a negotiation of meaning. At this time, meaning is anchored through reification and serves as the foundation for the next negotiation of meaning in which organization members actively participate and further create mutual experiences (Wenger, 1998). This cycle continues making the community's negotiation of meaning a dynamic one. In other words, through the complimentary participation and reification of practice, we can reexamine practice and find it is not merely something we do and do not think about. Rather, it involves doing and thinking at the same time. It is symbolic of the experience of practice and the continuous reflection on it.

Negotiation of meaning may be transformed as a result of contextual factors. At the same time, these changes occur, the individual will develop values different from his or her original ones concerning certain events, objects, people, and points of view as a result of this negotiation. Learning occurs at the moment of this shift. As previously stated, this study acknowledges an individual can take part in individual reflection and learning. However, the basis of this reflection and learning originates, as before, from social practice and the interaction of negotiations of meaning. This study refers to this as "learning moments in the negotiation of meaning."

3. Data Collection and Field of Study

3.1. *Data collection*

This research attempts to clarify how the process and details of how social learning constructs core competence in BS's realized community by analyzing field documents and utilizing the BS Supplementary Education Group's field data. As the process of organization core competence construction is a dynamic one, this cannot be adequately described through linear relationships. For this reason, it utilizes interviews in examining the learning and development process of BS senior tutors. In this way, we hope to dig more deeply into its social context and relationships to provide a clearer explanation of how learning within the COP influences the dynamics of core competence construction.

Table 1 is a precise listing of interview data.

Board Chairman Wang is also the founder of BS, and all of BS's managers who are middle or higher level must be proficient in these various positions; they must go through a series of trial job changes, from tutor to cram school manager. After attaining experience in attracting students, administration, and operations, they can then continue to be promoted as managers. As such, in addition to abundant operations experience, they also have ample teaching experience, as well as great faith in BS's teaching

Table 1.   Interview listings

Person interviewed	Number of interviews	Approximate duration of interview
Board Chairman Wang	3	3 hours (total)
General Manager Yang	4	8.8 hours (total)
Manager Cheng	1	0.6 hours
Co-manager Xie	1	2 hours
Co-manager Huang	1	1.6 hours
Tutor You	1	2.2 hours
Tutor Chang	1	2 hours
Tutor Liu	1	2.2 hours
Tutor Hong	1	1.8 hours
Tutor Fang	1	2.5 hours

system and core vision. In addition, to be a tutor at BS, it is necessary to pass a "teacher training appraisal," which is very strict, every year. Those who fail will not have their contracts renewed. According to the general manager (GM), tutors who have taught for more than one year become senior tutors. As such, the tutors I interviewed were all senior tutors with more than two years seniority.

The interviews were performed in a narrative manner and questions were not set prior to conducting the interview. Rather, the interview process was extremely open. An example question might be: may I ask you to speak about what impressed you most concerning entrepreneurial operations? How do you teach? How do you operate a school? These questions allowed the person interviewed to recall related memory fragments and start to elaborate on them. This study talked with every person interviewed for more than 2 hours on average and created a verbatim transcript to be analyzed.

3.2. *Study field*

BS Supplementary Education Group was founded in 1988 by Board Chairman Wang and his partner. At the outset, elementary school students were the focus of their teaching. At this stage they are one of the few supplementary education providers of gifted math courses for elementary and middle school students which has expanded to become a chain system. In 2009, they acquired an over-the-counter (OTC) technology company through mergers and acquisitions, and became the first OTC supplementary education company.

Previously, Board Chairman Wang worked for an educational cassette company which went bankrupt. At that time, Wang, who was excellent at math, actively taught the children of clients as a supplement to subscribers who had not yet received their product, and this was the genesis of good fortune in BS's founding, as it was Wang's start in supplementary math education. However, because it is so easy to start a cram school, many well-known tutors went off and formed their own schools later on. Because of this, Board Chairman Wang started considering the positioning of his own cram school. Originally, BS was one small cram school. Under the auspices of "supplementary education," it opened new school branches at an average rate of 24 schools per year over the course of 20 years, spreading from the south to central Taiwan, and then to the north. The BS cultural enterprise, which thrived under their gifted mathematics education brand name, also continued to widen their operational scope in the process of expansion. At present, their group includes the four departments of supplementary education, digital resources, cultural publishing, and lifestyles. In addition, they also have schools in Malaysia and Canada, thus expanding their brand of gifted mathematics education overseas. This chapter takes the BS Gifted Mathematics Cram School, which is a department of BS's Cultural Enterprise and Supplementary Education Group, as its research object. At present, it has 80 directly operated branches, and 200 exclusively employed tutors (including administrative employees) (Yang, 2013).

4. Cases

4.1. *Teacher training*

There was a low threshold with respect to conditions of establishing a cram school. Later, this led to one well-known tutor after another becoming independent. In order to allow BS to operate effectively in the future, W considered the possibility of BS having its own tutors.[2] He did not feel they had to rely on renowned tutors. W started recruiting tutors who would work exclusively for BS, and which BS would train. Through frequent discussion meetings with tutors, he taught them the teaching and problem explanation methods he knew. Gradually, these discussion meetings became a fixed training method within the organization — "teacher training."[3]

Teacher training is very important to BS's tutors, and this is particularly the case with newly arrived tutors. If they have just recently become a part of the BS organization, there is a large volume of proprietary teaching knowledge and skill which must be learned and made applicable; unique among these is "diagram explanation method."[4] If new tutors have not

---

[2]Tutors may only teach at BS, and may not teach part time anywhere else.

[3]Broadly, tutor training is divided into the middle school team, the elementary school team, and the special instruction team. The elementary school team is divided into lower grades (first grade, second trade), intermediate grades (third grade, fourth grade), and higher grades (fifth grade, sixth grade). The middle school team is divided by subject. The special training course is divided on the basis of courses created in accordance with need, and which require particular training for the related teaching material.

[4]Diagram explanation method was a problem explanation method which was created from learning from Japanese textbooks. In Taiwan's formal education system, fifth grade elementary school students do not learn the concepts of algebra

learned diagram explanation, in many cases, they cannot use traditional algebraic logic in making inferences, let alone teach elementary school children.

In BS, both junior and senior tutors must participate in teacher training, as this provides the opportunity for them to learn the teaching and problem explanation experiences of other tutors. Tutor C remembers when she was just beginning to teach and still did not know how to prepare for class. She would only practice the class problems beforehand in order to prepare to teach them to the students. At the outset, she would simply solve the problems one time and look at the answers to make sure she had solved them properly. C thought this was the proper way to prepare for class. However, she discovered that during class, her explanations lacked fluency and students could not understand her lecture method even though she had prepared. Later on in tutor training, GM Y made a suggestion concerning new tutors in preparing lessons: "when new tutors prepare lessons, they should make an effort to use diagram method logic and "think" about the problem three times. The first time is to solve the problem properly. The second time the tutor should think of how to explain the problem's solution. The third time the tutor must think of how to explain it so that the students will understand." After listening to GM Y's explanation C discovered this manner of preparing for class improved her teaching. She started to consider how to use logic the students could understand in teaching them rather than simply solving the problems for the students in a way they could not readily understand. From that time, this method became the main work flow for C in preparing classes.

In teacher training, there are many discussion meetings which inspire thought in tutors. Elementary school teacher training takes part twice a week with each session lasting 2.5 hours. Teacher training is performed in meetings at set times and in which grade level is divided into low, intermediate, and high. This training, which strengthens tutors' lecturing style, also provides an educational atmosphere in which tutors can continue their training. At the teacher training site, many different problem solutions

---

or unknown numbers. That is, if there are certain problems which cannot be solved without the use of the concepts of algebra, and algebraic logic is generally the commonly accepted mathematical teaching method. However, in BS, it is possible to use diagram explanation method logic to explain problems which originally required algebraic assumption to solve. (Later in this chapter, there is an example.)

can be presented, and the only principle is that explanations should use the diagram explanation method. At each grade level, senior tutors, who have already been exempted from teacher training, act as conveners and provide the itinerary for teacher training. Hereafter, demonstration teaching is undertaken in teacher training. In these demonstrations, the responsible tutor starts to write the problem-solving process he or she uses on the blackboard while explaining the logic involved. Senior tutors and others watch from downstage. After the tutor who is speaking has finished, everyone takes part in suggestion exchanges. Because not every tutor has the same strengths or weaknesses, some tutors might be good at diagrams, while others are good at application, with different types of problems being presented on stage, senior and junior tutors, as well as conveners, all provide their own opinions or solution methods. They can explain to the tutor onstage which concepts or teaching methods are most likely to cause students to make mistakes, and how to provide a more appropriate explanation. Finally, the convening tutor will sum up everyone's thoughts. The tutor who is being provided with these suggestions must record them and, after returning to their cram school, are required to consider these new concepts and practice them, as they will utilize them in demonstration lessons at the next teacher training session. In this manner, tutors can continuously try out these teaching methods and practices. For this reason, there is a strong impression concerning the problems tutors are responsible for. In addition, after sessions every tutor fills out a learning questionnaire in order to record the teaching methods and they use in class, as well as their explanations. These are archived once every teaching period for each grade, and are set into a book so that tutors can look at other tutors' teaching methods and explanations.

For example, such as Fig. 1, Tutor C was assigned to one math problem at one time: lines a and b combined have a length of 20. We know the end section of line b is 4. What is the length of line "a"?

C, who was still a new tutor, did not know how to use diagram explanation logic to explain the answer. As such, she only used traditional algebraic logic concepts which supposes "a" as x, with the front section of b

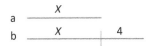

Fig. 1.   Line diagram explanation

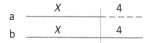

Fig. 2.   Line diagram explanation

also being x. Therefore, line b was $x + 4$, and a + b = $(x + x + 4) = 20$, and this allows us to arrive at a = $x = 8$. In traditional algebra, this is a standard way of answering the question, and is it not incorrect. However, senior tutors offered their own insights: because the target students were in elementary school, lower than fifth grade, they had not learned the notion of an unknown number. Thus, they had no way of understanding this explanation. For this reason, the senior tutors suggested using the diagram explanation method to explain the problem. As in Fig. 2, first extend an imaginary line from "a" so that it is as long as "b." Elementary school students have learned the concept of averages, so it is only necessary to make a and b the same length $(20 + 4)/2 = 12$, and say $12 - 4 = 8 = $ a. Thus, it is possible to arrive at the length of "a."

This is a transformative process. Tutor C originally used her own problem explanation logic and methods. Through the process of attending teacher training and discussing these methods with others, C discovered the algebraic method she found convenient previously was a concept elementary school students could not understand. Thus, she needed to use concepts closer to their conceptual understanding in teaching. Through this process, C changed her way of teaching. In teacher training, in a similar mode, senior and junior tutors provide their own solution methods and explanations with respect to the same problem. If three people provide explanations for one problem, and each of them possess sound logic, then tutors will have three ways of solving and explaining that problem.

Many new diagram methods were discovered in the process of these discussions. For example, BS has a diagram explanation method called the "scale method,"[5] which Board Chairman W happened across in a Japanese book. Later, Board Chairman W discussed it with GM Y. However, afterward Board Chairman W forgot about it after the discussion, while Y

---

[5]This used in the lever principle in physics. $F_1 D_1 = F_2 D_2$. It is a diagram created based on concepts of mathematical inverse. Finally, the equilibrium concentration is the level fulcrum with the mixed solution being placed into the two sections.

remembered it and brought it to the teacher training meeting in the north, where he taught it to other tutors.[6] The tutors from the north looked at it and discussed it. They felt this method would be good for solving more complex problems, as it would not be necessary to use formulas for concentration in explaining.[7] As such, the tutors from Northern Taiwan learned how to use the scale method in teacher training. In the south, Board Chairman W was responsible for teacher training, and he did not instruct the tutors there on this explanation method. Later, at one point, Tutor C from one of the northern school branches oversaw a special instruction session for math tutors with Manager L.[8] Tutor C taught class B, while Manager L taught class A, with both dealing with equally difficult problems. As a result of the screening process for students, the level of students in class A was generally higher than that of class B. As such, its average score should also naturally be higher than that of class B. On the contrary, Tutor C used scale method concepts in teaching complex problems. In final tests, the students in class B who learned scale method had higher general scores than class A. In one teacher training session in the south, Manager L angrily asked: "Why was this wonderful diagram explanation method not taught in southern Taiwan's teacher training sessions?" Hereafter, tutors from northern Taiwan traveled to the south to share scale method. After discussions and explanations on its logic, the tutors from the south became acquainted with this new method of explanation.

4.2. *Entering new markets — The case of GM Y's entrepreneurial story*

GM Y (hereafter Y) started as a lecturer, and then was promoted in succession to the Xiaogang branch school manager in Kaohsiung and, later, area manager, and finally, he became GM. In the process of being promoted up,

---

[6]Chairman W was responsible for teacher training in the south, while teacher training in the north took place under General Manager Y.

[7]In Taiwan's school system, percentage concentration is taught in the second year of middle school. However, this second year middle school physics and chemistry problem can be taught to elementary school students through scale method diagram explanation.

[8]The special instruction class is made up of students with excellent qualifications in school branches. More gifted students are placed into class A, and the others in class B.

he accumulated a great deal of teaching and managerial experience. At that time, the branch was in danger of closing. However, under Y's direction, the number of students increased by several magnitudes within a half year, and within a year, they were making a profit. His outstanding performance won him the praise of the Board Chairman, who wanted him to become the northern region manager and increase market share there. Y's assignment was to find new areas for branches, and bring in students, so that BS could expand profitably. With capital raised jointly by shareholders and the company, BS opened four branches in the north. What is more, Y was made responsible for coordinating the operation of each branch. However, at that time, BS could not provide a great deal of resources to assist Y.

BS encountered an operational bottleneck within one year as the competition in the Taipei market was intense, and Y was forced to spend advertising money at a rapid pace. He managed to completely spend the 8 million in advertising fees allotted to him. After six months, one school was forced to close because of deficits. A meeting was held with Y and other managers to determine why the first branch was unable to attract more students and grow. After discussing the matter, Y came to several conclusions: (1) the school was located in an area where it was not easily visible, and there was a limit to capital. In addition, the rent for first floor store fronts in Taipei is relatively high; so most branches are on the second floor; the entrance is in an alley which is extremely difficult to get to, and many potential customers could not find it. (2) Management lacked managerial experience, and the branch manager had not been on the job long enough, and did not know how to operate the branch. (3) The regional manager plays a critical role and should assist the branch manager. However, while Y was an excellent manager in the south, he did not know how to disseminate his managerial experience in instructing managers in school branch operations. Faced with the above problems, limited resources, and the necessity of leading a new group of branch managers, Y considered how to delegate his responsibility to others, as well as the possibility of allowing branch managers to learn branch school operation methods. Y suddenly realized he could create "assignment groups,"[9] and this method would allow Y to conveniently teach all involved the sales method he had invented.

---

[9]The assignment group method involved managers with varying skills working together (branch school managers are not necessarily chosen from those in administration, as some were previously lecturers. As such, these managers' tend

Faced with the density of schools involved in the supplementary education industry, and the extremely competitive environment in the north,
Y discovered that the generally used advertising flyers were a waste of paper
and did not necessarily have the intended effect. Thus, he decided to use a
method which would leverage greater effect with less resources expended to
advertise for BS. He invented utilitarian tissue packages for advertisement.
First of all, the BS advertisement was printed on the tissue package. These
tissue packages could be placed in many places of business. For example,
noodle stands and convenience stores, where those passing by could pick
them up. Tissue is a necessity of life which most members of the public will
take, and when they use the tissue, they will see the BS advertisement, and
this more likely to achieve the goal of advertising. Later on, other school
branches started to utilize this method as well. In addition, BS has an internal magazine entitled "BS Education." Originally, this magazine was circu-
lated within the company for reading by members. One day, Y had a sudden
thought: these magazines could be placed in beauty shops or clinics. At first,
many female branch managers thought this was not a good idea and told Y:
"This idea will not work. As a woman I know. No one who goes to the beau-
tician to have our hair washed, get a facial, or get a permanent will want to
read such a serious magazine. Most look at gossip magazines." Y explained
he knew clients would not look through the magazine. However, they could
see the cover and this would provide exposure for BS. As a result of this
short dialog, the managers started to reexamine the function of printed
advertising in attracting students. In addition, Y observed mothers were
the potential customers to advertise for, because they had more opportunities to go outside to buy breakfast or lunch or go shopping. For this reason,

---

toward being stronger in the area of education, and are unfamiliar with branch
management). Group activities are set up based on assignments. For example, if
the topic is attracting students, a manager for whom this is a strong suit will
be chosen as committee leader. Such a manager will have his or her own way
of attracting students and thus will be tasked with planning the overall activity,
and Y will assist from the side. During group discussions, the group leader will
share the plans he or she used to attract students and advertise for classes in the
past. This method of dividing groups can allow each manager to feel that he or
she has been acknowledged. At the same time, new managers who have trouble
attracting students can learn from observation. Conversely, if that day's group
leader's strong suit is education, this method can be used to strengthen lecturer
training for branch schools.

they were more likely to see BS's advertisements, while fathers were only responsible for providing the tuition. Mothers became the main medium of activities to attract new students. Finally, Y believed students should only have to travel a short distance to go to school. Because BS did not have an additional budget to provide transportation for students, they would attract students in areas where transportation to and from the schools was the most convenient. Y said that BS locked in on a 5-mile walking distance radius of 5 miles as their core area for attracting students. He discovered that this method clearly raised BS's visibility and increased effectiveness in attracting new students. While it was not possible to teach all of these methods to every manager, new managers could learn his sales methods through the function of assignment groups very quickly. These activities for attracting students, and related skills, became the "community strategy" for BS. According to new or junior managers, these practices were all the personal managerial experiences of Y and other managers, and it was questionable whether they could write a work instruction manual about it. However, through group discussion, it was possible for these managers to personally learn and carry out the duties of managing a school branch and understand "community strategy."

5. Narrative Analysis

5.1. *Germinal learning is formed within the teaching and operational community*

As Teacher C and GM Y both had the same perception after they engaged in teacher training and the assignment group. "If we had known about this great thing, I would have been better at math," teacher C said, and GM Y said: "Because I got to know them I found how to cultivate and lead a team." They arrived at this reflection primarily through in teacher training and the assignment group, as well as mutual engagement, discussion, interaction, and negotiation. This is necessarily linked with the social relations and practices of people, and based on Wenger's (1998) social learning theory; the proposed COP provides learning path to learning through consideration.

The participants who mutually engaged in teacher training and the assignment group naturally established a teaching (teacher training) and management (assignment groups) COP. Within the teaching community, if only a traditional top–down way of training teachers how to do problem-solving skills, this will become hegemonic, and non-innovative. If the novice teacher, however, stands on the teaching stage, and the other teachers, including senior and junior teachers, are under the stage to perform the role of consultants in discussion, the problem-solving approach will no longer be singular and more teaching experience can be utilized in leading discussion, which leads to logical thinking innovations making the graphical method more diverse in field training. For the operation community, since BS uses chain operations, the cumulative operational experiences of novices in and of itself will be insufficient. However, if the community operates interactively, senior directors can utilize their operational and practical experience in the discussion process. An example is GM Y, who brings out the concept of community strategy through regular seminars. The junior director in this environment learns how to think and use BS's peculiar mode of operation. Through ongoing practical interaction, community participants will link with each other to convert the significance of self-awareness and naturally negotiation of meaning by practice and synchronized learning. Therefore, the meaning of teacher training and task grouping is no longer that of a simple organizational system, but rather is the teachers' learning experience community.

Through senior and junior teachers and managers mutually engaging in practice, each participant in the community uses their own imagination (imagination) and alignment (alignment) in practice within the communities. The concept of imagination refers to participants' ability to imagine the practice form and guess how to perform these. Because imagination has many possibilities, it is of assistance in breaking through the limitations of the self-thinking framework. Thus, it is possible to create new practice. Alignment is a part of imagination within the process of trying to imitate a senior member or other participants' actions in adjusting to the practical state.

When teacher C was a novice, she was an outsider and had now memory or teaching experience with regard to BS. In addition, her understanding of the methods required for teaching at BS was vague and she relied on teaching methods used in the past (algebraic solution) in the framework of the education system. While utilizing this previously learned logic in interacting with senior and junior instructors, she found her teaching logic and direction were insufficient. First, she did not know what the graphical method was. However, when she actually became involved in teacher training, she obtained a fragmentary image of what it was. She then continued to participate in teacher training and self-training in which she tried to align graphical method with the many solutions the teachers provided (especially senior teacher) in constantly repeated likeness — align — imagining — and then aligned. Teacher C began to understand the BS graphical method, and develop her own graphical method. By COP approach, graphical method became creative, and allowed participants to be more logical and creative in practice. Participants could also continue to provide feedback in the form of new creativity to the community. The operation community also operates in a similar manner to develop community strategies. They are not kinds of objects or knowledge we can learn, but logic. Because the customer base of every BS branch office in the region is unique, the operations must also be based on differences and are subject to changes and adjustments. Therefore, as long as a member understands the logic of community strategies, he or she would be able to modulate their own admissions policies, including enrolling new students and others support activities. For the novice director, however, the community strategy is a very vague concept, so they must try to imagine the picture of community strategy and attempt to align the practices and ideas of senior directors, gradually learning what the community strategy logic is and how to use it. He or she must even, under this logic, create their own admission methods.

When members join the community, however, the practices of alignment and imagination are not like the "sending — accepting" of information, or an absolute one-way relationship. Rather, it refers to the multiple perspectives of members' interpretations and their convergence at that moment. Through participation mutual discussion, teachers and directors in the community begin to find sense in meaning through negotiations. In the COP, practice is not always rigid, but in constant negotiation, ongoing, and endogenous. That is, a senior member is never, in fact, absolutely right because there may be new entrants with new inspirations and elements affecting communities and senior's practice. Via engagement, BS's teaching and management experience is constructed, continuously invested in, and learned. The meaning of this negotiation process and its results are stored in the COP, and members of the community must be involved and engaged for it to be harvested.

Whether it is teacher C or GM Y, if the COP does not provide a route through which encounters and interactions evoke new practice, ideas cannot change and new understandings cannot be formed. Hence, from another perspective, when member practice transformation also represents a change in the meaning of the group's self-identity (due to self-identity changes practice). In this sense, the process of becoming through practice is learning.

5.2. *Participation in and stages of the negotiation of meaning*

Through participation in the COP tutors and managers continuously negotiate meaning within the community. Tutors' notions of meaning concerning
diagram explanation, and managers' ideas of meaning concerning operations, continuously transform with respect to how they are imagined as a
result of involvement. There are two necessary conditions for negotiation
of meaning: participation and reification. These items mutually assist each
other so the learner can more clearly anchor the educational meaning created in his or her COP.

For C, there are three stages involved in teacher training's negotiation
of meaning. The first is the **blind learning meaning negotiation**. This
stage involves forced participation in the organization. Prior to teacher
training, it is necessary to first obtain BS's lecture topics and think about
how you want to explain the problem. Afterward, tutors prepare to give a
teaching demonstration on stage. During teacher training, it is necessary to
lecture in front of other junior and senior tutors, to answer questions, and
to take directions from these tutors. This routine made C feel that teacher
training participation was simply another part of work. What is more, she
did not understand the meaning of teacher training participation. However,
since this phase involves legitimate peripheral participation, we cannot say
it held no significance for her. Rather, it provided her with the first visu-
alizations of the COPs. With the accumulation of teacher training participation experience, C entered the second stage: **alignment learning
meaning negotiation**. C still held onto the traditional algebraic logic in
teaching and describing how to answer questions. She believed if problems
could not be solved through algebraic logic, then they could not be solved
period. In teacher training, she wrote out the solution process and logic concerning the problem in "see details in the story" in detail on the blackboard
and explained it. When the senior tutors started discussing the problem
with C, learning was triggered. The senior tutors also provided feedback on
her teaching commentaries, and wrote down the methods for carrying out
diagram explanation method. For C, who brought her long-held problem-
solving logic when she started to participate in teacher training, the diagram explanation method provided a spark which allowed C to see and
consider problem solving from a different perspective. C started to record
the explanation methods, as well as the methods from the other tutors in
tutor training. After training finished, C used this logic to reconsider the

problem discussed in class, as well as other problems related to it. In this stage of meaning negotiation, C started to move away from the first stage of negotiation concerning blind study, as she had experienced that BS's actually was unique from what others thought.

The third stage is **reflection learning meaning negotiation**. Through teacher training class notes and recordings, C was able to anchor the logic of diagram explanation method. She used this logic to continue solving other problems in the lecture as well. Afterward, she attempted to explain it to herself and imagined she was talking to an elementary student and asking herself whether or he or she would understand her explanation. During this stage, C attempted to transform the diagram explanation method she learned during teacher training into something of meaning to her. In addition, in the following teacher training session, she further discusses diagram explanation logic with other tutors. Hereafter, she continued to participate in teacher training.

Y also went through similar learning stages, starting with the blind learning meaning negotiation stage. At the beginning, Y was "tasked" with developing the northern market. He did not know where to start when faced with this market, nor did he know how to teach the branch school managers. He could only use standard methods such as A4 advertising flyers and have the branches make advertisements. This method wasted money and was ineffective. This led to branch schools closing in the end. He saw his relationships with workers as a stratified one, and did not have any concern for them. For him, being the northern region manager was an assignment he was especially tasked with. At this stage, Y slowly started to involve himself with other members and the market. His failure and the actions which had led to his sadness, as well as his experiences gave him a new way of thinking about developing the market and teaching workers. In the alignment learning meaning negotiation stage, Y started to reconsider, in a new manner, past ways of doing things because of experiences of failure. For example, he started thinking about whether or not his past advertising methods were wasting money, and whether or not they were effective. As a result, he began to desire to find different modes of advertising. He forced himself to participate in the first branch school closing. He found through the process in which schools closed that, while he could manage, he did not know how to teach management. In addition, Y started to consider how to achieve great results with little effort in his consultations with new branch school managers. There were limited resources with which to interact with new managers, and Y came to realize the "assignment groups" were an excellent solution to this problem. Y also discovered the cohesiveness of organization members was insufficient. These setbacks sparked Y to develop a new kind of learning for the northern market, which he hoped would allow him to find new solutions from his failures. In the reflection learning meaning negotiation stage, he started to reconsider his involvement. He attempted to find solutions which would provide effective feedback from his failures. Y invented advertising tissue packages, the BS Education Magazine advertising method. He also observed mothers were the main object of student recruitment efforts, developed the idea of core student recruitment regions, and implemented other measures as well. These strategies were integrated to form the "community path strategy." Because of his involvement in interactions with his workers, he slowly came to understand what his workers needed was not simply spiritual demands; they must have demands concerning their interest as well. He actively created cohesiveness among the northern branch school managers and hoped to provide tutors a sense of belonging as well. When Y started these marketing strategies, his relationship with members, and his marketing activity teaching were not part of Y's initial plan for reform. Rather, Y had to experience continual interactive involvement with members, and negotiations of meaning, before he could arrive at the present meaning.

Stated further, in both communities of education and management, the negotiation of meaning within these communities is temporal and dynamic; meaning it is not fixed. For the individual, the negotiation of meaning temporarily serves as learning orientation "ability," and for the COP, this negotiation serves as its temporary competence. The individual's learning and the community's regime of competence will expand and improve based on time and the entrance of different members; examples include various tutors who are good at solving different types of problems and managers who have different expertise in management and instruction. As such, the regime of competence is the result of negotiation of meaning. The individual and community's learning move parallel as both the members and the community interact with respect to competence.

5.3. *Negotiation co-constructs the formation of a regime of competence*

Community members continue with regular and routine activities, and continue to be entrepreneuring, to aggregate, and to anchor every stage of meaning negotiations. The community co-constructs a tentative and unique meaning through negotiation which is significant and dynamic. This is then embedded within the community and becomes its regime of competence. This would include diagram explanation and community path strategy. With respect to the community, and the practice within it, a concrete learning track or track paradigm is created for members by this practice (Wenger, 1998), and members continue to negotiate competence based on this path. As such, the learning track is an important factor in meaning negotiation becoming a regime of competence. In each stage of meaning negotiation, the learner gradually modifies, carves out, and reforms the regime of competence as a result of his or her contact with meaning negotiation at each stage facilitated by the learning track.

In teacher training, this competence is none other than diagram explanation method. While the logic concept behind diagram explanation came from a Japanese book, the version of it BS uses integrates the community's junior and senior members' creation through learning in nature. This led to the development of BS's unique diagram explanation method. Senior tutors use BS's its own self-compiled problems in utilizing diagram explanation method in discussions with junior tutors. As an example, at the outset, BS did not possess scale method. When Y discovered it in a book, it was simply a logical concept. However, after Y started using it to instruct tutors in the northern region, the members of this community started using this notion with respect to BS's problems, thus carrying out a negotiation of meaning. In the end, scale method became a commonly used diagram explanation method for BS, and teacher training competence was modified and reformed. By contract, the regime of competence for assignment group tasks was community path strategy. Y and the managers in the assignment group were anchored by every observation of salesmanship strategies in the northern market. For example, advertisement tissue packages, the location of printed advertisement, the choice of student recruitment object, branch school location choices, core areas for student recruitment, and other strategies. While this might seem like a standard operational flow, in fact, it subsumed within it is the core regime of competence.

Diagram explanation method and community path strategy are BS's competitive advantage as a community. This competency is what distinguishes them from other competitors in the supplementary education business. It is also the critical factor which separates it from "remedial education" which is not part of a school curriculum. For members of this community, and for new comers specifically, following the learning track in learning the regime of competence is the source of difference between those just beginning and experts (Fuller, 2007). However, while experts may be able to gain approval through the accumulation of time, they still must seek recognition based on the depth of their learning and advancements as in the past. Different learners will experience different degrees of progress. This leads teacher training participant C to state "every tutor has a different understanding of learning the same diagram explanation method. Some tutors can utilize it right after they use it, while others have to learn several times before they understand." Therefore, it is necessary to see whether someone has skillfully grasped these competencies, in addition to the accumulation of time, in order to determine whether he or she will become an expert within the community.

6. Conclusion

Learning is sparked by interaction and meaning negotiations with others in the practice of everyday life, and allows the individual to have reflective experiences. It also creates the inspiration for the individual to revise his or her potential values and awareness. The learners in our study commence through their contact with the COP. It is the community which provides legitimate peripheral participation (the admittance to BS). The COP allows those newly entering the community, or those without a community track, to participate. These newcomers participate through observation or involvement. At the outset, C and Y entered into the COP's first stage through organization regulations and institutions in their learning. For them, this was the threshold for the experience of learning about BS.

Through the interactive involvement of members practice within the community creates concrete learning tracks or paradigm tracks. The learner may understand the community's conventions or routine activities through these tracks, in addition to following, aligning, and providing feedback in meaning negotiations with other members within the activity contexts. Negotiation of meaning necessarily relies on the reciprocal benefiting from growth provided by members' active participation accompanied by reified objects. Both of these are required. With this prerequisite, learners are not necessarily those with less experience. Those with greater experience can also learn from the former. An example of this would include Y's learning how to lead new managers through his contact with them. For this reason, a negotiation of meaning occurs through the co-construction of community members and learners. In addition, through interactive participation learning continues to occur. In other words, learning cannot be accomplished by the learner acting according to his own notions or intent. It is still necessary for the learner to form social connections and interpersonal relationships with the resources and other members of the community. Peer recognition is also required.

When members anchor the negotiation of meaning, a regime of competence is created and embedded within the community. This also becomes the organization's competence. In the cases this study presents "diagram explanation method" and "community path strategy" are the critical concepts which provide BS with its own unique station in Taiwan's market, a market in which "remedial teaching" prevails. The core competence of these two possesses both dynamic and tentative characteristics; they continue to be reformed and transformed as a result of the participants, dialog, and discussion, as well as spatial and temporal differences in the community. An example is the introduction of the scale diagram explanation method. These processes can occur either rapidly or slowly. These core competences are extremely important to the community. Internally, it is the subject of community member learning. Competency learners display the development and change of the community through continuous contact. An example includes a novice becoming an expert. Externally, this competence becomes critical to the community competing or interacting with other communities of practice, such as distinguishing one's own market within Taiwan, and being hard to imitate.

Individuals are transformed into new people as a result of the community's social relationships and learning which occurs through interaction (Lave & Wener, 1991). Through the recognition of core members, the learner continues to move toward the organization's core. This process also implies the transformation of individual identity. This can be adjudicated from two central factors. First is vocational advancement and, second, are the abilities and experiences of the member in interacting with the organization's resources and members. From the perspective of the organization, changes in vocational position represent leadership or management's acknowledgement of the learner's abilities and experiences. Within two years, C went from being a lecturer to being a branch school manager and BS's overall planner. Y went from being a lecturer to being a branch manager; he then went on to be a district manager, and later became BS's GM. These advancements not only represent the notion of moving toward the organization's core, but are also part of the process by which a person is transformed from a novice to a senior member.

References

Aurini, J. (2006). "Crafting Legitimation Projects: An Institutional Analysis of Private Education Businesses," *Sociological Forum*, 21(1), pp. 83–111.

Fenwick, T. (2008). Understanding Relations of Individual–Collective Learning in Work: A Review of Research, *Management Learning*, 39(3), pp. 227–243.

Fuller, A. (2007). Crtitiquing theories of learning and communities of practice, in J. Hughes, N. Jewson, & L. Unwin (eds), *Communities of Practice: Critical Perspectives*, London: Routledge, pp. 17–29.

Hamel, G. & Heene, A. (1994). *Competence-Based Competition.* New York: John Wiley and Sons.

Heo, G. M. & Breuleux, A. (2008). *Three Planes of Learning in COP: Exploring an Online Community of Chefs at the Community Plane.* Paper presented at the American Educational Research Association 2008 Annual Meeting, New York, US.

Kimble, C. & Hildreth, P. (2005). Dualities, Distributed Communities of Practice and Knowledge Management, *Journal of Knowledge Management*, 9(4), pp. 102–113.

Kwok, P. (2004). Examination-Oriented Knowledge and Value Transformation in East Asian Cram Schools, *Asia Pacific Education Review*, 5(1), pp. 64–75.

Lave, J. & Wenger, E. (1991). *Situated Learning: Legitimate Peripheral Participation.* Cambridge: Cambridge University Press.

Ljungquist, U. (2007). Core Competency Beyond Identification: Presentation of a Model, *Management Decision*, 45(3), pp. 393–402.

Prahalad, C. K. & Hamel, G. (1990). The Core Competence of Corporation, *Harvard Business Review*, 68(3), pp. 79–91.

Shiahhou, H.-P., Yang, B.-C., & Teng, M.-F. (2010). The Study of Prioritizing the Influential Factors of Choosing Core Competency and Core Organizational Capability, *Chung Yuan Management Review*, 8(1), pp. 89–122.

Wenger, E. (1998). *Communities of Practice: Learning, Meaning, and Identity.* Cambridge: Cambridge University Press.

Yang, B.-C. Shiahhou, H.-P., & Teng, M.-F. (2010). The Explanatory Study of the Content of Organizational Capabilities, *Management Review*, 29(3), pp. 45–63.

Yang, J. W. (2013). Recognizing the Six Math Tutoring System in Taiwan, *Parenting*, 44, pp. 154–160.

8

Pioneering Social Entrepreneurs in Japan: Financial Performance and Social Achievement

Akira Sawamura
Niigata University

Satoshi Arimoto
Niigata University

1. Introduction

This chapter aims to clarify that pioneering social entrepreneurs in Japan are also sound in their financial performance, which forms the basis for their social achievement. We first describe the history of social entrepreneurial theory in Japan and subsequently discuss three representative organizations: Daichi Co., Ltd.; Swan Co., Ltd.; and Florence, an incorporated non-profit organization (NPO). Daichi was the first to offer home delivery of organic foods in Japan. Swan was founded by a charismatic manager who filed a complaint with the Ministry of Transport (currently part of the Ministry of Land, Infrastructure, Transport, and Tourism) when he started his home-delivery business. He founded Swan to employ disabled people who lacked support. Florence is an NPO that helps working women by providing care for their sick children; the founder is well-known as one of Japan's representative entrepreneurs.

The three organizations are representative companies that enjoy stable management, and they have been discussed in various ways. However, these discussions have focused only on social significance, and none have examined management infrastructure, which is vital for keeping an organization going. In this chapter, we analyze the financial positions and social impacts of these companies to determine whether they can be evaluated as corporate bodies helping to reform Japanese society. To evaluate a profit-making enterprise, such outputs as value produced, profit and loss, and sales should be considered. To evaluate a social entrepreneur, however, not only outputs but also outcomes showing how much he or she has affected society should be considered.

In this chapter, we analyze the financial aspects of businesses operated by Japan's representative social entrepreneurs with the help of their business reports. Sales trends, the number of customers, and the number of employees can be used as indicators of output.

A social entrepreneur founds a company to solve a specific social problem that interests him or her. He or she will dissolve the company and look for another challenge once he or she solves the problem. Even if the entrepreneur fails to solve the problem, he or she will branch out into a new business field. Otherwise, it is necessary to see whether a policy was formulated to solve the specific social problem. That is, the social impact, or the social entrepreneur's desired outcome, exceeds the limits of what a person or company can achieve. To evaluate a social entrepreneur, therefore, it is necessary to confirm whether the entrepreneur gained followers or whether a policy satisfying his or her mission was enacted.

2. Input, Output, and Outcome

In this chapter, we introduce the concepts of *input*, *output*, and *outcome* to evaluate social entrepreneurs. These concepts are used in new public management theory, which asks government departments to adopt a management perspective. We expanded the scope of these concepts and applied them to the evaluation of entrepreneurs. Input refers to the management resources that an organization uses, output is the amount of goods and services the organization provides, and outcome refers to the organization's social achievements and its non-financial performance. It can be hard to differentiate between output and outcome, and most existing entrepreneurial theories do not make such a distinction. In this chapter, however, we define output as that which is directly provided by the organization while outcome refers to results produced outside the organization. For example, we judge that a social entrepreneur has produced an outcome and affected society if he or she attracted followers and if a policy was formulated to address the targeted social problem.

Using input, output, and outcome for analysis suggests that only organizations with social significance are being analyzed. Today, however, it has become important for general profit-making corporations to be socially responsible. With the advent of environmental accounting and the growing importance of the report on corporate social responsibility (CSR), for-profit corporations are now expected to produce outcomes (i.e., social results) in response to input. It is worth noting that the analytical viewpoint we adopt in this chapter is a generalized analytical viewpoint in current corporate analysis.

3. History of Social Entrepreneurial Theory in Japan

Industrialists regarded as social entrepreneurs have existed in history. After the modern age, we can identify social reformers like Toyohiko Kagawa who addressed improving shanty towns in Osaka and founded Kobe Consumption Association, which is the parent of today's Consumer Co-operative Kobe, in 1921. However, their actions were based mostly on socialist and Christian mindsets, and they did not give high priority to solving social problems as today's entrepreneurs do. Even before the modern age, Sontoku Ninomiya famously devoted himself to improving living standards in many villages, pursuing both moral and economic ends. His business was inherited as the Hotoku Undo (gratitude business), and several associations are active even today, mainly in Kanagawa and Shizuoka prefectures.

The system for founding non-profit corporations engaged in public-interest activities has existed since the 19th century, and many schools, museums, foundations, and medical institutes were founded through it. However, a large sum of capital is needed to found such an organization, and the standards for foundation are obscure, making the system irrelevant to organizations based on grassroots public campaigning. Under such circumstances, many volunteers got together for rescue and reconstruction efforts in response to the Great Hanshin Earthquake in 1995. Japanese society recognized that a volunteer organization for rescue and reconstruction could be called NPO. In 1998, the legal system established the corporate status of NPOs. This enactment made people think of NPOs first as organizations to solve social problems.

In contrast, it can be said that Yoji Machida (2000) first introduced the concept of the social entrepreneur in Japan. In the database of the *Asahi Shimbun*, the term *social entrepreneur* appears in a review of Machida's book, *Social Entrepreneur*; a term with a similar meaning had never appeared before that. Machida said he discovered the term *social entrepreneur* in a report published by British think tank DEMOS.

Accordingly, the term and concept of social entrepreneur, as used in Japan, was imported from Great Britain; it described people starting business to solve social problems both at home and abroad. Subsequently, people who started unprecedented businesses were called social entrepreneurs. The term first appeared in English in 1911 (Mair, 2011).

As described above, it is easy to define a social entrepreneur. The trend toward calling companies devoted to supporting the socially vulnerable *social enterprises* was imported from Europe and the United States to Japan. However, defining a social enterprise in this way is problematic. That is, it is impossible to tell how a social entrepreneur company differs from a company engaged in CSR activities or a company that contributes to society through its main business (e.g., by developing more convenient products and providing more efficient services). If an organization is founded to solve a social problem, it will lose its reason to exist as soon as it solves the problem successfully. It is interesting to consider what an organization should do when it loses its existence value. In this chapter, however, we focus only on social entrepreneurs without touching on social enterprises that exist on the assumption of the going-concern principle.

In the 21st century, researchers on NPOs and management scholars have accumulated studies of social entrepreneurs; such work is epitomized in books by Kanji Tanimoto (2006) and Tsukamoto and Yamagishi (2008). These two books are based mainly on case studies, and they discuss cases both in Japan and abroad. However, the cases in these books are mostly designed for qualitative analysis, and they simply offer a summary of organization, the content of the business, and the motivation for and significance of the start-up according to the founder. This chapter conducts management analysis using the statement of accounts and confirms the business' impact on society. We draw upon Steyaert and Katz (2004), Kerlin (2010), and Gawell (2012) as the preeminent studies on social entrepreneurs in the world, mainly the US and Europe.

4.   Case 1 — Daichi Co., Ltd.

Daichi Co., Ltd. (hereafter referred to as Daichi; the materials for discussion came from Kazuyoshi Fujita (2005) and from Daichi's business reports and website (www.daichi.or.jp)) offers home delivery of organic vegetables, mainly in the Tokyo metropolitan area. Originally founded as Daichi Wo Mamoru Shimin no Kai ("Society to Protect Land"), which was a civil movement started in 1975, the company played an intermediary role between producers and consumers in providing a stable supply of safe and pesticide-free agricultural and livestock products. In those days, however, corporate status was not available to civil movements, and Daichi faced various difficulties in concluding contracts while it remained a voluntary association. To overcome this problem, it incorporated its distribution division in 1977. Fujita, a representative of the civil movement, said he would have transformed the movement into an incorporated NPO if the status of NPO had been available in those days (Kazuyoshi Fujita, 2005). Some involved in the movement left in protest of the plan to incorporate, saying that a for-profit corporation is an advanced capitalist organization and therefore hostile to the civil movement. The period from incorporation until 2010 was dedicated to designing the organization so that people who joined the civil movement could use the delivery system of Daichi. Enrollment charges automatically allow new members to become single shareholders. Once membership is granted, new members can place orders for Daichi's safe foods, like organic vegetables, through its catalog once a week and have the food delivered to their homes the following week.

Daichi and the civil movement body "merged" in October 2010 with a view to achieving success in the market economy as a social enterprise. That meant the virtual dissolution of the civil movement body, but the reality was that the incorporated company succeeded the activities of the civil movement body. As far as we know, the brochure of the general meeting of shareholders and the business report were sent to the members of the civil movement annually, but a report on the civil movement was never sent in the middle of 1990s. From this, we can gather that Daichi and the civil movement were virtually united.

On the occasion of incorporation, Daichi had planned to make an initial public offering (IPO) in the future. To realize the plan, it was decided to base the stock price on the market price and ask the civil movement members to pay the difference between the old stock price and the market price should they wish to become shareholders. Because the new stock was more than JPY (Japanese Yen) 100,000, while the old stock was JPY5,000, the number of shareholders decreased greatly from more than 19,500 to 874. The drastic decrease can be attributed to the fact that many of the members joined the movement not because they agreed with its objective but because they wanted to purchase safe, pesticide-free agricultural and livestock products. (Members can still purchase through the home-delivery service even if they are not shareholders.) Daichi also exerts a great deal of energy on its web-based mail-order business. Therefore, Daichi can be

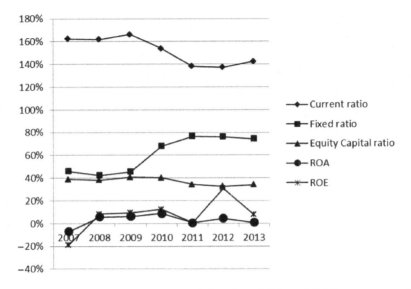

Fig. 1.   Indexes of Daichi's safety, ROA and ROE

said to have changed its attitude from that of a civil movement of public interest to a growing social enterprise.

Let us consider Daichi's financial condition from its statement of accounts. Unlike a general for-profit corporation, a company managed by a social entrepreneur is obliged to continuously provide outcomes. That is, such a company must be managed in a stable manner to keep providing outcomes. Therefore, it is important to confirm the safety of the organization. Figure 1 shows that Daichi, which is evaluated as a successful case that has been providing outcomes, remains sound in terms of safety. Based on this financial condition, it is necessary to analyze how much output Daichi has been providing. Daichi's statement of accounts shows that the company has expanded its asset size over the past seven years. It increased its total assets from JPY (in units of million) 3,477.43 in the fiscal year ending March 2006 to JPY4,474.96 million in the fiscal year ending March 2013. Because the equity capital ratio remained unchanged at about 35%, the business expanded without unreasonable borrowing. Although sales increased steadily until the fiscal year ending March 2010, they decreased slightly after the fiscal year ending March 2011. The decrease is partly due to the Great East Japan Earthquake. Whatever the case, Daichi enjoyed stable business expansion until at least 2010.

Figure 1 also shows that the return on assets (ROA) and the return on equity (ROE) remained stable until the fiscal year ending March 2009. Because Daichi is evaluated by both output and outcome, it can be said that Daichi maintained a reasonable level to date even if it is evaluated only by output. However, ROA and ROE both started decreasing in 2010. The fiscal year ending March 2010 was the period in which Daichi clarified its objective to increase outcome and output simultaneously with a view to making an IPO in the future to transform it from a civil movement body to a for-profit corporation. Daichi built a prepared foods booth inside the premises of Tokyo Station in March 2010 and opened a directly managed restaurant in Marunouchi in July of the same year. It can be said, therefore, that Daichi was transitioning from a social organization producing outcomes to a company pursuing outcomes and outputs simultaneously. Daichi was still unsuccessful in showing a clear trend of improving its ROA and ROE in the fiscal year ending March 2013; it entered into a new stage as a limited company because it had concluded a business collaboration agreement with Lawson, one of the major convenience store corporations in Japan. It is necessary to keep watching how the company improves its profitability, but its safety, as mentioned earlier, remains stable. We are concerned about whether Daichi will grow from being a company with a stable management infrastructure to a company that can provide outputs at the same time.

Next, we will discuss Daichi's social impact (i.e., its outcome). Fujita proposed his ideas to co-ops in the initial stage, but the co-ops declined saying his prices were too high. That is why he built a distribution channel by himself. Later, co-ops carried pesticide-free and decreased-pesticide vegetables, and for-profit food stores followed suit. Although it is unknown whether Daichi was motivated by this trend, Daichi's policy was clearly right, and the company took the initiative in the business to distribute organic products.

One of Daichi's outcomes in policy formulation is that the Ministry of Agriculture, Forestry, and Fisheries launched the certification system for organic foods in 2006. Some point out that the certification system for organic foods is not satisfactory and that gray and unsafe foods are being sold on the market. Regarding this issue, producers who are serious about selling organic products first think of Daichi and Radisshu Bo-ya ("Radish Boy") as companies for consultation. These companies are evaluated highly because they have been handling organic foods for a long time and have established self-developed know-how for examining foods.

Daichi faces three challenges, though it enjoys a stable managing status with increasing customers. First, when it goes public as planned, new shareholders will not necessarily keep its management policy as a social company in mind. They may be concerned only about its ROE. Daichi may not be able to adhere to its corporate philosophy of sticking with the "stable supply of safe and pesticide-free agricultural and livestock products" should it place a high priority on increasing ROE. Daichi was involved in founding another company in the same trade, Radisshu Bo-ya, in 1988. Radisshu Bo-ya became a consolidated subsidiary of another company in 2000 and later became a company within another corporate group. Subsequently, it was listed on the JASDAQ in 2008 but became a subsidiary of NTT DoCoMo through TOB in 2012. Daichi is not immune from the possibility of following Radisshu Bo-ya's path.

The second challenge is that Kazuyoshi Fujita, who is a founding member and served as representative for a long period, was born in 1947, and he will have to transfer management rights to the next generation sooner or later. A social company risks becoming a general company unless the aspiration and mission of the founder are inherited.

The third challenge concerns the present state of the primary industry in Japan. Workers in the primary industry are aging and continuously decreasing in number. Some statistics indicate that the majority of workers in the primary industry are over 70 as of 2010. In addition, trade liberalization causes domestic agricultural and livestock products to compete with imported products, and Japanese fisheries are about to be outdone by foreign fisheries. Daichi will face a big challenge in continuing to secure stable supply sources in the present circumstances, even though organic vegetables and safe marine products are value-added high-end products.

5. Case 2 — Swan Co., Ltd.

Swan Co., Ltd. (hereafter referred to as Swan) was founded with the objective of employing disabled people. (Information on Swan was obtained from Masao Ogura, 2003; Setsuko Makino, 2003; a personal interview with Ayumu Kaizu, January 22, 2013; and Swan's website (www.swanbakery. jp).) Besides running directly managed bakeries and bakery cafes, it operates bakery cafes nationwide through a franchise system. Seeing that the average monthly salary of workers in the welfare facility was JPY10,000, Masao Ogura, who was then representative of Yamato Transport, which is known in the home-delivery business, founded Swan in 1998 to show that even a welfare facility could be profitable (Masao Ogura, 2003). However, because it was in 1989 that Swan was registered as a company, it is possible to say that the registration aimed to transform the business of the existing company. However, no one in the present organization knows how or why. After opening a directly managed Ginza store in 1998, it opened three directly managed stores and 29 franchised stores by 2012. (Of the 29 franchised stores, three were closed and one is scheduled to close.) Swan is a wholly owned company of Yamato Transport, and it is a special subsidiary of Yamato Transport under the Handicapped Person's Employment Promotion Law. It is partly responsible for fulfilling Yamato Transport's obligation to employ handicapped people.

Swan has obviously been producing the direct outcome of employing disabled people, but it is necessary to confirm that it has the organizational infrastructure vital for providing this outcome. Swan's equity capital ratio is nearly 100%; the high ratio indicates that Swan is different from limited companies doing business for profit. The high ratio naturally has something to do with the fact that Swan is a wholly owned subsidiary of Yamato Transport. According to the official gazette, Swan increased its assets from about JPY (in units of million) 100 in the fiscal year ending March 2003 to JPY345.72 million in the fiscal year ending March 2012. It is hard to analyze Swan's business trend in detail because it does not release sales, but it has apparently been expanding its management size successfully. The expansion trend is not due to excessive borrowing, even though the support from Yamato Transport should be considered. The ROA and ROE results indicate that Swan had a bad period, but it recovered after hitting bottom in 2010.

Today, Swan is widely recognized as a social company. For example, Representative Umezu was elected as a member of the "new public" round table meeting that the democratic cabinet established in 2010, and Swan Bakery was introduced as a case in the declaration of the meeting. At the same time, it is rumored that it is easy to obtain social welfare corporation status if a company operates a franchised bakery of Swan Bakery. Swan's current status largely depends on the abilities of Kaizu. He was originally employed by Yamato Transport as a part-time worker. After he became a full-time employee, he became an influential figure competent enough to conduct various operational reforms. In fact, he successfully restructured the office that had been operating in the red. That is, he was the most suitable candidate to succeed the charismatic entrepreneur Ogura.

Next, we will discuss Swan's franchisees. Swan has a total of 26 franchised bakeries, of which 16 are managed by social welfare corporations or voluntary organizations of the same kind, two by one NPO, one by a co-op,

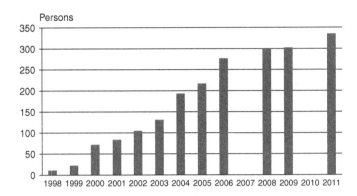

Fig. 2.   Number of disabled people employed by Swan Bakery
Source: Materials provided by Swan. No data are available for 2007 and 2010 because data are available only for years when new stores are opened.

one by the Japan Junior Chamber, and six by for-profit companies. The 26 franchisees employed a total of 334 disabled people in 2011 (Fig. 2), and an employee's annual income is little more than JPY1,220,000 on average.

Taking ex-franchisees that had closed stores in the past into consideration, Swan confirms that new franchisees should share the company's philosophy, faithfully observe sanitary standards, and be able to pay minimum wage. Swan extends technical guidance and introduces supply sources for raw materials to new franchisees but does not impose the franchise fee. According to Kaizu, the "strong will" of an autocratic owner generally allows a franchisee to continue business. On the other hand, a railway company became a franchisee because the president of the railway company had wanted it. However, the second-generation leader was an ex-conductor and did not have a strong enough will to continue the business. He only talked about why he could not continue the business. The president retired on the day it became a franchisee. This bakery was closed in about three years.

The interview with a franchisee revealed that some franchisees were operating in the red and unable to pay minimum wage to disabled people — the original objective of the organization. This franchisee lost about JPY10 million annually despite such measures as doing business inside the building owned by the parent company and having 90–100 loaves of bread purchased by Yamato Transport in the same prefecture. Under these circumstances, they are obliged to receive subsidies under the Services and Supports for Persons with Disabilities Act (Support for Continuous Employment Project Type A).

In the first place, the idea of franchising stores was formulated by the manager of a company. When he attended the opening ceremony of a welfare facility, he heard parents of children saying, "We wish the salary to increase from JPY6,000–7,000 to JPY10,000." He assumed they were talking about daily wages, but he was surprised to learn they were talking about monthly salaries. His surprise reminded him of Swan Bakery. In the initial stage, the bakery café was part of the main business. Because the business needed to become a welfare business to receive the subsidies mentioned above, it went independent in order to become a general incorporated company. Accordingly, it became harder to manage the business. Nonetheless, the management keeps the business running with the hope that the people surrounding the business might motivate the business. He further mentioned, "What we are doing cannot be a business model."

Two evaluations can be made of Swan's outcomes. The spread of franchisees can be regarded as an indirect outcome. Although the number of franchisees has steadily increased, Kaizu does not place the highest priority on increasing the number of franchisees. Instead, he closely examines the applicants' aspirations and their ability to run a business before granting franchising rights to them. The slow increase can also be attributed to the poor management of the franchisees. Nonetheless, he allowed a large corporation earnest about employing disabled people to open a store on a franchise basis, and he plans to develop foreign markets in the near future. His strategy can be characterized as slow and steady progress.

In contrast, if a Swan Bakery cannot be profitable unless it becomes a franchisee, and if a franchised Swan Bakery is hardly profitable, it is hard to say that Swan has an impact on society judging by Ogura's philosophy that even a welfare facility can be profitable. It is possible to say that Swan's business cannot be profitable without support from Yamato Transport. Organizations in the field of welfare mostly depend on subsidies from the administration to be profitable. That is, a welfare facility operates on the assumption that it will not be in the red. In this sense, it may be a problem with the system that does not motivate a welfare facility to aim for independence in management.

Swan can be said to have a sound financial infrastructure if it is analyzed from the viewpoint of output. However, because Swan is a special subsidiary of Yamato Transport, it is hard to evaluate Swan properly, even though Swan is a successful case in terms of both output and outcome.

It is Yamato Transport that delivers the products made by Swan Bakeries, including allergy-ready cakes. Yamato Transport receives words of gratitude for these products directly from the customers. (Yamato Transport applies only quantity discounts to Swan products, and it does not give more benefits because providing more favorable conditions is equivalent to profit sharing.) It is possible to evaluate Swan to a certain degree in that Swan provides outcomes to society as a special subsidiary by making the best use of the main business of its parent company. It will not create any problems as long as Swan is recognized as helping the parent company provide CSR and is evaluated highly inside the group. However, the quality of employees to dispatch and the reason for its existence may become unstable should that recognition change.

In addition, we cannot overlook the fact that each franchisee, which is an indirect outcome, is not profitable.

6. Case 3 — Florence, An Incorporated NPO

Incorporated NPO Florence (hereafter referred to as Florence) is one of the most famous Japanese social companies. (Information and data on Florence were obtained from Hiroki Komazaki, 2007 and Florence's website (www.florence.or.jp).) Representative Hiroki Komazaki is often discussed as a social entrepreneur. He is mentioned in Tanimoto (2006) and Tsukamoto and Yamagishi (2008). He wrote books, and he has appeared in many magazines.

Hiroki Komazaki founded an IT company when he was a University student and managed it for several years after graduation. Tired of making money, however, he went to the United States and learned about volunteer activities and NPOs (Hiroki Komazaki, 2007). After he returned to Japan, he knew the following situation in Japan: If a child left in a nursery or day-care center runs a fever, one of his or her parents customarily has to pick the child up. Many working women have to take off from work when their children get sick, causing them to risk losing their jobs. With this knowledge in mind, he founded Florence, which is devoted to caring for sick children.

Florence is not a limited company, but it started disclosing simplified income statements and simplified balance sheets on its website in 2008. This practice reveals Florence's awareness that it is a social company despite the fact that it is an NPO. As with the two previous cases, we examined the safety of its management infrastructure that allows it to keep providing social outcomes and found that it is sound in current ratio, fixed ratio, and equity capital ratio. However, considering that contributions and subsidies make Florence's balance of payments viable, it may not be a good idea to evaluate Florence in the same way as a general company.

Florence has steadily increased revenues and current net profit. In 2005, Florence's revenue and current net profit are JPY (in units of 1,000) 18,463 and JPY1,588. After that, in 2012, each of them increased to JPY517,073 and JPY31,537, respectively. These increases result from subsidies and contributions thanks to the evaluation by the governmental department; the business it develops with this revenue has recorded net income. This can be an evaluation of its outcome.

Florence started a complementary business that allows members to have their sick children cared for by certified contract nurses. In the initial stage, the company consulted with professionals in welfare and child care, but it received very little response from them. However, Florence came to an issue immediately after it was founded in Tokyo in 2004. As its business expanded, government officials visited the company for inspections and proposed a similar system as a policy.

This chapter does not touch on the business status of Florence because it has already been covered by various media. We analyzed its management with the help of its business reports after 2006. Florence was in the red in 2006, but it went into the black in 2007. It has been accumulating net assets year after year, and they reached JPY47 million at the end of 2011. Total revenue exceeded JPY400 million, of which JPY260 million was business revenue. In this sense, Florence is a typical NPO business, and it is a case of the commercialization of an NPO. It increased its membership ninefold from 174 in 2006 to 1,600 in 2010. Likewise, the number of sick children cared for increased by more than 10 times from 286 in 2006 to 3,026 in 2010 (Table 1). As for the membership fee, each member pays JPY21,000 (per child), and the initiation fee that ranges from JPY5,000 to JPY20,000 depending on how old the child is. The monthly fee includes a usage fee for one care each

Table 1. Membership trend and the number of sick children cared for (2006–2010)

Year	2006	2007	2008	2009	2010
Membership	174	298	683	1,094	1,600
Number of sick children cared for	286	1,060	1,232	1,832	3,026

month, and a member pays JPY2,100 per care on and after the second care. The renewal fee is JPY10,500. The membership fee is reviewed depending on the situation or utilization, but Florence's membership is by no means low.

As for Florence's outcome, we introduce the following fact. Affected by Florence's results, the government created a system to support similar businesses and incorporated small-sized nurseries commercialized by Florence in the Law to Support Children and Child Care enacted in 2012. In this sense, Florence's outcome set a precedent for a solution to a social problem. However, another NPO was founded with the same objective of caring for sick children, Byoji Hoiku wo Tsukurukai ("Society to Found Incorporated Nonprofit Organizations for Caring Sick Children"), and it is unknown whether this trend can be attributed only to Florence. Rather, it is natural to evaluate highly the management abilities of the founder, Komazaki.

We can point out two issues in the case of Florence. One pertains to distributing net assets that accumulate continuously. Because Florence is an incorporated NPO, it is prohibited from profit sharing. Florence expanded its business into fields other than caring for sick children and introduced new low-priced services for low-income families. Nonetheless, Florence's net assets have been accumulating continuously. A case existed in which a corporate tax was imposed on a membership-based volunteer organization because its retained earnings grew enormous due to a repetition of carrying forward. Because Florence has become a famous organization, it may receive the same tax treatment. (In 2012, however, Florence made an investment for the following year and reduced its net assets.)

The other issue is that the entrepreneur Komazaki plans to leave Florence sooner or later. (Tsukamoto & Yamagishi, 2008 wrote on page 71 that Komazaki is scheduled to leave Florence in March 2013, but he remains the representative director as of July 2013.) As we pointed out in the case of Daichi, it is an issue whether people succeeding the founder will inherit his or her aspiration and mission. Florence has clearly defined the mission and action guidelines for employees, but it is not clear whether the followers can maintain the mission and action guidelines. In the United States, an NPO was in the news because it spent a large portion of retained earnings on fringe benefits. In this case, the mission established by the founder was lost, and the organization lacked flexibility as management changed. It is impossible to say that the same will not occur with Japanese NPOs.

7. Conclusion

In this chapter, we analyzed the financial aspects of three businesses run by Japan's representative social entrepreneurs based on their business reports. All three businesses were found to be financially stable, and all had established infrastructures for carrying out their missions. As for output, both Daichi and Florence are growing steadily in terms of customers and members. Swan has a problem with the management of its franchise system, though it enjoys stable business in terms of employing disabled people.

It is true and recognized socially that these three companies have built stable financial infrastructures and have continuously solved social problems. While past research has mostly focused on their sociality, we clarified the stability of management in the three companies.

None of the three companies are completely free of problems. In particular, it is a big issue for a social company whether the mission and aspiration established by the founder will be transferred to the succeeding generations; even Drucker spends one chapter discussing this issue (Drucker, 1990). All the three companies are being managed by the founder or a representative close to the founder, and their evaluations as social companies will not be established unless they undergo generational changes.

Fujita, Ogura, Kaizu, and Komazaki are excellent managers and full of aspirations, but it is necessary to consider whether they are competent enough to do business in a calm manner. Will their succeeding managers inherit their missions and aspirations? The selection of their successors will fix their evaluations as individuals.

In this chapter, we did not discuss a social company as we mentioned in Sec. 2. However, the concept of a social company is defined in Europe and Korea. In Japan, there is a draft law that allows the government to subsidize businesses that support the socially vulnerable, and the social company will be defined in that law sooner or later. When it is defined, research on the social company in the context of the definition can be conducted. However, it will remain controversial as to whether the legal definition is appropriate from an academic viewpoint.

References

Drucker, P. (1990). *Managing the Nonprofit Organization*, NY: Harper Collins Publishers.

Fujita, K. (2005). *A Revolution from a Radish*. Tokyo: Kousakusha (in Japanese).

Gawell, M. (2012). Social Entrepreneurship: Action Grounded in Needs, Opportunities and/or Perceived Necessities? *Voluntas*, Published Online June 9, 2012.

Kerlin, J. (2010). A Comparative Analysis of the Global Emergence of Social Enterprise, *Voluntas*, 21(2), pp. 162–179.

Komazaki, H. (2007). *Changing the Society is My Work*. Tokyo: Eiji Press (in Japanese).

Machida, Y. (2000). *Social Entrepreneurs*. Tokyo: PHP Shinsho (in Japanese).

Mair, J. (2011). Social Entrepreneurship: On Origins and Future of a Concept, *Planned Administration*, 34(3), pp. 31–37.

Makino, S. (2003). *Fly Swan Bakery*. Tokyo: Choubunsha Publishing (in Japanese).

Ogura, M. (2003). *Management to Change Welfare*. Tokyo: Nikkei Business Publications (in Japanese).

Steyaert, C. & Katz, J. (2004). Reclaiming the Space of Entrepreneurship in Society: Geographical, Discursive and Social Dimensions, *Entrepreneurship and Regional Development*, 16, pp. 179–196.

Tanimoto, K. (ed.) (2006). *Social Enterprise*. Tokyo: Chuokeizai-Sha (in Japanese).

Tsukamoto, I. & Yamagishi, H. (eds.) (2008). *Social Enterprise*. Tokyo: Maruzen (in Japanese).

Daichi Website: http://www.daichi.or.jp.

Florence Website: http://www.florence.or.jp.

Swan's Website: http://www.swanbakery.jp.

9

The Socially Constructed Industry Landscape through Entrepreneurial Practice Innovation: Health-Care Product Industry in China

Stephen Dun-Hou Tsai
National Sun Yat-sen University

Meng-Chen Wu
National Sun Yat-sen University

1. Introduction

After 1976, China has become the world's manufacturing hub due to the opening up as a result of globalization. Many of the technologically advanced countries have located most of their manufacturing centers in China, by transferring their production methods and managerial technologies to China. Even though people then focused on how to "learn capital management and marketing approaches of foreign enterprises" (Deng, 1994), a fact that cannot be ignored is that China started to show its capability in building the industries with Chinese characteristics. Along with these changes, the Chinese also began to gain wealth in the market economy. In the early 1990s, many civilians were able to accumulate considerable wealth due to strong economic reforms in China and started to display an ability to purchase consumables other than the basic necessities. As the common people started to purchase commodities other than essentials, health-care products that claimed to be able to strengthen people's physical health opened a new market in China. Within as short as three years, this market tripled, with the number of manufacturers increasing over 30 times. This led to the emergence of the first batch of well-known millionaires in modern China. Most research holds that the advent of the consumer market was the result of China's amazingly growing economy in the wake of globalization, whereas few studies have viewed this phenomenon from the social, cultural, and humanities-related respects of China, and even less from the process of construction of the newly emerging industries.

This study explores the relationship between entrepreneurial practices and health-care industry's development through an entrepreneurial narrative delivered by a Chinese entrepreneur who started to engage himself in health-care products in 1997. This study combines his experience in taking part in the health-care industry in China with the historical background of the health-care product industry in the country to scrutinize the industry that "initiated a quick consumable market with great momentum." It explores the way how the entrepreneurial practices in the industry constructed a new market in such a special social, economic, and cultural circumstance of an old country like China. The reason why we choose health-care product industry as the empirical context is because this industry not only merely "launched a quick consumable market with great momentum," but also gathered remarkable passion of many entrepreneurs of that time. It progressed with such momentum that it became a trillion-dollar value industry from a small market scale of only million dollars' value within two decades. Without a shred of doubt, entrepreneurs have played a crucial part in that process of construction.

In this study, we seek to shed additional light on the role of entrepreneurial practices in the formation of health-care industry in China. We do so through a longitudinal case study of the health-care product industry in China and a narrative inquiry of an entrepreneur who founded his health-care product company. The entrepreneur surveyed in this study, Mr. Toong, was a futures exchange man before delving into the health-care industry under the enthusiastic atmosphere among the industry in 1997. He created his own company, Longevity, and it has become one of the famous firms in health-care market now. We explore how Mr. Toong constructed the business landscape and organized the way to participate in the industrial practices, how the innovation occurred to the practice, and how the practice engagement constructed the configuration of industry.

Through the entrepreneurial narrative given by Toong, the study found that initially entrepreneurs constructed the images of business landscapes of the industry on their own, and deliver their own entrepreneurial practices within the ambit of the already constructed business landscapes. Second, although most of the entrepreneurs would not have sufficient information to imagine and construct this industrial business landscape, such lack of information lent more space for them to imagine and led to a wide variety of possibilities and necessities of the new practices. Through engaging in practices in the real business world, entrepreneurs were able to fill the gap in their insufficient industrial knowledge and brought about new possibilities for innovation in the industry. This seemingly lack of information and knowledge appeared more obvious in the initial phase of the industrial development. Third, in the intense developmental phase, entrepreneurs could very easily deliver their subjective ideas into the industry and leave an imprint in the developing industry.

From this study, we suggest that a proactively developing industry would help entrepreneurs to open up their imagination for the business, which would trigger entrepreneurial development further and facilitate advancements in the industry. Meanwhile, the study suggested that new entrepreneurs put forth efforts in entrepreneurial practices based on their imagination, and start a series of constructions on new practices, thus attracting more people to join, reviving the energy of the industry, and leading to a change in the logic of the industry. This is contrary to the past ideas that "opportunities for enterprises" motivate the development of the industry, put differently, more entrepreneurial activities are equivalent of more innovative practices and more growth and transformation in the industry. During the process, the entrepreneurs would materialize their cultural tendencies and preferences into entrepreneurial practices, and thereby construct an industry that boasts local features.

2. Research Field: Health-Care Product Industry in China

Before 1994, there was no so-called health-care product industry in China, but only state-run pharmaceutical companies producing pharmaceutical products, which was also the situation faced by the majority of the people's livelihood industry. Majority of peasant-workers had no idea of health-care product consumption although they accumulated wealth in the market economy. Until 1993, a world famous Chinese track coach endorsed traditional Chinese self-cultivation physical health drinks in television commercials, which instantly detonated the Chinese public's enthusiasm for health-care products. According to statistics, there were only over 100 health-care product manufacturers in China before 1994, but the number surged to more than 3,000 by 1998 within five years, and the products categories also jumped to about 30,000. The amount of sales also increased

12-fold, reaching RMB30 billion. Health-care product industry was the fastest-growing and a spectacular industry in China at that time, and many of "the richest men" were born during this trend. Due to the problems such as exaggerated propaganda and curative effect of false advertising, the Chinese health-care product industry faced a serious consumer confidence crisis after the contention at the beginning, but the desire of Chinese people to sustain their health continuously increased and the health-care product companies were also actively looking for a way out. In 2013, the overall size of China's health-care product industry reached RMB600 billion, and the annual growth rate was about 20%, and is expected to reach a trillion RMB by 2015 (Hong Kong Trade Development Council, 2013).

2.1.   *Richest-men era of health-care industry in China*

After China's reform and opening up in 1978, people's livelihood consumption patterns changed a lot. By the 1990s, most of China's major cities had been out of poverty; after 1993, China entered a "whirlwind Rich Era" (Wu, 2008). One was health-care product industry which started its "Golden 10 years" since 1994. These health-care product companies with the rebellious spirit used advertising bombardment as the primary means to "thoroughly launch China's fast-moving consumer goods market" (Wu, 2008).

2.1.1.   *Health-care product booming in 1994*

Chinese people's eagerness to longevity and life succession (Li, 1998) and these two thirsts combined with the growth of economy became a powerful consumer force. In 1993, impacted by a sporting event,[1] the health-care products and Chinese people's desire for life were sketched together to make health-care product industry become the arena for the most ambitious entrepreneurs in China.

---

[1] "Ma Gujun" led by Ma Junren broke the records in 1993 world championship and 1996 Olympics, and became a widely known hero. One month after the 1993 world championship, Ma Junren, in an advertisement, holding up a box of health-care products and in Liaoning mandarin said: "we drink the China turtle liquid." Its formula was sold to the drinks company Robust at the price of RMB10 million, which announced that its "nuclear energy of life" oral liquid developed according to the formula will go public two months later. Since then, Robust became one of the most famous companies in China, snapping up the market. During the spring of 1994, people were immersed in passion from "nuclear energy life."

But in 1998, the number rapidly surged to more than 3,000, and the product categories boomed to 30,000. The amount of sales increased by 12-fold, and the scale reached to RMB30 billion. The health-care product industry soon became the fastest growing and most compelling industries in China. Well-known health-care product manufactures rapidly grew in that time, including robust selling "nuclear energy of life," with Apollo and Feilong selling medicines for kidney ailments, Sanzhu selling health liquid for gastrointestinal ailments, etc. Their bosses have become the richest persons widely known.

These health-care product companies used advertising bombardment as the primary means to open the market. At that time, the information in China's rural areas was underdeveloped. Television and radio were the main sources for people to get information. Health-care product manufacturers, through advertising, unscrupulously exaggerated the efficacy of their products, and achieved great success. Owing to the geographic distance, these health-care product sales channels were routed mainly through provincial distribution system. The agency referred to the local dealer for sales and marketing, and this exaggerated advertising and marketing methods, in the countryside, achieved great success. Health-care product companies put all their efforts in the marketing channels and promoted innovatively to seize the new market. For example, Sanzhu launched the "encircling the cities" strategy, and designed a four-level marketing system in the rural markets. They were not only having a very intensive distribution channel but also sent the "volunteer medical consultants" to the rural areas to sell their products. Their promotion was a huge success. In their second year, the sales of their single product reached RMB2 billion.

Feilong and Sanzhu both rapidly rose by strong advertising and marketing. The success of health-care product providers was so "dazzling" that it attracted the attention of enthusiastic entrepreneurs, like the Chinese beverage magnate CW Lee, as well as Shi Yuzhu who made his fortune by doing computer boards. For Li Jingwei, the success of Feilong and Sanzhu was very random, and he could replace them. And at the same time, China's economy continued to heat, the public consumption kept increasing, and almost all the consumer behavior presented a thriving and prosperous scene. These phenomena also fostered the growth of the entrepreneurship in China's health-care product industry. Sanzhu reached the highest point in 1996 with a sales value of RMB8 billion, and became one of China's most high-profile companies in mid-1990s.

Li (1998) argued that this kind of irrational purchase in health-care products was a kind of "disconnected" consumption, because shopping was not for them. For example, middle-aged people bought health-care products for their parents and growth liquids for their children to get stronger. This belief in health, in case of an emergency, would rapidly shatter. Health-care product market constantly exaggerated the features of their products while advertising, which placed their products on the poor quality credit situation and collapsed in 1997. Giant Shi Yuzhu fell in 1997, and Sanzhu collapsed in 1999 under a series of lawsuits. Apollo began to go from bad to worse. Health-care product industry, after the initial passion, went into consolidation stage.

2.1.2. *The health-care product industry in Shanghai*

Shanghai is a city with long history. In the mid-19th century, Shanghai was one of the earliest trading ports, and laid a solid business foundation for local development. By the 1930s, Shanghai had become an international city and the Far East Finance Centre, the landmark of Shanghai headquarters of HSBC stands in the Huangpu River, the Paris of the Orient. Although, during the years from 1949 to 1976, the economies were depressed due to the communist policy, Shanghai soon recovered after the reform and opening-up policy. The development of Pudong area led the entire development of Shanghai and the Yangtze River, and glittered in the world again.

Shanghai was China's largest "integrated economic zone" after the opening-up policy (Lu, 1988). Industry and commerce were in the first place in the whole of China, besides, the first modern stock exchange market and Future Trade market in China were set in Shanghai during 1990 and 1992. The per capita income in Shanghai area was also the highest one in China, US$2,038 in 1995. In 2000, Shanghai was the only one city whose per capita income was over US$3,000. So, Shanghai people's purchasing power has been the best in China. For neighboring hinterland, hundreds of millions of population in Shanghai, its consumption for the whole of China accounted for 3%. The transportation, educational, and commercial circulations are also the highest in the entire China. Since the Qing dynasty, it has been the most important and leading foreign trade city.

Glamorous Shanghai paid attention to life-talk especially to health-care even after experiencing economic and cultural sluggishness. Shanghai people have "very deep traditions" (L686, Toong) in the concept of self-cultivation health. When the Chinese economy began to take off, these once bustling traditions were trapped. In the cultural revolution period, even the official policies denied the contribution of the Chinese ancestors, but now many Chinese would acknowledge their ancestors when they become rich, and would say that their ancestor was wisdom and wonderful (L727, Toong). With the economic recovery, health consciousness also came back to their lifestyle. However, early large-scale health-care product companies put their eyes on the national market, especially the vast rural market, but their price and brand images were relatively rough. All his (Shi Yuzhu) advertisements seemed so vulgar for Shanghai people, but lively and colorful for rural people (L274, Toong). For merchants, health-care product markets in Shanghai aiming at high-end products would be new business opportunities.

2.2. *Toong's entrepreneurship*

When Shanghai established the first stock exchange in 1990, Toong was majoring in Industrial Management in Shanghai Jiao Tong University. Toong kept up with the trend of the first wave of stock warrants in China, while in that time, majority of people still had no idea of a stock, and made his first fortune. After graduating from college in 1991, Toong was assigned to the Materials Bureau. Next year, China's first futures exchange center "Shanghai Metal Exchange" was established in the same building where the Materials Bureau was located. Toong was assigned to the Shanghai Metal Exchange Bureau to be the sales representative of a futures dealer. In 1995, Toong with rich experience in futures founded a future brokerage company with his friend, and made a large fortune.

High-risk of futures industry also made Toong feel precarious. In mid-1990s, the health-care product industry in China became an entrepreneurial fashion and became the birthplace of zillionaires. Many little-known bosses and companies, who took turns into health-care products industry, became well-known richest persons and companies in the health-care product industry in two or three years. Toong was also attracted by the promise that this entrepreneurial trend in health-care industry held. Although Toong had never run a production-based company like this, nor engaged in the industry related with health-care product before, he was confident in this investment because of his past successful life experience and big fortune. He employed three employees and started his health-care product company "Longevity" in 1998.

For Toong used his contacts with other bosses to make a big fortune for himself. "Longevity" aimed to become a high-order health food brand which distinguished from the mainstream in rural market and Shanghai. For his market positioning, Toong implemented good manufacturing practices (GMPs) in the pharmaceutical sector, which was considered a very advanced action at that time. Since 2005, health-care products in China must pass the GMP authentication. This strategy also showed in the raw materials which he used in his product, he believed "it is ok to use more expensive ingredients, . . . , just use good materials," and said "it is meaningless for me to save one cent or two cents," because he thought "my products are for use by the elites," and "if you ask me to sell a product which only priced one dollar or five cents, . . . I would never consider it."

Although Toong started his new enterprise with confidence, he realized that he was just a layman during the actual operation. For example, he could start futures business in the past just employing two or three friends, but in the health food industry, that was far from enough. He needed to establish and maintain the relationship to practically run and manage the factory, marketing, finances, and also needed a team to establish relationship with various advertising channels, and to coordinate with suppliers in marketing and credit to deal with credit sales and payment in arrears. Apart from these management problems, he also faced some problems in the production. Toong soon found that the GMP-oriented pharmaceutical factory that he ran was "in fact, very backward in terms of facilities and its machines were all out of use." Toong had to build another two new factories. And owing to the fact that the GMP factory he bought was once state-owned pharmaceutical company, he had to deal with 60–70 labors whose management skills and quality were not satisfactory. Toong had no operational experience in health-care industry. Thinking alone cannot resolve. At that time, the health-care industry was so much in a mess, Toong had to learn how to survive in the existing conditions.

Toong felt "the game is going to be over." The turning point came up that was to graft "citron tea" to health-care products. Toong saw in a supermarket "citron tea" which was all imported from Korea and was expensive and strange to Shanghai people in that time. This successful experience transferred Toong's identity about health-care product from drug to diet. Supermarkets were also surprised at the success of "Longevity citron tea," because the ones that were imported from Korea sold 1 to 2 bottles at most a day, while they could sell 100 to 200 bottles a day when coordinated with "Longevity citron tea."

Another important turning point in Toong's entrepreneurial process was the changes in his marketing channels. Toong had not thought about mechanisms to sell his product on "new channels," like on-line shopping or TV shopping and thought that neither others did. One of Longevity products which had begun to slide gained huge unexpected success with TV shopping. This experience led him to reflect his prejudice and to think about the strength of TV shopping. Toong found that the products on TV shopping could be introduced very thoroughly, for example, "who should eat this health-care product? What kind of effect it would provide?" This experience made Toong realize that health-care product was "knowledge marketing," which means allowing consumers to "understand you" And led to a successful trial and helped Sung Wei become more organized and to gradually understand the operations of health food business. Longevity finally began to make money and became a well-known health-care products brand in Shanghai.

3. Analyses

In this study, we shed additional light on the role of entrepreneurial practices in the formation of the health-care industry. We do so through a longitudinal case study of the health-care product industry in China and a narrative inquiry of an entrepreneur, Toong, who founded a venture by engaging with the industrial practices. We explore how the entrepreneur participated in the industrial practices, how the innovation occurred to the practice, and how the practice engagement constructed the configuration of industry.

3.1. *Socially constructed business landscapes*

In the entrepreneurial study, the acquisition of industrial knowledge of the entrepreneurs is considered a prerequisite knowledge to starting an enterprise and spotting an opportunity when it arises (Cope, 2005). The recognition and understanding of the business landscape of the industry is especially considered the basis through which one may be equipped to analyze the overall phenomena of the industry and recognize any threats to opportunities for the industry. Such knowledge set limits to the industrial territory the entrepreneurs are taking activities, and frames the ways the entrepreneurs engage in business practices. In theory, a description of business landscapes is a very serious and meticulous task that requires collecting data and doing research in an elaborate way before analyzing the practitioners, including suppliers, consumers, and competitors and delineating a boundary for one's own territory. By so doing, they can find their own position in negotiating prices (Ghemawat, 2006). From the perspective of entrepreneurial strategies, the more one is able to analyze the business landscapes, the better one may grasp opportunities and win success in the industry they are in.

In Toong's narrative, we discover a new way to initiate an enterprise and depict business landscapes. When Toong intended to change the track of his career in 1997, he found that "many big privately held firms are engaged with health-care commodities." His eyes were diverted to health-care products and found this a worthwhile business after doing some research work. Toward the end of the 20th century, there were some 3,000 health-care business agents. It seemed impossible for Toong to make a comprehensive research on the business landscapes of the 3,000 health-care companies. Matter-of-factly, Toong only imagined that health-care product firms were large-scaled privately owned enterprises. This image of a large-scaled privately owned enterprise became the basis for his construction of health-care product business:

> At that time, I heard about some big names such as Sanzhu, Apollo, Wahaha, Giant and Angli, and discovered that they were all in the health-care product industry. After some thought and research, I took a keen interest and founded my own company, Longevity.

From the operating models of these big companies and the discourse on such an industry, Toong was able to conceive a plan for the business landscape of the health-care product industry. It has created many millionaires; it is related to health care; it has a rather high net profit rate; it is an enterprise that focuses on production and sales; health-care products can be sold out overnight with advertisements; and the current promotion ways are very clichéd in the eyes of the Shanghai people.

The operating model of "big privately owned health-care product companies" became the subject of Toong's imagination. Toong found a "high-class," "for wealthy people," and "Shanghai-oriented" niche in this industry, and decided on a type of practice that he intended to engage himself. For instance, on the business landscape of the "big privately owned health-care product companies," he thought about "opening a pharmaceutical factory" as a health-care product firm which in his opinion would produce capsules, tablets, or other forms of medicine. Toong bought an old state-run pharmaceutical factory in the very early stages of setting up a firm of his own.

He also decided to use the best possible material to manufacture medicines at a higher cost. In the meantime, Toong extended great efforts to set up marketing/selling channels, such as building a relationship with convenience stores. He copied the example from other big health-care product firms, although Toong took it to a step further. He said laughingly that if these companies made a budget of the scale of the "grenade," then he adopted a budget of the scale of a "rocket" to enhance the brand image of Longevity. He also learned from Wahaha by buying extended hours of TV commercials. After he decided to delve into the health-care industry, he "watched TV all the time." Then he became determined to give up on noisy, low-class commercials of the past and used a poem composed by a famous politician of thousands of years ago, Cao Cao to be a spokesman for his commercials on TV and radio stations all over Shanghai.

In the process, Toong played a crucial role in turning societal resources into a business landscape. This business landscape had an origin from the industrial network and practices from 1995 through 1998, and was reconstructed to appeal to the Shanghai consumers who loved higher-quality products and who tended to enjoy luxury. This special niche found by Toong was a discourse on health-care product industry, also created by Toong.

In the process of Toong building this business, we also found that business landscapes were changing from time to time. When Toong saw a brand of pomelo tea in a Carrefour store in Shanghai in 2006, and decided to introduce pomelo tea into his production line, his conception and construction base about a health-care product firm changed. In the past years, Toong had regarded "medication" or "tablets and capsules" as the main line of health-care products. Thereafter, he pushed his boundary beyond, and stepped into the territory of "dietary therapy." In 2011, with the sudden success of the TV channel, Toong switched his business landscape from physical channels to "knowledge marketing channel" and put in more resources in TV and online channels where "he could better communicate with consumers."

From seeing health-care products as an "enterprise," to buying a pharmaceutical factory and manufacturing tablets and capsules, to making commercials on TV, to turning to "dietary therapy," Toong experienced a huge transformation in his concepts in the construction of his business's landscape. In addition, his notional change from using physical channels to employing knowledge-based marketing has proved a widening conception on health-care products. Presently, he focuses on knowledge and stresses the importance of conveying such knowledge to consumers. This manifests that for Toong, a health-care product enterprise is not a fixed, priori-objectivism knowledge, but a transformative process of business landscape which consists of at least three phases so far.

This means that when Toong constructed a business landscape of health-care products, he inherited some of the current practices of that time, being a part of the health-care product industry, while adding some of his interpretations and constructive notions into the construction of business landscape so as to bring about transformations and innovations into this industry. This process was a socially constructed process initiated by the entrepreneur, in which the business landscape was transformed and reconstructed.

3.2. *New entrepreneurs' learning and innovations*

The operating models and pace of the pioneering entrepreneurs have inscribed the now established business landscapes and have left the new-generation entrepreneurs with a stigma that they are not innovators, but merely "followers" who could only imitate the pioneers' doings and actions. Imitation and innovation, in the past research literature, were regarded as oppositional concepts, which suggested a hierarchical order. Innovation brings value to the society, whereas imitation makes lesser contribution to the society (Johansson, 2010). This led to a dilemma to entrepreneurial learning in past years: What is entrepreneurial learning? What is the relationship between the learning of entrepreneurship and innovation? Does such learning lead to innovation?

In the process of Toong's building his business, he emulated many of the old "big privately-owned health-care product enterprises" by building pharmaceutical factories, pharmaceutical license, producing tablets and capsules, creating marketing channels, making commercials, starting pomelo tea (copied from a Korean brand) and even cooperating with TV channels to boost sales. Even though all this seemed emulation from old big firms, Toong had had a different touch to this approach. Yet, he demanded his factory correspond to GMP standards, which was rather new in 1998. Unlike old firms such as Wahaha, which pinched on the cost, Toong insisted on high-quality materials to manufacture good medicine, and shooting high-quality commercials to please the Shanghai people and create the image of a top brand. If the dichotomy of innovation/emulation is correct, then were all the efforts to make tablets/capsules, pomelo tea, and vertical channels only emulation without a shred of innovation in them?

The dichotomy of innovation/emulation is a much simplified carrier that ignores the creativity of human beings in social life. For Northern European scholars such as Berglund and Johannisson (2012), everybody has an enterprising capacity in their own familiar field, and "everybody is born as an entrepreneur" (Johannisson, 2011). They believe ever since the beginning of mankind, "everybody has tried to organize and develop new ways to improve life conditions for individuals and for the whole society" (Berglund & Johannisson, 2012). In other words, people invent new ways to improve their life when engaging in some kind of practice. Take pomelo tea as an example. When Toong introduced pomelo tea, he considered that this product was strange to the Shanghai people and would find the price spiky; therefore, he decided to give an old-style Chinese saying "relieving inflammation and making one's complexion better" on the cover. By doing so, the Shanghai consumers, who had known the brand Longevity, would know more about pomelo tea. He also decided to manufacture pomelo tea in China without importing Korean tea, which considerably reduced the price of pomelo tea. Such efforts to create differences by paying attention to the details in daily life were a dynamic invention on the part of an entrepreneur who made dialogues with the society s/he was living in, and created social transformations through their actions.

From the story of Toong, we may easily discover that the latter entrepreneurs are not followers, but are innovators who learn current practices and gain knowledge while endeavoring to produce innovations in starting their enterprises. By using human instincts, they have created differences by taking small steps to work on consumer's lifestyle. Toong's example reminds us that entrepreneurship is not merely an intense process of innovation that the rich partakes in, but a dynamic dialogue between entrepreneurs and the societal life space.

3.3.   *The industrial structure created by entrepreneurship*

From the standpoint of social learning, when people stay and act in a social context, they interact with others in dual ways. This suggests that under participation and materialization, everybody forms a special track to learning and identification (Wenger, 1998). As a modern health-care product businessman, Toong is also a Shanghai-born person who was raised in a Chinese-cultural background. With this multiple-membership, his participation consisted of action and connection (Wenger, 1998). As Toong began to dedicate himself to the practice of health-care product industry, he tried to materialize his tendency and knowledge in the practice of health-care product industry:

> *When I started to open a business, I found myself greatly in love with Chinese traditional culture, and therefore I thought about old names for medicine shops in China. There were very renowned shops called Tungzentang and Huxingyutang, so I thought about using Tang as the last word. Then it occurred to me that "shou" (in Chinese, it means longevity) sounds good. That's why I named my firm as Longevity.*

Toong combined the experiences and practices from other companies of differing periods of time, and created a special meaning of his own in the new dominion of practice. The uniqueness of his firm was also hidden in his context of entrepreneurial learning and subsequent development. He insisted on using traditional Chinese characters and old thread-bound books to make a catalogue of Longevity, which shows Chinese herbal medicine knowledge, an introduction to diets, and all its products:

> *Longevity published a thread-bound book that is worth collection. We introduce our top-quality products in this catalogue and insist on using traditional Chinese characters.*

Toong also emphasizes Chinese traditional products in his development of health-care products, such as caterpillar fungus gift boxes, swallow's saliva drinks, or high-class sea cucumber gift boxes. All these top-quality gift boxes are a combination of the old health-care concepts in China and the 21st century health-care products:

> *I discover that the Chinese people have had a long, excellent tradition of health care. Huangdi Neijing could be dated back to more than 2500 years ago. I just want to make modern health care medicine on the basis of traditional wisdom. The last thing I want to do is to create another Viagra. The more traditional, simple, and familiar the products, the better the sales.*

The reason why Toong's inclinations for and imagination about starting a business could well connect with the top niche of health-care industry in Shanghai lay in the fact that he won consumers' appreciation by using traditional herbal drinks such as caterpillar fungus and swallow's saliva. Such herbal drinks were not strange to the Shanghai people. Toong employed a modern-style package and marketing channel, on the other hand, and left his own inscription in health-care industry. Hence, we may suggest that when consumers' imagination is materialized, and the industrial community (consumers included) gives its consent, the entrepreneurs would exert more influence over the industrial community, and incorporate such materialized affairs into their imagination for the industry's business landscape. Thus, the territory and landscape of the industry would be transformed. That explains why the health-care industry in China deviates from that in the US, Taiwan, and any other country in the world.

In summation, Toong employed products, concepts, and discourses to create an innovative significance for health-care industry out of his own life experience and inclinations which were molded by tradition and the societal, cultural, and historic circumstances. With such actions, he then created a new entrepreneurial practice for health-care industry with huge success.

4. Conclusion

In this study, we investigate Chinese health-care product industry with an entrepreneur's narrative as well as historical documents, to explore the development of Chinese health-care product industry.

Unlike traditional institutional and resource-based views that limit the retribution of industry entrepreneurs, or the individualism perspective to undervalue the power of structure, we use the social constructive perspective to investigate the configuring process of an industry. We found three factors. First, the industrial dominant logic is social-constructed by the entrepreneurs. When time goes by, the entrepreneurs would learn more about the competence of the industry and encounter newer practices; this newness would lead to different depictions about the business landscapes. When the entrepreneurs' depictions about the business landscapes change, their imagination about the industrial dominant logic would be transferred at the same time, too.

Second, when entrepreneurs engage into the industrial practices, they could learn the competence of the industry and reorganize their resources and capabilities which would lead to an entrepreneurial innovation. And third, those entrepreneurial innovations would leave an imprint on the configuration of industry and create a special locality of the industry.

References

Cope, J. (2005). Toward a Dynamic Learning Perspective of Entrepreneurship, *Entrepreneurship Theory and Practice*, 29(4), pp. 373–397.

Deng, X. P. (1994). *An Anthology of Deng Xiao-ping.* Beijing: Jen Min Publishing.

Ghemawat, P. (2006). *Strategy and the Business Landscape.* NJ: Pearson/ Prentice Hall.

Hong Kong Trade Development Council (HKTDC) (2013). Chinese Health Food Review. http://china-trade-research.hktdc.com/business-news/ article/%E4%B8%AD%E5%9C%8B%E6%B6%88%E8%B2%BB%E5% B8%82%E5%A0%B4/%E4%B8%AD%E5%9C%8B%E4%BF%9D%E5% 81%A5%E9%A3%9F%E5%93%81%E5%B8%82%E5%A0%B4%E6%A6% 82%E6%B3%81/ccm/tc/1/1X000000/1X002L54.htm.

Johansson, A. W. (2010). Innovation, creativity and imitation, in F. Bill, B. Bjerke, & A. W. Johansson (eds.), *(De)mobilizing the Entrepreneurship Discourse,* Cheltenham UK: Edward Elgar Publishing Limited.

Li, C. C. (1998). *China: Consumer Revolution.* HK: Joint Publishing.

Lu, F. Z. (1988). *A Discourse on China's Economic Development.* China: Nan Fang Tsung Shu Publishing.

Wenger, E. (1998). *Communities of Practice: Learning, Meaning and Identity.* Cambridge: Cambridge University Press.

Wu, H. P. (2008). *The Age of Speedily Accumulated Wealth in China: 1993–2008.* Taipei: Yuan-Liou Publishing.

10

Contiguous Entrepreneurship in a Modern Food and Beverage Business Group — the Perspective of Complex Adaptive System

Shang-Jen Li

Meiho University

1. Introduction

In recent years, the hospitality business has become increasingly popular and has facilitated the social economy in a number of ways. This chapter mainly explores how a single-brand restaurant builds up the mechanism of contiguous entrepreneurship and becomes multiple-brand hospitality group via the perspective of Complex Adaptive System (CAS).

Through the case study, two major issues are investigated: (i) how sustained momentum in contiguous entrepreneurship emerges along the developmental process and (ii) how members conduct innovation and value creation activities collectively inside the group. The findings show that the Wang's hospitality group builds a mechanism to encourage internal entrepreneurship and by doing so, it aids the integration of internal resources and capabilities in responding to the market dynamics. Through internal entrepreneurship mechanism, the Wang's hospitality group provides the likelihood to grab market share rapidly in a short time and crafts the capacity to initiate new business successively. Through contiguous entrepreneurship, the Wang's hospitality group can deploy measures for risk aversion based on the respective knowledge of its members. Factors such as capital deployment and human resources are also significantly affected.

1.1. *Research background*

The very last decade of 20th century has seen the advent of technology shift and global economic integration, which nourished the "new economy" that made a difference among all industries around the world. Ventures and start-ups, benefiting from new economy, rapidly turned out to be multinational giants such as Microsoft and Google. According to Peter Drucker (1992), start-ups launching out into business in the United States every year have increased to 600,000 — a number that is seven times greater than that of the start-ups during the 1950/1960s economic boom. Taiwanese version of the same story depicts the rise of Quanta Computer and HonHai/Foxconn founded by Barry Lam (林百里) and Terry T.M. Gou (郭台銘) respectively.

Starting a company in the time of new economy is something significantly different from equivalent activities in the industrial age. Globalization and its momentum have made it a prerequisite for any newly founded business to take up market share worldwide as quick as it can. That means, when dealing with ever-changing environments, independent inventors and research prodigies do not always have an edge on existing enterprises, if the latter establish certain venture mechanism integrating all internal resources and capabilities that are necessary. 3M exemplifies this mechanism by encouraging individual employees to innovate, thus spawning new branches, affiliates, and in-house ventures out of project teams. On the other hand, Cisco applies to the operation pattern of a third dimension value matrix, entrusting some R&D, testing, manufacturing, and outsourcing to specialized contractors and contract workers. In this way, diverse functions are combined into a seamless platform, giving support to Cisco's efforts in various countries.

1.2. *Managerial scenarios in the age of new economy*

That said, we may as well argue that new economy brings forth opportunities for entrepreneurship, either conducted by independent technology developers exploring novel areas or utilized by large companies with internal entrepreneuring systems to take up modern challenges and evolve along the way.

First-rank employees, such as brand managers and sales managers, are often the most keenly aware of market opportunities. Rapid reporting of market conditions by these employees must be utilized by a conglomerate if it wishes to be innovative. This requires a degree of cooperation between top management and its branch employees. To facilitate this cooperative effort requires the smooth connection and communication among its subordinate units.

Because of all that, it is a must for an enterprise to adapt itself to the new economy environment, to adjust its configuration to the optimized extent that upholds both the flexibility and creativity of a small company and the exclusive resources plus sheer size of a corporate Hercules, and to make continual improvements within a knowledge economy. What happened in Intel was a typical case. Its top management, Andy Grove, was concentrating on taking the memory chip-related technology to the next level. On the contrary, the project managers and sales executives were fine-tuning the strategy and shifted their focus to the processor business. These first-rank employees were the most keenly aware of market opportunities. By shifting Intel's focus, they kept up with the market. For these crews in the front line, innovation and enterprising spirit were learned from the market, and this helped them expand the scope and scale of Intel's business to be the greatest. Similar formations could be observed in 3M and Canon, to name a few.

Let us take a look at 3M and its "15% rule," which sanctions 15% of employees' working — hours to be diverted to any promising research project of their own choice. Once proven successful, such projects will be turned into serious business, and the stories and experiences of the project initiators will become lesser paragons to their peers. 3M emphasizes on the entrepreneurial potentials of employed individuals, and preserves its organizational culture in an entrepreneurship-friendly manner. While other big companies regard their component units as the sums of malleable sub-units, 3M encourages sustained innovation and entrepreneurial spirit inside these sub-units, and gradually reorganizes creative squads and project teams into departments and divisions.

Certain Taiwanese businessmen have fulfilled sustained innovation and long-term evolution in the same way. The CID Group was founded in October 1999, and rapidly raised approximately NT$4.4 billion for four separate venture capital funds it controlled in less than a year. The total market value of the funds increased to NT$10 billion by 2003, and reached NT$25 billion 12 months later. Strategically speaking, the portfolio team's venture motto is to attend to the purposes and logic of both financiers and industrialists. That way the team plays the role of capital raisers and market opportunity hunters, and swiftly acquires winning technology for the selected industry in order to strike at the root of the business and enhance its vertical development. In consequence, the CID Group expanded its business in a very short time and amazing profits become theirs to take. As a PhD candidate under my advice, Tzu-tang Lan (2005) concludes that owner-managers in charge of such a venture capital group possess the advantages of seizing precise opportunities, high initial public offerings (IPO) efficiency, and strong teamwork/coordination. By such doing, the company can earn enough return on its investment in shorter time spam.

On the other hand, Wang's Restaurant Group comes up with this operating goal of launching at least two new brands per year under the patronage of its chairman Steve Day, a true believer in the value of entrepreneurship within the existing group. His "Project Dancing Lion" aims at 30 upcoming brands with 10,000 outlets in the next 30 years. Besides, he encourages senior executives to find their own duchies within his kingdom, calling it "organic growth" of the group. For the past three years, two restaurant chains established that way, namely Tasty Steak and Taoban, have earned acclaims all over Taiwan. In addition, Day's men had more than two ideas to submit, which gave birth to later restaurant chains such as Yuanshao and Giguo. The proliferation of outlets and the evolution of the group go hand in hand.

1.3. *New configuration of enterprises in the age of new economy*

So far it can be concluded that an organization promoting contiguous entrepreneurial activities often relies on the following:

(1) The idea of decentralization. The centralization of the headquarters is downplayed, which enables a decentralized decision model that promises the devolution of powers and responsibilities.
(2) The heterogeneity of subsidiaries and their dynamic self-adjustment in response to the environment. To pursue as many market niches as possible, subsidiaries must elevate the heterogeneity and diversity of their specialized areas.
(3) High autonomy enjoyed by all subsidiaries. For delegation and heterogeneity can only be completed if different subsidiaries are allowed to customize their own rules of engagement and operating principles dealing with specific situations.

With those in mind, the concept of Horizontal Enterprises brought up by Castells (1998) is actualized. He argued that, in the age of new economy, global economic evolution is accompanied by the strengthening of relatedness among peer organizations, turning their mother enterprise into a hub of the multifunctional decision-making network. To prevent articulation errors in such a network, a new management pattern has to be formulated, so that the multifunctional decision-making network is effectively reinforced by the integration of existing resources and capabilities, while the flexibility of decision-making and the advantage of coordinated efforts are retained, ensuring innovation and sustainability the enterprise seeks in an ever-changing environment.

An organization involved in sustained entrepreneurial activities is bound to face an environment with industry-wide challenges such as:

(1) **Chaotic markets**: Due to the development of information and communication technology and Internet media, the asymmetry of available information no longer exists between the firms and their customers. The latter becomes thoroughly aware of all product/market-related information and trends, stimulating changes in demand. Therefore, the uncertainty of the market drastically rises, and market situations become blurred and unpredictable for suppliers/providers.

(2) **Keener competitions**: Aforementioned blurring and unpredictability intensify struggles and dogfights for resources and market niches, which promise sustained market advantages and maximized profits, among competing firms. Bitter battles against rival companies can be expected in an industry/market going in that direction.

(3) **Higher dynamics**: Setting foot in a market full of chaos and competitions, the enterprise must cope with higher dynamics of its market environment.

The above descriptions focusing on sustained entrepreneurship organizations configured in new economy systems and the environment they encounter, illustrate the research background of my studies concerning the strategic evolutionary mechanism of sustained entrepreneurship. The theories I am about to discuss with you, though adequate in the aspect of explaining how an organization evolves in a dynamic environment, have not put into consideration the fact that the scope of operation of an enterprise itself has to evolve accordingly and continually, to the extent that starting up new business frequently is regarded as an integral part of the enterprise's main business. Thus, my thesis applies to the viewpoint of CAS and concentrates on how an enterprise keeps on starting up and developing new businesses in an unstable environment, to achieve better understanding of the issues and phenomena related to the strategic evolutionary mechanism of sustained entrepreneurship.

2. Literature Review

Traditionally, theories on organizational/strategic management were based on hierarchy mechanism (as opposed to market mechanism) advocated by scholars preferring the transaction cost approach. Under the rules of comparative institutional theory (Hennart, 1994), the decrease in transaction cost and the increase in transaction efficiency in an economy system were possible only because of the hierarchy that exploits the presence of the firm to substitute one single long-term transaction contract for several short-term ones for simplicity. That explains the existence of organizations as governance mechanisms in the market where transactions take place (Coase, 1937; Williamson, 1985; Rindfleisch & Heide, 1997).

Since the birth of the theory that treated the organization as another governance mechanism, scholars specializing in organizational/strategic management have directed their main concerns, from the choice between two external governance mechanisms; that is, the question of "make or buy" (Williamson, 1991; Hennart, 1993, 1994; Chi, 1994), toward the solution dimension that deals with the differences of destinations and risk-bearing potential of principals and agents belonging to the same organization (Eisenhardt, 1989; Bergen & Walker, 1992).

Under such heritage, those who studied organizational/strategic management might occupy themselves with internal or external issues, but they shared the same final purpose of clarifying effective strategies of development that helped firms reduce costs while strengthening competitive capacities. Whatever their arguments might be, their basic logic was derived from the age of old economy, during which efficient mass production and cost reduction were considered priority.

Organizations afterward started to notice the gradual changes of customers' needs, the rising heat of market competitions, and the participation of emerging industrial technologies. As a result, topics concerning organizational/strategic management relocated their focus on industry structures and the acquisition of competing positions. That was prominently exemplified by the school of Industrial Organization (IO), which accentuated the analysis of external situations for enterprises and the detection of opportunities and menaces, in order to make use of the advantages and weak points of the enterprises to construct appropriate strategies for them. However, IO was predisposed to strategic analysis of industry structures and competing positions (Porter, 1980; Spanos & Lioukas, 2001), and thus insufficient for specifying why there were strategically correct corporations with authentic industrial positions ending up failing the market. Besides, various scholars have begun to learn the fact that the basic strategy (and the main profit driver) of a company is determined by nothing but the resources and capabilities it possesses, and the accumulation and cultivation of its internal resources and capabilities promise sustained competitive advantages for the organization itself (Wernerfelt, 1984; Barney, 1991). Thus, the core resources and capabilities shall be the critical elements for company to scheme long-term strategies and as the nexus that a company exercises strategic thinking (Grant, 1991).

Due to the formerly neglected factors mentioned above, a new point of view with consideration for technologies and resources was brought to the spotlight, which focused on the concept of core competence in order to figure out how a firm with core capabilities and resources could outshine its competitors. It is known as the RBV, or the Resource-Based View (Wernerfelt, 1984, 1989; Barney, 1991), which argues that a competing organization must acquire key resources and capabilities that are valuable, imperfectly imitable, rare, and non-substitutable (V.I.R.N.) to maintain its core competence, optimizing its operating efficiency to achieve sustainable competitive advantages over its opponents (Barney, 1991; Collis & Montgomery, 1995). Although this viewpoint enriches the theories of organizational/strategic management and explains how an organization fulfills efficiency/effectiveness with improvised strategies responding to the immediate environment, the fickleness/complexity of the environment, the continuous development of technologies, and the ever-changing customer demands are not significantly addressed. While RBV highly values the sustainable competitive advantages, the drastic change in its strategic basis and the abrupt increase in the industrial dynamics it faces pose more and more of an obstacle. Aside from the features of core resources and capabilities it depicts, RBV provides little concrete or executable know-how as to the establishment of such resources and capabilities. Therefore, RBV simply gives us a glimpse of the attributes of core resources and capabilities. It has not submitted the best solution for firms to construct sustainable competitive advantages in the new economy environment.

As a matter of fact, the school of IO and the school of RBV share the same basic hypothesis that believes in the singular core around which the strategies are made certain and planned out. It is the analysis of external environments and the study of the competitive position of an enterprise that distinguish IO from the inward approach RBV takes to comprehend how new strategies are possible via internal resources and capabilities. Nevertheless, the examples of the strategic evolutionary mechanism of sustained innovation have shown to us that an enterprise is not an organization with one single core. Furthermore, strategies do not evolve in a predictable manner, for they are the consequences of struggles among diverse judgments made by different action-takers.

Yet, researches on dynamic evolution are not unprecedented. Some scholars have noticed the special features of unique environments and market competition patterns in a new economy system, and their scrutiny into these features has come to the conclusion that, in order to grasp the competitive advantages for an organization, the prior task is to build up dynamic capabilities that quickly answers to environmental changes and briskly detects market opportunities.

Teece and fellow researchers were the first to advance the theory of dynamic capabilities. It suggests that, when exposed to the highly dynamic market nowadays, companies need their managers to integrate and recompose all internal/external resources and capabilities, so that dynamic capabilities can be established to conquer the ever-changing market (Teece, 1993, 1997). It also holds that companies have to adjust their internal process of management and organization according to the immediate environment, update their technologies, enhance their connections, refine the market positions of their brands, and expand/enlarge their path of research and development. In a word, the establishment of dynamic capabilities enables not only new products but also new process and routine of production, service and management that evolve along with the constantly changing market situations (Helfat, 1997), guaranteeing the competitive edge and market value of the companies. The ongoing integration and re-composition of the three P's (path, process, and position) represent the planning and constructing strategy of dynamic capabilities.

On the other hand, Bartlett and Ghoshal (1995) have indicated that, in an ever-changing environment, management team leading a large-scale international enterprise should not confine itself to managing its strategies, structures and systems, for there are crucial factors such as objectives, processes, and individuals at its service. The latter, especially front-line executives in large organizations are the ones that catch up with latest information and devise effective management strategies out of it. Their superiors in the headquarters must make unconventional use of them to maximize their contributions to collaborated decision-making.

Still, certain things remain unsolved. Researches on dynamic evolution, with their main concern fixed on the scopes of operation of enterprises, provide little new points of view. For example, the thinking of dynamic capabilities explains the improvement and sublimation of internal processes, positions, and paths for an organization, yet it only applies to the organization with one single core. Precious as Bartlett and Ghoshal's theory may be, it has not gone far enough to include enterprises with multiple operating cores under examination. Some enterprises situated in dynamic settings, with their scopes of operation evolving on and on, even regard the constant starting-up of new ventures as their main business. To address that, I would like to concentrate my observations on how enterprises in fickle, chaotic environments start new business on a frequent basis.

Decentralization, multiple cores of decision-making, emphasis on participation and coordination, and dynamic network out of joint efforts by independent units are common among organizations familiar with strategic evolutionary mechanism of sustained entrepreneurship. With a little help from the theory of CAS, such organizations can be better understood.

3. The Perspective of CAS

The year was 1984. Santa Fe Institute, founded in New Mexico, dedicated itself to the study of CAS including complex biology, computation, and attributes, behaviors and evolution of technology/economy systems. These scholars tried to describe non-linear systems, and appealed to evolutionary and cognitive science to construe the origin of lives and intelligence. Also known as complexity science, the subject invoked interdisciplinary ideas, methods, and experiences from almost every department of knowledge (Anderson, 1999). Academic masterminds such as Arthur, Holland, Kauffman, and Anderson, hailing from the worlds of economics, biology, computer science, politics, anthropology, and social studies, devoted their efforts one by one. The sum of their dedications can be roughly stated as the findings below.

(1) *Self-organization of a system*: The fountainhead of a CAS is usually random and chaotic at best. However, the comprising agents of the system spontaneously assemble themselves. This bottom-up behavior motivates unexpected development of the system, and the consequence

can be either desirable (such as the growth of an economy) or unwelcome (such as the crash of a stock market or the maturity of a tropical storm).

(2) ***Non-additivity***: A CAS cannot be simply interpreted as the additive result of its comprising elements. For instance, the capabilities of a human brain are beyond the sum of the functions of different brain cells. Similarly, an economy system is always more complicated than the aggregation of the institutions and individuals that reside in the system. Simple as the components may be, they combine to form a new machine of complicacy. In his "Complexity: The Emerging Science at the Edge of Order and Chaos," Waldrop (1992) borrows Langton's assertion concerning computer-simulated physics models, indicating that complicated behaviors do not necessarily derive from complicated origins, for it is possible to elaborate intriguingly complex activities from pure and simple elements.

(3) ***Edge of chaos***: In CAS, behaviors of order and chaos co-exist, alternately showing themselves. It is referred to as the edge of chaos, a status between order and disorder, conservativeness and innovation, stabilization and transformation. Just like Brown and Eisenhardt (1998) have described, it is a gray area mixing up regulatedness and anarchy, capturing behaviors of complexity, uncontrollability, unpredictability, and self-organization at the same time. The edge of chaos does not only benefit the creativity (adaptivity) of human brains (living species), but also supply enterprises with core kinetic energy of sustainable innovation.

The theory of CAS proposes that actors in the systems realize co-evolution and, as time goes by, adapt themselves to their respective environment to strive for higher rewards or adaptation functions (Holland & Miller, 1991). Moreover, the reward for a certain actor is influenced by decisions made by other actors. In other word, the adaptive landscapes of actors are ceaselessly shifting/drifting (Levinthal, 1997). That results in some kind of dynamic equilibrium standing on the edge of chaos (Kauffman, 1992). Simply put, CASs operate far from the global optimum of system performances (Holland & Miller, 1991). As the systems distance themselves from equilibrium, small initial changes are amplified by the effect of positive feedback, causing unexpected, important impact. When every system involved becomes sensitively dependent on initial conditions, the cause-and-effect connections will be lost. That is to say, there are no linear relations between individual actions and global consequences. The long-term consequences basically emerge out of the blue from the organization. Therefore, while persons and groups in the organization are able to choose, plan, and manipulate their interfering actions, the outcome of the actions cannot be chosen, planned, or manipulated (Stacey, 1996).

In short, the CAS see the world as a systematic entity composed of related heterogeneous actors regarded as the combinations of individuals uphold different strategies. Interactions between the actors constitute the global environment in the system, in which both independent and collective operations incur only unpredictable outcomes, or time-dependent emergent. And that is how the system makes its way to innovation (Coleman, 1999; Kelly, 1994; Lissack, 1999; McKelvey, 1999; Muffatto & Faldani, 2003).

To sum up, the highlights of the theory of CAS are:

(1) All actors are independent agents, with their strategies distinct from one another.
(2) As a whole, the strategy of a CAS cannot be pre-planned or foreseen, for it is emergent during the evolution.
(3) Strategies taken by the actors evolve with the scenarios/situations till they reach optimum, so that the actors respond better to the challenge of competitions and environments. Such procedures promise the effect of fitness landscapes for the evolutionary mechanisms of the actors' strategies (Beinhocker, 1999).

4. Contiguous Entrepreneurial Organizations under the Perspective of CAS

The study of CAS, derived from the complexity theory, actually provides a relative simple structure to examine systems discussed in social science (Stacey, 1996; Beinhocker, 1997; Anderson, 1999). Dooley (1997) also believes that CASs are capable of self-organization and learning, creating a holistic viewpoint for those who wish to analyze the organization or society to which they belong. Hence, an organization engaging in contiguous entrepreneurial activities can be looked upon as a CAS, with four primary features. They are:

(1) Full of specialized and independent business units doing different business. As decentralized as a constantly entrepreneuring organization is, it consists of specialized, heterogeneous, and highly self-ruling bodies running on their own. Under such a structure, autonomy can be witnessed in every comprising unit in the organization.

(2) An environment of discrete equilibrium. Organizations involved in sustained entrepreneurial activities are usually situated in industries of chaotic conditions, fierce market competitions, and intense dynamics.
(3) Adoption of emergent, instead of pre-planned, strategies. Holistic strategies of such organization take shape as units subordinate to the organization interact with one another while coping with their respective industrial environments that evolve at their own paces. Emergent strategies like those are too spontaneous to be worked out in advance.
(4) Complex network and co-evolution. Though autonomous and heterogeneous, units engaging in continuous entrepreneuring are still closely tied to their headquarters. Analogically, however diverse and loosely related their new business are, these units support one another financially and materially when necessary, creating a highly connected network of affiliation.

Henceforward, it would be safe to say that the organizations we have been analyzing conform to the requisites of CASs. I will further resort to what the CAS discourse has observed to discuss the mechanisms linking independent units in an organization and the roles they play.

Aforementioned cases of the evolutionary processes of modern organizations devoted to sustained entrepreneurial activities, including those of 3M, Cisco, Wang's Restaurant Group and CID Group, have showcased notable qualities such as:

(1) Never stop venturing into new business. CID, for example, takes into account both the responsibility of a financier and the purpose of an industrialist, to stick by its strategic venture motto, and thus invests in three to five newly created technology business every year. Wang's Restaurant, with its "Project Dancing Lion" thrusting for 30 new brands with 10,000 outlets in the next 30 years, manifests the same spirit.
(2) Tightly associate the headquarters with all the affiliated start-ups, yet do not compromise individual autonomy and specialized heterogeneity. In Taiwan, gentlemen in power at Wang's have resoundingly standardized the managerial systems throughout the group, even though they allow subordinated restaurant chains to develop their own tactics and ideals. Besides that, all top executives leading different brands under the flag of Wang's gather to exchange opinions and experiences on a weekly basis.

(3) Delegate the rights of conventional strategy-contriving/decision-making to all business units in the organization, and provide them with incubation of talents and assistance of various kinds after delegation. Specifically speaking, it involves turning the headquarters into a dispatch center of funds, instructors, and training sessions, to incubate quality labor. That is how CID employees advance their insights into different industries, which helps to single out potential investment targets and pour in the capital in no time.

Exploiting those novel approaches to achieve ceaseless evolution under unstable conditions, enterprises engaging in sustained entrepreneurial activities become challenge-proof even when being surrounded with complicated fickleness. The following directive purposes are common among these organizations.

(1) Sustained evolution of all business units. That is to say, the headquarters must be ready to launch into emerging business foreseen to be prosperous at any time, and not afraid of dumping outdated business in time. Such practice relies on the independency of all affiliated business units as self-sustained institutions, sometime even with dissimilar equity structures. Therefore, when the market mechanism declares the destined downfall of a certain unit, it can be closed without endangering other units.

(2) Sustained evolution of capital and governance mechanism. Legal distinctions between business units define their independent existences, but do not refrain them from sharing compatible governance mechanism or drawing from the same capital pool. Cooperation like that helps negate different risks happening in different timeframes. The story of CID Group has proven that, with its highly associated, seamlessly integrated capital pool and governance mechanism, the core strategy of "best of both worlds" (referring to their double concerns as financiers and industrialists) does bring about sufficient funds and precious information, ensuring widespread success for its independently operating portfolio teams.

(3) Sustained evolution of human resources. For large enterprises devoted to sustained entrepreneurial activities, the persisting thirst for innovation and leadership must be quenched. The acquisition of capable managers is also an evolutionary process, either via promoting worthy employees or by recruiting talents from the outside. In this aspect,

Wang's Restaurant does an excellent job by searching for outstanding personalities with "venture factors" among its employees, which authorizes outlet managers scoring growing sales to start anew as project leaders/outpost founders.

5. Strategic Evolutionary Mechanisms of Contiguous Entrepreneurship

To fulfill those directive purposes mentioned above in a continuously evolutionary frame, organizations engaging in constant entrepreneurial activities should prepare themselves to answer these questions:

(1) **How is it possible to build up common recognition for the integration of different business units into a low-risk, substantially consolidated organization?** Gentlemen in the headquarters must realize that, units under their rule, though formally independent, still need basic consensus and mutual recognition on certain levels to make a difference.

(2) **How to establish platforms benefiting effective information exchange and knowledge deposit?** Entrepreneurial know-how is dynamic, and can only be perceived during actualization (Krizner, 1973; Minniti & Bygrave, 2001). Every enterprise has to find their own mechanism of knowledge-brewing/brain-storming that promises a better chance of successful entrepreneuring attempts.

(3) **How to manage risks in unknown, swiftly changing environments?** Predicting possible market fluctuations is always the opening act in conventional risk management, right before countering strategies can be outlined. However, enterprises in the age of new economy face a different story of fickle, complicated environments that are difficult to prevision. Operating risks have become even more irregular to be held under control these days, especially for large enterprises. Hence, a more flexible mechanism of risk management is necessary for organizations frequently starting up new business.

Instead of returning to the same old strategy–structure–system model of traditional strategic management, we believe that it takes the logics of CAS to construct new strategic mechanism solving those questions. The following are the strategic evolutionary mechanisms of sustained entrepreneurship we suggest.

(1) Building up organizational identity to promote sustainable innovation that enhance integration of business units, reduce operating risks, and heighten consolidation among comprising agents of an organization.

Brown and Eisenhardt (1997) has pointed out the possibility of combining organizational structures (which help define respective duties and straighten out priority of missions), extensive communications, and unbound, situational creativity to develop organizational reform. Under such existed structures of an organization, its members are encouraged to detect any quick-paced change in the market, and cultivate insight benefiting innovative reform of the organization through massive external/internal exchanges of information and market perception evolving with situations. This method of operations eliminates obstacles to most reforming acts and avoids chaotic reform without any guidance. It also symbolizes the transformation of organizational development from observing pre-regulated formulation of solutions to adjusting evolutionary formulation of countermeasures to multiple tasks and situations.

In brief, managers should embed specific assignment of duties and intensive communications in the adaptive, flexible organizational structures they created for continuous improvement of individual projects, in order to establish organizational recognition of sustainable innovation. Once these principles are maintained, there will be neither lack of creativity nor anarchy inside the organization. Moreover, the constantly entrepreneuring organization will confront little difficulty in integrating various business units, reduce operating risks, and heighten consolidation among its members.

(2) Building up knowledge sharing platform that accumulates and shares entrepreneurial knowledge.

Krizner (1973) has argued that the knowledge of enterprisers is not static or fixed. They do have access to market-oriented and technology-related information beneficial to their newly created business, yet it does not mean they are fully aware of the ultimate action that helps them seize opportunities on the market. Their knowledge is dynamic, subject to changes, and can only be empirically accumulated via their direct experiences in launching new business. What they uncover in the knowledge are probable market opportunities, which in turn reinforce the evolution of their entrepreneuring knowledge, continuously expanding their knowledge pool.

Therefore, Minniti and Bygrave (2001) further implies that the act of entrepreneuring is a learning process, and entrepreneurs launching new business make the most out of their experiences from the past and in the making to pile up more and more entrepreneuring knowledge. While the new ventures are being founded, the cumulative amount of entrepreneuring knowledge climbs up accordingly. Still, in most organizations, there may be merely one entrepreneuring team that exclusively enjoys the experiences and/or knowledge in question. In an organization utilizing strategic evolutionary mechanisms of sustained entrepreneurship, however, there are multiple entrepreneurs acting separately on their own entrepreneuring knowledge that lead to different market information, different allocations of resources, and different market opportunities for development. Besides, the headquarters of such organizations are able to integrate communicative platforms for different kinds of entrepreneuring knowledge, maximizing the accumulation of all related knowledge. In Taiwan, Wang's Restaurant Group has made it a rule for the venture committee of the "Dancing Lion Project" to dine at 100 or more rival restaurants famous for their peculiar cuisines or exceptional services every year, so that future discussions by the committee members are based on actual surveys and empirical investigations that essentially accelerate the accumulation of entrepreneuring knowledge, which becomes their most precious assets when they start even more new business in the depths of the restaurant industry.

(3) Building up business risk aversion mechanisms of optimal maneuvers.

Conventional strategies of risk management are preceded by the prediction of forthcoming market fluctuations, and provide solutions to these problematic changes. Nevertheless, predicting market status has become more and more infeasible for enterprises facing perplexed, uncertain environments in the age of new economy, making it more difficult to manage the potential operating risks that can be extremely troublesome for companies of larger sizes.

With the perspective of CAS, Beinhocker (1991) has made an enlightened analogy between the formations of operating strategies of enterprises and the evolutionary process of coming to a climax in fitness landscapes. As the enterprises keep moving forward, making multiple explorations of areas for future development, and fine-tune their long-term and short-term investments in new business, they are also capturing best market positions for themselves. Thus, during their constant, recurring starting-up of new business, these enterprises neither expect nor have to be successful at their very first attempt of multidimensional investments in various new markets. Sometimes, loss-making ventures reveal key clues concerning the most probable target for future investments once the withdrawal of resources is completed.

Hence, it can be inferred that, organizations adopting strategic evolutionary mechanisms of sustained entrepreneurship, with their headquarters capable of running multiple investing projects in diverse industries at the same time, are in touch with potential future developments of different markets. Such mechanisms help evade the tragic domino effect of the failure of a certain business unit undermining the operation of the whole group or collapsing the ongoing innovation of the organization, which illustrates how the feasibility of modern age risk management can be retained.

Taiwan-based CID Group, for instance, has noticed that, in the high-tech world, the advent of new products usually marks the rise of several corresponding component suppliers. Inspired by the fact, the group broadens its investing scope to cover IC packaging/testing services, semiconductor assembly, telecommunication component makers, and so forth, taking up larger market share at the headstream of pioneering business including 3G cellular phone manufacturing. While the financing experts of the group raise capital with professional efficiency, its portfolio teams hunt for various market opportunities and promptly acquire crucial technologies in promising industries, initiating both vertical and horizontal development to ensure its investing advantages. With numerous investing targets diversely and diffusely picked out, CID effectively averts from the risk of concentrated investment in homogeneous industries. And the portfolio teams also do a terrific job replenishing working funds and uncovering remunerative opportunities hidden in the market, which deepens its success and charts out more critical paths toward further development of existing business.

6. Conclusion

The common strategic concept of earlier theories of IOs, resource-based view, and dynamic capacities, hypothesizes that the confirmable pairing of specific causes/effects or actions/consequences does exist in the real world. They all regard an organization as a system, but they overestimate the power of choice (enjoyed by external consultants and internal executives) over the organization's objectives and directions that employees are supposed to pursue/defend. Strategic theories of this kind have been taken for granted. However, the strategy–structure–system model of conventional strategic management turns out to be insufficient when applied to interpret the evolutionary process of modern organizations engaging in sustained entrepreneurial activities, for the process involves continuous evolutions of business units, capital, governance mechanisms, and human resources over time.

Another defect of those decades-old theories lies in their limited descriptive ability beyond linear, equilibrium-oriented issues of strategic management. For modern enterprises comprising several highly-connected, co-evolving heterogeneous business units, the theories barely provide any account of how to establish collective recognition to integrate different units, how to effectuate risk management in unknown, ever-changing environments, or how to enhance association between all business units to maximize the synergy under a decision-making mechanism of multiple cores.

To complement the precedent theories, my study appeals to the views introduced by the CAS, achieving better understandings of organizations devoting themselves to sustained entrepreneurial evolutions. Such organizations are identical to CASs in appearance, and the essence and process of their entrepreneurial activities do conform to the features of non-linear evolution, which can be fully elucidated by the theory of the CAS. The findings of my research indicate three distinct qualities observed in the process of starting up new business inside such organizations. They are:

(1) Units within the organization are always in the process of starting up new business.
(2) Start-up units maintaining intensively close association with their headquarters, without compromising their autonomy and specialized heterogeneity.
(3) Headquarters turning itself into a consultant, talent-incubating, capital-supplying center.

As the entrepreneurial activities go on and on, the organizations themselves evolve along on three different levels. They are:

(1) Sustained evolution of all business units.
(2) Sustained evolution of capital and governance mechanism.
(3) Sustained evolution of human resources.

Such organizations also make the best of the strategic evolutionary mechanisms mentioned below to solve problems standing in their way of evolution.

(1) Organizational recognition mechanisms of sustainable innovation.
(2) Communicative platform mechanisms that accumulate entrepreneuring knowledge.
(3) Risk management mechanisms of optimal maneuvers.

This study focuses on the strategic evolutionary mechanisms of contiguous entrepreneurship and the emerging organizations that adopt these mechanisms. It adheres to a softened, nimble, organic management pattern, pointing toward a previously overlooked yet potentially promising direction in the field of entrepreneurial studies. Furthermore, the management of top executives in such organizations should place emphasis on different ways of assisting these executives in working out long-term perspectives of organizational development and leading the organizations in new and hopeful directions, instead of meticulously analyzing the environment to respond to it with proper strategies in a conventional manner. It may exactly be what most Taiwanese enterprises are looking for as they improve their outdated management methods.

References

Anderson, P. (1999). Complexity Theory and Organization Science, *Organization Science*, 10(3), pp. 216–232.

Barney, J. B. (1991). Firm Resources and Sustained Competitive Advantage, *Journal of Management*, 7, pp. 99–120.

Bartlett, C. A. & Ghoshal, S. (1995). Changing the Role of Top Management: Beyond Structure to Process, *Harvard Business Review*, January–February, 16, pp. 120–132.

Beinhocker, E. D. (1997). Robust Adaptive Strategies, *Sloan Management Review*, 4(3), pp. 95–106.

Bergen, M., Dutta, S., & Walker, O. G. (1992). Agency Relationships in Marketing: A Review of Implications and Applications of Agency and Related Theories, *Journal of Marketing*, 56, pp. 1–24.

Brown, S. L. & Eisenhardt, K. M. (1997). The Art of Continuous Change: Linking Complexity Theory and Time-Paced Evolution in Relentlessly Shifting Organizations, *Administrative Science Quarterly*, 42, pp. 1–34.

Brown, S. L. & Eisenhardt, K. M. (1998). *Competing on the Edge.* New York: Harvard Business School Press.

Castells, M. (1998). *The Rise of Network Society.* Oxford and Malden, MA: Blackwell Publishers.

Chi, T. (1994). Trading in Strategic Resource: Necessary Conditions, Transaction Cost Problems and Choice of Exchange Structure, *Strategic Management Journal*, 15(4), pp. 271–290.

Coase, R. H. (1937). The Nature of the Firm, *Economica, New Series*, 4(16), pp. 386–405.

Coleman, J. H., Jr. (1999). What Enables Self-Organizing Behavior in Businesses, *Emergence*, 1(1), pp. 33–48.

Collis, D. J. & Montomery, C. A. (1995). Competing on Resources: Strategy in the 1990s, *Harvard Business Review*, July–August, 73(4), pp. 118–128.

Dooley, K. J. (1997). A Complex Adaptive Systems Model of Organization Change, *Nonlinear Dynamics, Psychology, and Life Science*, 1(1), pp. 69–97.

Drucker, P. (1992). *Managing for the Future.* New York, NY: Truman Talley/E.P. Dutton.

Eisenhardt, K. M. (1989). Agency Theory: An Assessment and Review, *Academy of Management Review*, 14(1), pp. 57–74.

Grant, R. M. (1991). The Resource-Based Theory of Competitive Advantage: Implications for Strategy Formulation, *California Management Review*, 33, pp. 114–135.

Helfat, C. E. (1997). Know-How and Asset Complementarity and Dynamic Capability Accumulation: The Case of R&D, *Strategic Management Journal*, 18(5), pp. 339–360.

Hennart, J. F. (1993). Explaining the Swollen Middle: Why Most Transactions are a Mix of Market and Hierarchy, *Organization Science*, 4(4), pp. 529–545.

Hennart, J. F. (1994). The Comparative Institutional Theory of the Firm: Some Implications for Corporate Strategy, *Journal of Management Studies*, 31(2), pp. 193–207.

Holland, J. & Miller, J. H. (1991). Artificial Adaptive Agent in Economics Theory, *The American Economic Review, Papers and Proceedings of the Hundred and Third Annual Meeting of American Economic Association*, 81(2), pp. 365–370.

Kauffman, S. A. (1992). *Origins of Order: Self-Organization and Selection in Evolution.* Oxford: Oxford University Press.

Kelly, K. (1994). *Out of Control: The New Biology of Machines, Social Systems, and the Economic World.* Reading, MA: Addison Wesley.

Krizner, I. (1973). *Competition and Entrepreneurship.* Chicago: The University of Chicago Press.

Lan, T.-t. (2005). The Owner-managers of Information Technology (IT) Entrepreneurial Businesses — An Explorative Case Study on Electronic Components Manufacturing Companies, unpublished dissertation, National Sun Yat-sen University, Taiwan ROC.

Levinthal, D. A. (1997). Adaption on Rugged Landscape, *Management Science*, 43(7), pp. 934–950.

Lissack, M. R. (1999). Complexity: The Science, its Vocabulary, and its Relation to Organizations, *Emergence*, 1(1), pp. 110–126.

McKelvey, B. (1999). Complexity Theory in Organization Science: Seizing the Promise or Becoming a Fad? *Emergence*, 1(1), pp. 5–32.

Minniti, M. & Bygrave, W. (2001). A Dynamic Model of Entrepreneurial Learning, *Entrepreneurship Theory and Practice*, Spring, pp. 5–16.

Muffatto, M. & Faldani, M. (2003). Open Source as Complex Adaptive System, *Emergence*, 5(3), pp. 83–100.

Porter, M. E. (1980). *Competitive Strategy*. NY: The Free Press.

Rindfleisch, A. & Heide, J. B. (1997). Transaction Cost Analysis: Past, Present, and Future Applications, *Journal of Marketing*, 61, pp. 30–54.

Spanos, Y. E. & Lioukas, S. (2001). An Examination Into the Causal Logic of Rent Generation : Contrasting Porter's Competitive Strategy Framework and the Resource-Based Perspective, *Strategic Management Journal*, 22(10), pp. 907–934.

Stacey, R. D. (1996). *Strategic Management and Organizational Dynamics: The Challenge of Complexity*, San Francisco: Trans-Atlantic Publications, Inc Berrett-Koehler.

Teece, D. J. (1993). The Dynamics of Industrial Capitalism: Perspectives on Alfred Chandler's Scale and Scope (1990), *Journal of Economic Literature*, 31(1), pp. 199–225.

Teece, D. J., Pisano, G., & Shuen, A. (1997). Dynamic Capabilities and Strategic Management, *Strategic Management Journal*, 18, pp. 509–533.

Waldrop, M. M. (1992). *Complexity: The Emerging Science at the Edge of Order and Chaos*, NY: Simon and Schuster.

Wernerfelt, B. (1984). A Resource-Based View of the Firm, *Strategic Management Journal*, 5, pp. 171–180.

Wernerfelt, B. (1989). From Critical Resources to Corporate Strategy, *Journal of General Management*, 14, pp. 4–12.

Williamson, O. E. (1985). *The Economic Institutions of Capitalism-Firm, Markets, Relational Contracting*. NY: The Free Press.

11

How Cultural Product Could Re-create the Representation of Region: A Story About Organizing

Ted Yu-Chung Liu
National Pingtung University

Jung-Chih Hung
National Sun Yat-sen University

1. Introduction

Since the 1990s, cultural economy has become a major issue in academic research, and culture industries are seen by many countries as the important strategy for local and regional redevelopment. However, most research focuses on industry clusters, value creation, and business administration (Caves, 2000; Crossland & Smith, 2002; Power, 2002); comparatively, there has been little work addressing on the local economic dynamics, in which the process of organizing brings about the development of local or regional cultural industries and the recreation of representation of region.

According to Hall (1997), culture industries have great importance to local economies and urban policies, and offer significant economic and cultural benefits. In the 1970s, many Western cities gradually became aware of the benefits of mobilizing culture as a form of capital, and actively enlisted the assistance of business leaders and urban planning professionals in efforts to expand their artistic infrastructure in order to reduce levels of unemployment. Regardless of whether culture plays an economic role, provides software, or is seen as a capital inducement, all these directly or indirectly represent local economic development. This process of representation is not a mere reflection of local economic development, as in a mirror, but rather plays an active role in constructing local economic development.

The current mainstream organizational perspective is derived from open systems theory, and regards organizations as independent entities with clearly-defined boundaries that interact with their "environment." This perspective regards organizational actions chiefly as means of adapting to changes in the environment. However, as Czarniawska (1997) noticed, in view of the innumerable phenomena connected with large and small organizations in today's world, the open systems organizational perspective is inadequate to deal with all the organizational matters that are constantly occurring, and thus suggests that organizational theory should make a shift from structural aspects to constituent aspects, which is equivalent to a shift from "organization" to "organizing." In an investigation of organizational issues from a social construction perspective, Czarniawska (2008) also suggests that, from an organizing perspective, an organization by no means is an independent entity with a clearly-defined boundary from the outside world, and in fact, when viewed from the perspective of society, the boundaries of organizations are frequently changing. Organizational actors are not as independent of their organizations as the traditional viewpoint would have it; instead, organizational actors are constantly constructing their organizations via their actions and interpretation of the meaning of their actions. In light of these circumstances, organizational research on "organizing" should focus on actions, and not on the behavior corresponding to actions. MacIntyre (1981, 1990) believed that while behavior is the consciousness of sense-data, actions have their intentions, their goals, and their underlying logic. The meaning of actions requires a setting in order to be manifested and grasped. Schutz (1973) consequently claimed that "We cannot understand people's actions if we ignore their intentions, and we cannot understand actors' intentions if we ignore the settings that they endow with meaning." Any effort to understand the meaning of an action must also understand the setting in which that actions takes place. As a consequence, the process of investigating "organizing" must proceed from tracking and recording actions to "sensemaking." According to Czarniawska (2008), meaning is not something given in advance, but is rather the reorganization of the fragmentary events of daily organizational life into meaningful knowledge, and the sharing this knowledge with others, through sensemaking process. The linking of meaning and reality is the act of representation. We use language, written words, or images to understand, describe, and define the world we see. The material world acquire meaning only via representation systems, and we also employ representation systems to construct meaning from the material world. Representation is therefore a process in which we construct the world around us, while generating meaning as we go (Sturken & Cartwright, 2000). This study therefore employs actor-network theory (ANT) as a framework in investigating the organizing process of the Anping district of Tainan city in Taiwan to understand how the representation of region is recreated via the process of organizing by means of the development of cultural products.

2. Research Method

Although the application of the ANT theoretical perspective in research on organizations and cultural economics is only just getting underway, many scholars believe that ANT's core concepts and value will make it a mainstream research tool in this field (Gherardi & Nicolini, 2005; Steyeart, 2007). Employing field research and analysis, this study tries to examine the relation between the development of Tainan's Anping district and the becoming of cultural product sword lion by various relevant network and actants.

2.1. *ANT as the perspective*

While the social sciences formerly generally took humans as the central actors, and clearly distinguished technology and society, human and non-human, and micro and macro, the ANT regards this dual thinking as an inappropriate way to analyze our world. Not only does the composition of the world include many non-humans possessing agency, such as matter and technology, at the same time, technology and society are embedded in a common network, and are thus co-formed and co-constructed. Because of this, what is truly deserving of attention is not "micro" or "macro," but rather a "social process of circulating entities," or in other words, a network.

Since a network of actors invariably contains both human and non-human actants, ANT suggests that the construction of scientific knowledge and technology are not determined solely by society (benefit), but are also jointly determined by a "heterogeneous actor network" composed of humans (society) and non-humans (tools, objects, research subjects, etc.). In other words, ANT is a technique for describing how a heterogeneous actor network is interactively constructed, forms, exists, evolves, and even faces dissolution (Law, 1999).

ANT also emphasizes that both human and non-human entities or actants are in an anti-entatitive state, which has prompted researchers to employ the concepts of relational materiality and performative to investigate the development and evolution of the relationship between the two. According to Law (1999), so-called relational materiality refers to the perspective that no actants have a real inner nature, and their form and characteristics are the results of their relationships with other actants. In this model, actants have no endogenous, inherent nature, but are rather the effects and outcomes of interactive convergence.

Performative aspects refer to an actant's outward appearance, which is shaped by the actant's position and relationships. We can also say that actants' performative aspects are derived from the interaction of the relationships that they are involved in, rely on, and use. The question that concerns us here is how things are performed or perform themselves, resulting in a state of contingence wherein "all things are uncertain and reversible" (Law, 1994), and not the given object order. Because of this, from the ANT perspective, the nature of actants is changeable, and their forms are also changeable — these things depend entirely on the actants' relationships and mutual interactions. In other words, the unique feature of ANT is that it has no pre-existing frameworks, but is instead produced from interaction between humans and non-humans, and reflects the diverse linkages in society.

As described above, actants are endowed with positioning and character from the links between their relational materiality in the course of their performance. This process of naturalization is changeable due to the development of relationships; actors are continuously displaced in time and space, and their original contexts may expand or evolve. We must therefore use special methods to deal with actors in order to stabilize them and cause them to have recognizable "features." This method is known as translation. In other words, the form, outward appearance, and essence of an actant may change because of changes in the actant's position in time or space. Linguistic and textual translation is therefore required, along with transformation of benefit and goals, in order to express the actant's temporarily stable identity, which can be used to extend the linking context.

2.2. *Adopting Callon's analytic framework of translation*

How do scholars put ANT into practice? While the answer varies from person to person, as an example, in 1986 Callon using the scallop-raising process in France's St. Brieuc Bay to explain how scallops, fishermen, scientists, and researchers could achieve a stable character via the process of translation. According to Callon's account, translation results in an actor network; different actants emerge from an action network with a huge structure, engage in mutual translation, and cause each other to form a "unitary" macro actor network. It can therefore be said that an actor network is a potential result of an action network. Callon also proposed that translation has the following four important moments of opportunity:

• **Problematization, or how to become indispensable**

At the start of problematization, a certain actant possessing a specific intention proposes or announces a period that is hard to solve or able to attract others' interest. At the same time, the actant also provides all actants with a preliminary solution, and the actants then reach a certain consensus, the goal of which is to cause other actants to become aware of knowable definitions, and in the process form an "obligatory point of passage" (OPP). Under conditions acceptable to all, this constitutes a preliminary screening standard, while also causing other actants to walk into the trap, so that good and bad alike become indispensable links in the process on the basis of their mutual definitions.

• **The devices of interessement or how the allies are locked into place**

Each actant that passes the OPP will be pushed or pulled by others into a preliminary position, which will facilitate the establishment of mutually beneficial relationships with other actants. This, in other words, makes it look as if everyone has benefited. This process is also partly motivated by the need to purge other temptations outside each actant's circle. As soon as relationships are specificalized, the actants can begin negotiating a transaction model among themselves, and can obtain the repayment that they expect from involvement in the network. The main task of the actants is to eliminate the possibility of other options through mutual benefit. Locking in each actant's position in this way also clarifies problems. Because different actants have different checklists of needs and criteria, they must negotiate cautiously concerning their mutual identities, goals, and alliances in order to achieve an arrangement beneficial and satisfactory to all.

• **How to define and coordinate mutual roles: enrollment**

A network gradually emerges as actants coordinate with each other and form alliances. The formation of each network link is accomplished through negotiations that consolidate the individual benefit of each actant. At the same time, this is also a continuous process of trial and error, which continues until the group achieves answers that are mutually acceptable to all. ANT usually refers to the changes that occur during this pivotal period — namely the formation of alliances through strategy, tricks, and negotiation — as the process of organizing or orchestrating.

• **Mobilization of allies: Is the spokespersons representative?**

Actants within a network can use networks established jointly with others as intermediaries in order to regulate the entry or attention of even more actants, and can influence the external environment through announcements, which indicates that a network has already taken shape. At this time, as a group of actants conscientiously perform their assigned duties, these actants will ultimately form a recognizable macro actor network, which will speak out in many directions via a spokesperson. This symbolizes a stable but unfixed state of cohesion, and simultaneously constructs an actant in the world. In the macro actant network, as the actants interact with each other, the actants mutually give rise to translation in their process of co-production, causing them to become actors with intentions and also defining their individual positioning. At the same time, the establishment of relationships between the actants ultimately achieves the overall translation of the network. However, these translations have no end points, and will churn and revolve endlessly. A macro actant at any one period may quite possibly become involved as an actant during the next period, and this process can continue to expand and develop.

2.3. *Research procedure and data*

This study relied on 12 field observation sessions at irregular intervals, 56 interviews with relevant individuals, and the collection of 38 sets of secondary data during a data collection period extending from July 2010 to 2012 to collect relevant information concerning the development of sword lion cultural products in the Anping district. The research team further wrote the story and research paper following discussion and analysis.

This study employed both formal interviews and face-to-face/telephone informal interviews at total of 56 person-times to collect information from an individual in Tainan city government (one person-time), personnel in the Tainan Bureau of Cultural Affairs (five person-times), personnel at the Anping district office (19 person-times), cultural workers (14 person-times), Anping sword lion cultural product entrepreneurs (10 person-times), the Anping district borough warden (two person-times), and Anping district residents (five person-times). Apart from 32 news articles from the *China*

Times, China Daily News, and *Liberty Times* concerning Anping sword lion cultural products and cultural activities, secondary data also included six items of literature, namely *Homeland of the Sword Lion: Anping* by Tsai Chin-an, *Record of the Yanping Street Incident* by Wu Chao-ming, the Tainan city government's *Enter Spring in Tainan Activity Plan,* the Anping district office's *Anping Sword Lion Fair Activity Plan,* and the academic research papers on Anping sword lion culture.

In view of the fact that one of the major aspects of ANT is its bestowal of equally importance on human and non-human actants, after collecting field observations, interviews, and secondary data, the study team decided after six discussion sessions to employ the ANT approach, attempt to assume the perspective of the Anping sword lions, and write the story of the becoming of Anping sword lion cultural products in the first person. After this story underwent five rounds of revision, the team then conducted five analytical sessions before finalizing its research findings and writing the research paper. The research procedures were as shown in Table 1.

3. Autobiographical Story of Anping Sword Lion

I have many different identities: a doll, a necktie, a hanging ornament, and many types of stationary articles. Apart from the local cultural museum, you can also purchase me at chain convenience stores and specialty stores. Beyond this, I am also very popular on the Internet — Just Google me, and you will easily find more than 600,000 of my pictures and pieces of information about me. However, this was not the case just a few years ago, and it even seemed that I might disappear completely. I have existed in Anping for over 300 years, and I have long been prominently displayed on the walls around the doorways of nearly every home. Because, when people see me, I am always holding a sword in my mouth, with the sword pointing either right or left, and sometimes I even have two swords, Anping residents have always called me a "sword lion."

It is getting hard for me to remember where I came from. Some people say that Koxinga brought me over from China. Others claim that, during the Ming or Qing Dynasty, when the troops stationed in Anping returned home to rest after drills, they placed their swords between the teeth of the lions on their lion-headed shields, which they hung in their doorways or on their walls to scare away evildoers, and I evolved from those lions. Although my origin is a matter of dispute, I could be seen playing the role of a talisman or suspicious object on the walls and lintels of many

Table 1. Research procedures

Research procedures		Data sources	Times/items
Research method	Field observations	Anping district	12 times
	Interviews with relevant individuals	Tainan city government, 1 person-time Tainan Bureau of Cultural Affairs, 5 person-times Anping district office, 19 person-times Cultural workers, 14 person-times Anping sword lion cultural product venders, 10 person-times Anping district borough warden, 2 person-times Anping district residents, 5 person-times	56 person-times
	Collection of secondary data	News articles, books, activity plans, academic research papers	32 news articles 6 items of other secondary data
Team discussions			6 times
Writing			5 story versions
Research analysis			5 times
Writing of research paper			

Source: This study.

of the houses in Anping during the Qing Dynasty and period of Japanese occupation.

How did I become a cultural product? I would better first explain the role of the "Yanping Street Incident." First built as early as the Dutch period, Anping's Yanping Street, which is also known as Taiwan Street, which not only Taiwan's first shopping street, but also the liveliest place in all of Taiwan during the late Ming and early Qing dynasties. Originally, you could see me on the walls near the doorways of all of the houses on this street. But because many people had moved away from Anping, the local economy had gradually gone downhill, and because Yanping Street was so narrow that even small fire trucks could not get through, in 1994 local residents asked the government of Tainan city for funds for street widening, which they hoped would improve the urban landscape and restore their former prosperity.

However, the plan to widen Yanping Street ran into strong opposition from culturally-minded parties. As a consequence, Tainan city government, the Anping district office, and residents of Yanping Street got involved in a one-and-a-half year struggle with cultural preservationists, which was known as the "Yanping Street Incident." In order to change the minds of Anping residents concerning widening the street and resolve the crisis concerning demolition along the street, the National Festival of Culture and Arts, which is directed by the Council for Cultural Affairs, Executive Yuan, was specially conducted in Anping in May 1995, and was accompanied by the "Discover the City of the King" activity series. It was hoped that processions along the old street would awaken Anping residents to the need to preserve their cultural assets. However, although the preservationists had given a lot of thought to the matter, their actions did not achieve the intended effect. Following the conclusion of the activities, at the end of July of the same year, after some residents took matters into their own hands by demolishing buildings on their own, Tainan city government embarked on the full-scale widening of Yanping Street on August 1, and the incident drew to a close. Of course, since I inhabited Yanping Street, the widening caused me to disappear as well.

Unexpectedly, following the widening of Yanping Street, the new city landscape did not bring Anping the desired prosperity. Later, starting in 2000, Tainan city government and the Anping district office began implementing an Anping commercial circle project that they hoped would restore Anping's prosperity. Over a nine-year period, with the city government's support and assistance, the Anping district office ceaselessly pursued central government funding for various commercial circle development assistance projects, including Anping image commercial circle, Anping charm commercial circle, and Anping brand commercial circle projects. However, because the central government officials reviewing the plans for these projects felt that because a commercial circle in Anping would only offer snack foods, and would have no distinctive local features, it would probably not be sustainable. After hearing this warning and taking it to heart, some district office officials started racking their brains to think up a solution.

Fortunately, cultural workers accidentally discovered me during the planning of the "Discover the City of the King" activity series. They felt that I looked quite attractive, and paid attention to me because the gradual destruction of the old buildings in Anping was threatening my survival. The preservationists therefore hoped to protect me prevent me from vanishing in Anping. The biggest problem was that the residents of Anping did not pay much attention to me at the time, and certainly did not understand me. The cultural workers begin studying me, and they interviewed some of the older residents of Anping. They discovered the significance of the direction of the sword I hold in my mouth: "Pointing left wards off evils, pointing right seeks blessings, and two swords block evil." They also started training cultural interpretive personnel, and hoped to enroll the support of even more people in protecting me.

Because the preservationists felt that Anping was the cradle of Taiwanese culture, and I symbolized the spirit of Anping, I possessed great cultural significance, and should be used more in everyday life with different appearances and appealing forms. As a consequence, using my image as a blueprint, cultural workers printed me on neckties and made die-cast metal belt buckles displaying my features. As a result, many products with me as the main actor appeared on the market, and were displayed and sold in the "Anping Sword Lion Local Cultural Museum." From that time on, I no longer existed solely on the walls outside the homes of Anping residents, but had also formally moved into some Anping stores and shops.

In 2005, the Anping district office, which had been trying to find some distinctive Anping features, felt that I, who had been introduced to them by the cultural workers, could become a representative for Anping's local character, and help stimulate the growth of a commercial circle. Officials from the district office first discussed this idea with cultural workers. After performing an assessment of Anping's three major cultural assets — me, the Wind Lion God, and Anping pots — it was discovered that the Wind Lion God was already being promoted on Kinmen, and Anping pots would be hard to market due to the limitations of their shape. So it was decided that I was Anping's most representative cultural asset. Tainan city government agreed with this decision, and so I obtained official status as Anping's cultural representative. But as the officials from the district office discovered, although the cultural workers had designed and manufactured cultural creativity products featuring me, they did not sell very fast, and sellers ended up with too much inventory. As a result, the officials wanted take over the task of marketing me. The cultural workers felt that, because the district office had more resources and adequate manpower, it would be easier for them to assume the responsibility of marketing me, and they handed over the work to the office, while voluntarily serving as assistants.

Starting 2006, the district office began a series of actions aimed at saving me, which marked a new milestone in my protection. In 2007, the district office held a marketing project conference to plan a series of cultural marketing activities intended to greatly increase public awareness of me. That year was also the Tainan city government's cultural tourism promotion year, and I served as a main character in the "Enter Spring in Tainan" activity held for three consecutive years on the occasion of the Lunar New Year holiday. Throughout this time the district office worked hard to make Anping my home and transform me into Anping's most distinctive feature. The cultural workers cooperated with a young designer to transforming into a modern doll, which was sold in convenience stores, and invited to participate in the 2007 Taipei Toy Festival. Cultural workers felt that, apart from being the guardian of Anping, I could even become Taiwan's international mascot, and could be Taiwan's representative to the world like Singapore's Merlion. They not only established a "sword lion shop" in the Kinmen Hall — one of the "Five Halls of Anping" originally on Yanping Street — to exclusively sell cultural creativity products connected with me, but also found professionals to design sword lion dances, sword lion banquets, sword lion colored embroidery, and carved brick sword lions, which have helped market me.

In 2010, the Anping district office proposed the "Anping Sword Lion Cultural Creativity Industry Assistance Project," which obtained three years of funding from the Ministry of Economic Affairs' local development fund. The district office not only found designers to design different looks for me, and asked the public to vote for their favorite, but also registered my trademark, which they freely provided online for use by cultural entrepreneurs. When Anping residents, who originally did not value me very much, saw the city government, district office, and cultural workers strenuously marketing me, and also notice that more and more tourists were flooding into Anping to tracking down, gradually realized my importance to Anping. This prompted them to stop deliberately stripping me off old buildings that were being renovated, and instead start to protect me and cherish me, and make sure my living environment was clean and neat. Local residents thus began participating in the various marketing activities arranged for me by the city government, district office, and cultural workers.

Nowadays, when one enters the Anping district, one will see sword lions everywhere, from the community entrance to the sword lion park to the electric poles and school walls. Anping has also become cleaner, brighter, and more orderly. In particular, the crowds of tourists flocking to Anping are giving residents new opportunities for recovering their past prosperity. I have not only become Anping's spokesperson, visiting tourists inevitably buy a copy of me to take home before they leave. Anping has changed because I changed, and has assumed an entirely new appearance.

4. Discussion

4.1. The organizational process of cultural product Anping sword lion

What the above story tries to explain is how Anping's sword lions were transformed from traditional talismans found on the walls of Anping homes to a variety of cultural products. This process does not just comprise local translation, but is also a process of organizing of cultural products. This study takes the four important opportunities for translation proposed by Callon as a framework for the analysis of the process of organizing in the development of Anping sword lion cultural products.

■ **Problematization**

In the story, the decline of the Anping district due to loss of residents and deteriorating economic conditions attracted the attention of the Tainan city government, Anping district office, and Anping residents, who hoped to resolve the community's problems and increase its economic vitality by widening Yanping Street and improving the district's appearance. Unexpectedly, this plan encountered strong opposition from cultural preservationists, and the two sides got involved in a one-and-a-half year struggle. After this period of antagonism, although officials and residents won a temporary victory, they failed to bring prosperity to the community, which gave the preservationists a subsequent opportunity to establish an OPP point of passage — "protecting Anping's cultural assets will stimulate local prosperity." This declaration attracted the interest of several main actants, including cultural workers, the Tainan city government, the Anping district office, and Anping residents. However, because the actants were unable to individually resolve the common problems that they faced, problem-solving required mutual negotiation and cooperation, and the assignment of preliminary identities. This is the meaning of mutual identification. The actants originally listened only to themselves, and tried to solve problems using their own methods. However, after "passing the OPP," they gradually

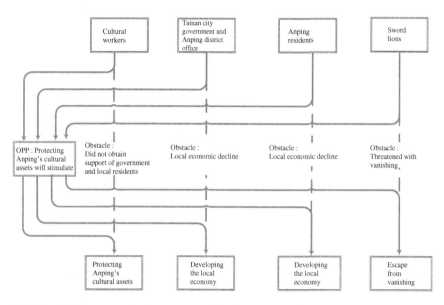

Fig. 1.   Chief actants in the process of development of Anping sword lion cultural products and their crossing of the OPP
Source: This study.

realized that their character was to participate in "protecting cultural assets and bringing prosperity to Anping." This process is shown in Fig. 1.

These definition procedures allow us to see the start of displacement among the actants, and their preliminary translation. For instance, the cultural workers were originally exclusively local cultural personnel, and had little interest in developing the economy, but nevertheless attempted to introduce small quantities of sword lion cultural products for sale. When the widening of Yanping Street failed to yield the expected economic benefits, Tainan city government and the Anping district office began wondering whether the protection of local cultural assets might stimulate economic growth in Anping's commercial circle. These actants did not exist exclusively for the sake of protecting cultural assets, and did not possess extensive relevant knowledge, but were rather acquired from their original contexts. As soon as they passed the point of passage, they begin transforming their individual identity into part of a collective problem-solving effort, and attempted to find roles that they could play in this effort. These actants, which originally remained separate from the "protection of Anping's cultural assets" (OPP), not only transformed their locations by crossing the point of passage, but transformed their identities and interacted with each other. Due to the results of this problematization, all parties were able to establish a consensus and find various possible methods of marketing Anping's sword lion cultural products. Not only did the cultural workers extensively research the cultural background behind the sword lions and train interpretive personnel in sword lion culture knowledge, but they also gradually introduced a variety of sword lion cultural products. For their part, Tainan city government and the Anping district office also held a series cultural promotion activities centered on Anping's sword lions.

■ Interessement

While each actant proposes various possibilities during the course of negotiation, a preliminary consensus concerning major principles has already emerged, which is the blueprint for solving the entire problem: "develop cultural products featuring Anping sword lions." Following negotiation concerning three Anping artifacts — sword lion, Wind Lion God, and Anping pots — the cultural workers and Anping district office ultimately decided that the sword lion could serve as Anping's representative cultural asset, and the two parties accordingly performed a mutually-beneficial adjustment of their individual objectives and desired benefits. The cultural workers conducted a series of sword lion cultural product development projects, and simultaneously held various activities to promote sword lion culture. This ensured that Anping's old sword lions did not disappear, while yielding substantial economic benefits. Tainan city government and the Anping district office shifted from their original role as destroyers of cultural assets into the role of promoters of Anping's sword lion culture, while relying on marketing project conferences to plan a series of cultural marketing activities enhancing awareness of Anping's sword lions. They further established linkage between the sword lions and Anping's commercial circle in order to develop the local economy. The growing numbers of tourists to the district prompted Anping residents to reconsider the importance of their sword lions, and they begin to protect old sword lions and neaten up their community and living environment in order to improve the appearance of the community. Following this process of negotiation and adjustment, each actant passing the point of passage was placed in a certain position that indicated its role within the group as a whole. At the same time, each actant's actions and linkages affected the process of negotiation within the group. Because this process involves placing beneficial relationships on the table and engaging in interactive, mutually-beneficial operations, some scholars refer to this process as the setting of boundaries, which implies the mutual assignment of the other parties' positions via negotiation. We can also say that actants are locked in by specific perceptions following negotiation, and the process of negotiation and positioning enables actants to find beneficial relationships, while also eliminating the temptation of other benefits. Because of this, the actants became involved in the organizing of Anping sword lion cultural products.

■ Enrollment

In the story of the Anping sword lion, we saw that the cultural workers continued to enroll the support of artists, designers, and restaurant operators in introducing sword lion dolls, sword lion dances, sword lion banquets, sword lion colored embroidery, carved bricks featuring sword lions, and many other cultural creativity products featuring sword lions. At the same time, Tainan city government and the Anping district office also registered the sword lion trademark, which they freely provided online for use by cultural entrepreneurs, while urging Anping residents to jointly protect surviving old sword lions. They also planned and implemented a series of cultural activities enhancing awareness of Anping's sword lions, which attracted tourists from outside and actively transformed the sword lion into one of Anping's local features. The various actants formed alliances through coordination and alignment, which led to the implementation of a series of sword lion cultural marketing activities, and a temporary stable state was reached.

■ Mobilization

At that time, we can regard the Anping sword lion network as a collective entity in action; the coordination between its key parts weaves the overall collective Anping sword lion network. Because this kind of collective network is a type of assemblage, and its scope is greater than that of the individual actants, it can be referred to as a macro network (Callon & Latour, 1981). However, a macro network is only a temporarily stable result in which the actants travel in the same direction as a consequence of their positions and mutual relationships, and there exists a common spokesperson who serves as the network's external voice (Callon, 1986). The spokesperson's declarations enable the macro network to announce to the outside world: "This is the Anping sword lion marketing network."

Through the foregoing analysis, we can sketch the organizing process of Anping sword lion cultural products as shown in Fig. 2.

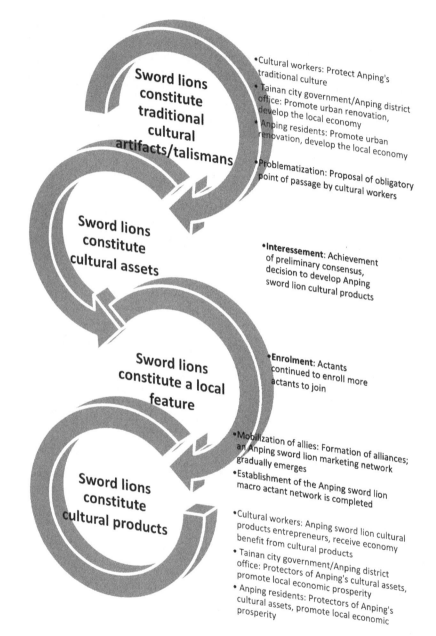

Fig. 2.   Organizing process of Anping sword lion cultural products
Source: This study.

The organizing of Anping sword lion cultural products begins from the "Yanping Street Incident." At first, the individual actants had tense, antagonistic relationships, which led to the gradual destruction of Anping's cultural assets. Afterwards, cultural workers adjusted their strategy in order to protect vanishing cultural assets. After the easing of antagonism, an OPP — "protecting Anping's cultural assets will stimulate local prosperity" — was established. Soon afterwards, the actants involved in this network — namely Tainan city government, Anping district office, cultural workers, Anping residents, and the sword lions — gradually strengthened their alliance through constant negotiation, adjustment, and enrollment. As a result, a macro actor network dedicated to marketing Anping's sword lions with the Tainan city government and Anping district office as spokespersons was ultimately established. The coming together of these elements constructed the entirety of the organizing process involved in the development of sword lion cultural products.

4.2. *Understanding the multiple displacements within the process of organizing*

■ The organizing of cultural product derived from the consequence of the collective displacement of actants from antagonism to cooperation

In an analysis of cultural products at the level of social space, Becker (1984) suggests that while it may be possible to momentarily see cultural products as independent works, they may still be the results of cooperation, even if they ultimately bear only a single producer's name. Artists do not operate in a vacuum, but rather occupy "central positions in networks of collaborating partners," where they engage in core activities. From the perspective of ANT, we also discovered that, in the becoming of Anping sword lion cultural products, in keeping with Becker's suggestion, the roles of individual creators weakened, and were supplanted by the cooperation of all actants in the network. However, this cooperation originally emerged from a state of tense, antagonistic relationships.

Prior to the development of Anping sword lion cultural products, Tainan city government and the Anping district office decided to widen Yanping Street in order to renovate the urban landscape. However, this action induced strong opposition from preservationists and cultural workers. The two sides became embroiled in a one-and-a-half year struggle, and conflict extended from the local level to the central government. But even though the Council for Cultural Affairs specially held the National Festival of Culture and Arts in Anping in hopes of encouraging residents to protect their cultural assets, this effort failed, and the widening of Yanping Street and demolition of buildings went forward.

However, although the buildings along Yanping Street were demolished, preservationists continued their actions to protect cultural assets, and after accidentally discovering the beauty of the sword lions in the wake of the Yanping Street Incident, embarked on a research campaign in order to protect the remaining old sword lions, and attempted to introduce small quantities of sword lion cultural products.

After a decade of hard work, research on sword lion culture and development of sword lion cultural products by cultural workers gradually bore fruit. In addition, when officials and local residents discovered that the widening of Yanping Street did not deliver the expected prosperity, Tainan city government and the Anping district office had to come up with a new strategy for achieving local prosperity. At that time, as the concepts of cultural industries and the cultural economy grew increasingly mature, cultural workers and preservationists finally obtained an opportunity to strike back. Targeting their former "adversaries," cultural workers dumped their previously antagonistic strategy and recommended to the district office that the sword lion could serve as Anping's distinguishing local feature, and could provide a new concept for the development of a commercial circle. This constituted the establishment of an OPP. Without any adequate counter strategy, the district office and city government performed a reassessment and adjustment, and, abandoning their past method of demolition and renovation, decided on a new policy of using the cultural economy to stimulate local prosperity. Anping residents followed suit by shifting from support for urban renewal and replacement of the old with the new to greater appreciation for old cultural assets.

At this stage, the cultural workers had learned their lesson from the failure of their previous antagonistic strategy, and made a new start. In addition, the city government, district office, and residents realized the emptiness of their brief triumph. All of the actants became aware of their erroneous strategies during their previously antagonistic relationships, and decided to make adjustments in order to achieve success in the subsequent stage. All of the actants finally joined forces in a cooperative effort, and constructed an Anping sword lion cultural product marketing macro actor network. Only because all actants had made a collective displacement from antagonism to cooperation, Anping district was able to develop various kinds of sword lion cultural products.

■ **The collective displacement of actants derived from the translation of actants' identities and benefits in the cultural product organizing process**

In our analysis, the identities and benefits of several main actants in the organizing of Anping sword lion cultural products have undergone some translation. For instance, while the Tainan city government and Anping district office were originally intent on renovating the district, which would make them destroyers of Anping's cultural assets, translation driven by the lobbying and enrollment efforts of preservationists and cultural workers made the city government and district office the protectors of Anping's cultural assets. The city government and district office also employed marketing project conferences to plan a series of cultural marketing activities boosting awareness of Anping's sword lions, they used the sword lion as a new symbol of community improvement, and they linked the sword lion with Anping's commercial circle in an effort to rely on cultural economy to foster local prosperity.

While the cultural workers were originally exclusively local cultural personnel, and had little interest in developing the economy, they later became Anping sword lion cultural product managers through a process of translation, and they designed various kinds of sword lion cultural products. In addition, they also held a variety of promotional activities connected with sword lion culture in order to ensure that Anping's old sword lions did not disappear, while providing tangible economic benefits.

Due to the growing numbers of tourists from outside visiting the district, Anping residents gradually shifted through process of translation from being accomplices to the government's renovation policy, which was destroying sword lions, to placing greater importance on the sword lions. Apart from starting to protect old sword lions, residents also participated in cultural activities marketing Anping's sword lions, and placed emphasis on improving and neatening the community environment, which brought the benefit of local prosperity.

After having been vanishing traditional artifacts, the Anping sword lions were gradually transformed into various kinds of cultural products through a process of displacement, and assumed the heavy responsibility for bringing prosperity to Anping. The translation of the actants' identities and benefits is shown in Tables 2 and 3.

Table 2. Translation of the actants' identities and benefits in the Anping sword lion cultural product organizing process

Actant	Translation of identities and benefits in the cultural product organizing process	
	Role prior to translation	Role after translation
Cultural workers	Local cultural workers	Developers and managers of Anping sword lion cultural products
Tainan city government, Anping district office	Destroyers of Anping's traditional culture	Protectors of Anping's cultural assets
Anping residents	Accomplices in the destruction of Anping's traditional culture	Protectors of old Anping sword lions
Anping sword lions	Traditional cultural talismans	Cultural products/cultural activities

Source: This study.

Table 3. Translation of actants' benefit in the Anping sword lion cultural product organizing process

Actant	Translation of benefit in the cultural product organizing process	
	Benefit prior to translation	Benefit after translation
Cultural workers	Protection of traditional culture	Receiving economic benefit from cultural products
Tainan city government, Anping district office	Renovation of the urban landscape	Creation of local economy prosperity
Anping residents	Renovation of the urban landscape	Creation of local economy prosperity
Anping sword lions	Vanishing traditional cultural talismans	Main actor in the restoration of Anping prosperity

Source: This study.

The foregoing actants eventually became a temporarily stable "single" macro actor through translation of identity and benefit. They could then continue to undergo translation and create other networks. Interaction during the previous stage inevitably influences the creation process, and the continuous enrollment of new constituent actants, such as artists, designers, restaurant operators, and tourists from outside the area, will cause a network to continuously expand. It is only thanks to the establishment of this macro actor network that sword lion cultural products will continue to develop and bring prosperity to the Anping community.

■ The displacement of representation of power in the midst of negotiation and competition

Spivak (1988) suggests that representation can be divided into the two issues of who is speaking and what they are speaking of. The issue of who is speaking involves a representer-centered perspective, while the issue of what they are speaking of approximates the other's political entrustment. Although the two approaches are different, they are related, and both involve power issues.

In hope of revitalizing Anping's commercial circle, Tainan city government and the Anping district office originally played the role of destroyers of cultural assets, but cultural workers proposed an OPP, and relied on lobbying to gradually shift their strategy for bringing prosperity to Anping from urban renovation to protection of Anping's cultural assets and development of the cultural economy. The Anping district office also employed marketing project conferences to plan a series of cultural marketing activities enhancing awareness of Anping's sword lion, and they further established linkage between the sword lions and Anping's commercial circle in order to develop the local economy.

Because the Anping district office had official local status, and possessed a relatively large amount of resources, it had powerful mobilization capabilities. Because of this, after they had become aware of the advantageous qualities of sword lion cultural products through their proposal of an OPP and attempts to develop small quantities of sword lion cultural products, cultural workers were willing to actively transfer command powers over the marketing of Anping sword lion cultural products after it was decided at negotiation meetings that sword lions would be Anping's representative local feature. This made the Anping district office the spokesperson for the Anping sword lion marketing macro actor network.

However, behind this superficially peaceful process of power displacement achieved through negotiation were the signs of power competition. In the Yanping Street Incident, Tainan city government and Anping district office were originally executioners bent on destroying Anping's sword lions. The city government and district office consequently joined forces with local residents in waging a one-and-a-half year battle with preservationist forces concerning the protection of cultural assets, and won a partial victory allowing them to demolish buildings along Yanping Street. Nevertheless, after only a few more years, the officials had taken command of the Anping sword lion marketing efforts. Such a large transformation of identity unsurprisingly induced many questions.

In the organizing of Anping sword lion, the relationship between the cultural workers and officials shifted from antagonism to cooperation, and the cultural workers even made the jump from establishing an OPP to actively supporting the Anping district office as the spokesperson of the macro actor network. This change occurred chiefly because the cultural workers realized that the Anping district office possessed official status, relatively abundant resources, and strong mobilization capabilities. However, the command of resources and possession of mobilization capabilities actually revealed as asymmetrical power relationship. To be fair, many of the actions taken by the officials after they took charge of marketing the Anping sword lions were questioned and disputed by cultural workers. However, in view of the lessons learned from the Yanping Street Incident and awareness that "you cannot fight city hall," those cultural workers who held opposing views had to remain quiet and maintain a low-key stance. This enabled the officials to consolidate their identity as spokespersons.

■ The becoming of cultural product resulted in the recreation of representation of region

In the Anping sword lion cultural product organizing process, the inherent uniqueness and excellent suitability for marketing of the Anping sword lions attracted the interest of cultural workers and the Anping district office, enabling the sword lions to defeat such local competitors as the Wind Lion God and Anping pots, and become Anping's representative cultural asset, making the lions Anping's leading local features. Furthermore, because of their plastic character and appearance, the sword lions could be transformed into tangible products such as neckties, belt buckles, and dolls, and even cultural activities such as sword lion dances and sword lion banquets. The sword lions thus shouldered the heavy responsibility of attracting tourists to Anping and inducing them to engage in consumption.

As a cultural artifact, the sword lion, in the cultural product organizing process, first established close ties with the locality via a series of cultural activities held by the Anping district office, Tainan city government, and cultural workers, establishing the proprietary localization of these cultural artifacts. During this period, the Anping district office and cultural workers not only held intensive cultural activities conveying the message that Anping is the sword lion's homeland, but also relied on the sword lion's inherent reputation of evoking safety and good fortune to polish its image as Anping's lucky talisman, and took advantage of the opportunities brought by the development of sword lion cultural products to engage in extensive marketing efforts.

As the bonds between the sword lions and Anping grew increasingly close, and various kinds of sword lion cultural products appeared, attracting more and more tourists to Anping, the Anping district office proposed that, since Anping was the cradle of Taiwanese culture, and the sword lion was Anping's lucky talisman, the sword lion should be considered a historic guardian deity of Taiwan. This line of thinking prompted the expansion of links between the Anping sword lion and Taiwan's history. It is expected that the sword lion's positioning as a historic guardian deity of Taiwan will attract even more domestic and foreign tourists, foster the development of tourism in Anping, create employment opportunities, and attract people back to the community.

In the transformation from Anping's lucky talisman to a historic guardian deity of Taiwan, we can further discover that the sword lion is no longer just a cultural product of Anping, but has rather become a representation of Anping. By assuming the positioning as a historic guardian deity of Taiwan, the sword lion's role was enlarged to that of a representation of Taiwan. In other words, the sword lion became a representation of Anping/Taiwan, and therefore became a symbol that could be constantly expanded and understood. The representation of the positioning of the sword lion began from that of a cultural artifact linked with the Anping district, and it not only expanded out of the Anping district into all of Taiwan, but even appeared in the international domain. It is hoped that, like Singapore's Merlion, the sword lion will represent Taiwan around the world. The creation of representations can amplify the displacement energy of cultural artifacts, and attract even more actants to enter the cultural product organizing process, yielding even larger macro actor-networks, and achieving the economic objectives of culture representations. The representation of the Anping district is thus recreated as the becoming of cultural product sword lion proceeds.

5. Conclusion: Seeing the Place of Power in the Process of Organizing and ANT

As explained above, the organizing process involved in the development of Anping sword lion cultural products cannot be attributed to the efforts of one person or a small number of persons, but was instead the result of the continuous collective displacement of the cultural workers, Tainan city government, Anping district office, Anping residents, and the sword lions themselves. Although several of the chief actants were initially involved in an antagonistic relationship, they subsequently changed their erroneous decisions and put an end to their antagonism, and eventually altered their identities and desired benefits through negotiation and lobbying. The actants also further enrolled artists, designers, restaurant personnel, and tourists from outside the area, and successfully constructed an Anping sword lion macro actor network. The ANT perspective not only lets us see how the Anping sword lions macro actor network was constructed, but also reveals how humans (cultural workers, Tainan city government, Anping district office, and Anping residents) and non-humans (Anping sword lions) had equal status in the network construction process, and exerted major influence on the network as a whole.

When we rely on the ANT perspective to avoid a focus on such traditional economic aspects as industry clusters, value creation, and business administration, we can follow the context of both human and non-human actants, and observe production of these actants and the changes that they induce, and can understand how the many actants that participate in the becoming of cultural products engage in organizing through enactment, revealing the subtle dynamics of social entrepreneurship in the organizing of cultural products.

We have also discovered that not only did the Anping sword lion cultural product organizing process follow the collective displacement of the actants from antagonism to cooperation, but several main actants' identities and desired benefits underwent translation, and power displacement also occurred simultaneously in the actants' cooperative/competitive relationships. The macro actor network constructed through the actants' collective displacement caused the Anping sword lion cultural product organizing process to have a uniform direction. At the same time, the actants in the network all performed their own duties and engaged in cooperation, which amplified the organizing energy of the cultural products.

In addition, we also saw that the representations of the positioning of cultural artifacts in the cultural product organizing process were achieved through the discourse constantly created by the actants. At the same time, this process expanded the displacement energy of the cultural artifacts, and induced other actants to join the network, which facilitated construction of an even larger macro actor network. Not only transforming the "sword lion" from talismans in traditional culture into cultural products, but further representing sword lions as "a historic guardian deity of Taiwan," the Anping district successfully stimulated local economic development and recreated its representation of local region. Furthermore, it is noticed in this study that the process of organizing not only involves the collective displacement in the development of cultural products, in which actants shift from antagonism to cooperation and the actants' identity and benefit are translated, but also the power is transferred as competitive relationships turn into of cooperative one. At the same time, the representation of region is recreated via the process of organizing by means of the development of cultural products.

The use of ANT to gain an understanding of the Anping sword lion cultural product organizing process allows us to find new research directions outside of the discussion of traditional cultural economics and cultural industry, and avoid discourse from the angle of conventional economic thinking. In other words, when using ANT to examine cultural economics, cultural industries, or cultural products, we can discover how individual actants engage in negotiation, calculation, plotting, mutual adjustment of benefits, and relationship building when facing common problems, and create new order in the midst of social life.

References

Becker, H. S. (1984). *Art Worlds*. Berkeley: University of California Press.

Callon, M. (1986). Some elements of sociology of translation: Domestication of the scallops and the fishermen of St. Brieuc Bay, in J. Law (ed.), *Power, Action and Belief: A New Sociology of Knowledge*, London: Routledge & Kegan Paul, pp. 196–233.

Callon, M. & Latour, B. (1981). Unscrewing the big Leviathan: How actors macro-structure reality and how sociologists help them to do so, in

K. Knorr-Cetina & A.V. Cicourel (eds.), *Towards an Integration of Micro- and Macro-Sociologies*, London: Routledge and Kegan Paul, pp. 259–276.

Caves, R. E. (2000). *Creative Industries: Contracts Between Art and Commerce*. Cambridge, MA: Harvard University Press.

Crossland, P. & Smith, F. I. (2002). Value Creation in Fine Arts: A System Dynamics Model of Inverse Demand and Information Cascades, *Strategic Management Journal*, 23, pp. 417–434.

Czarniawska, B. (1997). *Narrating the Organization: Dramas of Institutional Identity*. Chicago and London: The University of Chicago Press.

Czarniawska, B. (2008). *Narrative We Organize By*. Amsterdam/Philadelphia: John Benjamins Publishing Company.

Gherardi, S. & Nicolini, D. (2005). Actor-Networks: Ecology and Entrepreneurs, in Czarniawska, B. & Hernes, T. (eds.), *Actor-Network Theory and Organizing*, Copenhagen: Copenhagen Business School Press, pp. 285–306.

Hall, T. (1997). (Re)placing the city cultural relocation and the city as center, in S. Westwood and J. Williams (eds.), *Imagining Cities*, New York: Routledge, pp. 202–218.

Law, J. (1999). After ANT: complexity, naming, and topology, in J. Law and J. Hassard (eds.), *Actor Network Theory and After*, UK: Blackwell/ *The Sociological Review*, pp. 1–14.

MacIntyre, A. (1981/1990). *After Virtue*. London: Duckworth Press.

Peredo, A. M. & Chrisman, J. J. (2006). Toward a Theory of Community-Based Enterprise, *Academy of Management Journal*, 31(2), pp. 1–50.

Power, D. (2002). Cultural Industries in Sweden: An Assessment of Their Place in the Swedish Economy, *Economic Geography*, 78, pp. 103–127.

Schutz, A. (1973). *Collected Papers Volume 1: The Problem of Social Reality*. The Hague: MartinusNijhoff: MartinusNijhoff, Netherlands.

Spivak, G. C. (1988). *Can the Subaltern Speak?* Urbana and Chicago: University of Illinois Press.

Steyeart, C. (2007). Entrepreneuring As a Conceptual Attractor? A Review of Process Theories in 20 Years of Entrepreneurship Studies, *Entrepreneurship & Regional Development*, 19, pp. 453–477.

Sturken, M. & Cartwright, L. (2001). *Practices of Looking: An Introduction to Visual Culture*. Oxford: Oxford University Press.

12

Narrating an Entrepreneurial Process — A Case from Taiwan's Outlying Islands

Ming-Rea Kao
Wenzao Ursuline University of Languages

Shelley Hui-Yin Lin
National Sun Yat-sen University

1. Introduction

Entrepreneurship is usually seen as a solution to problems in community development — through new firms, new industries and community mobilization, stagnating regions and cities are expected to return to growth and prosperity (Cornwall, 1998). While this solution is almost undisputed, the question of what entrepreneurship is and how it emerges often remains unanswered or neglected (Spinosa *et al.*, 1997). This chapter focuses on exploring the initial entrepreneurial process of how the entrepreneur challenges and extends the boundary to promote the development of cultural industry.

Taking Taiwan's outlying islands as the focus areas to research on rural lands, the authors recounted the developmental progress of the cultural industry in Penghu Islands, and explored the points addressed by the authors at the research institute, and that is — entrepreneurship as boundary work. Through the lens of boundary work, it analyzes how the entrepreneurial actor deviated from the limitation of the knowledge, space, cultural, economic and enterprising thinking, and how it is brought into the new cultural industry externally. These have rarely been analyzed or discussed by the research community (Hjorth & Johannisson, 2003). Thus, through the lens of boundary work, this chapter tries to provide such traveling narrative of cultural park planner's mindset changed over the course of a full year as a planner, and to reveal how the entrepreneurial process is connected to boundary work based on the spatial practice of the site. At the end of the chapter, the researchers also points out the findings from the entrepreneurial story, in that entrepreneurship is the knowledge, space, cultural, economic and entrepreneurial thinking transforming process of the boundary work.

2. Narrative Entrepreneurial Knowing

Polkinghorne (1988) once mentioned in the preface of his book "Narrative Knowing and the Human Sciences" the two reasons why he wrote this book. Due to his role as a psychology researcher and a practicing psychoanalyst, when Polkinghorne was faced with personal conflicts, he was convinced that the perspectives of the scientific research and the professional practice could be integrated. However to his dismay, he found that the academic research had little assistance to his clinical works. On the other hand, he also found that "unlike the natural science, the social science could not pass with just a simple statement of the findings." Polkinghorne found that practitioners used narrative knowing in conducting their works — they cared about people's stories, they used narratives to explain. And so Polkinghorne turned to narrative knowing in his search for a solution for the plight of his experience.

Johansson found the dilemmatic issues, which Polkinghorne wrote in his book, seemed to be the same dilemma apparently faced by him when acting in his role as a consultant to small business managers and when writing his doctoral thesis. Therefore, he proposed that "a narrative researcher can play different roles to pull the widening gap between scientific knowledge and practical knowledge closer." In order to demonstrate the interactions between a researcher and a practitioner, Johansson proposed the following three roles that were not only very different but also had distinct characteristics: (i) inside researcher role (IRR), (ii) enactive researcher role (ERR) and (iii) follow research (FR) (Johansson, 2008). Compared to an IRR where he or she is a member of the research organization, an ERR is the initiator of a progress where they lead the others in joint effort to work together. These types of roles and methods can be found in the study of the entrepreneurship research scholar Johannisson (2005) where he developed these roles while participating in the practical project called "Anamorphosis."

Johansson further pointed out that the role of an ERR is not unusual; however, for those who intent to overcome the division between the practical and the academic knowledge, an ERR could perhaps provide better opportunities than any other roles. One of the authors of this chapter, being both an entrepreneur and a researcher, her entrepreneurial action is rooted in an urgent injection of new industry into the field of Penghu Islands. Through the invitation by a local public official, the researcher had the opportunity of a hands-on participation in the developmental plan of an originally idle space into a new base for a cultural industry. The planner, who had permanently resided in the city, was inspired and set off to participate in this project after reading about the dream of a Japanese curator for an Art Village. After being personally involved in the planning of the cultural park, and in the process of collecting local cultural resources, she discovered that Penghu had long been, in its developmental history for nearly 700 years, a relay station for the people in Mainland China to migrate to Taiwan. On the historical stage, it had experienced through such wars with Netherland, France and Japan. However, due to its inability to link up with the development of industrialization and globalization, the richness in its cultural heritage preservation was far more than what the planner had originally imagined. After nearly a year of participation in the planned implementation of the cultural park, she revealed, in a self-narrative way, the entrepreneurial process of how the role of an ERR can see, consider and think in the process of entrepreneurship. Through the first-person narrative in the role of an ERR, thus developed the following five-chaptered entrepreneurial narrative of "The Story."

3. The Story

3.1. *The beginning of a vision...*

It was early spring in April of 2010 when I had an opportunity to plan a cultural park for the Penghu Islands. The park's planned base area was originally a large idle military camp and military dependants housing quarters. The Penghu County Government hoped to activate this long idle space through cultural arts and cultural tourism, and to further promote the development of Penghu's cultural industry. Due to my passion and enthusiasm in the promotion of cultural industry, on impulse, I made a bold promise to the customer. As for how to go about it? It had me on a spot. This was the planning of a cultural park of which I have never done before. I can only start from imagination. . .

Whenever I have something, I really wanted to do but did not know where to start, I would go to a bookstore to find inspiration. Fumio Nanjo, the author of "From Art to the City," recorded his 15 years' path as an independent curator. Fumio Nanjo wrote at the end of that book, that if he had sufficient land and capital, his wish was to build an ideal art village. What would Fumio Nanjo's dream art village be like? This is how he described the ideal art village he dreamt of:

First at the center of the park is a building with exhibition space, a library and a Customer Service Center. It can be a single building or a multiple linked buildings. Not far from there is the restaurant. This is because if it is separated and independent from other buildings, then it would easily be accessible for people coming from outside. However, nowadays, the restaurants in Art Galleries must not only be delicious, but it must also be the best restaurant in the city. The restaurant is open until late at night and hopefully it will attract crowd. Then in a corner or somewhere else, a cozy bar that would be open for business until past midnight can be established. Here, the local residents can converse and get in contact with the artists, or even better, a traveler from afar paying a visit after hearing about this unique styled bar.

Nearby, there will be apartment hotels. This would be the living quarters of the resident artists and at the same time, accommodation for the visitors. From time to time, poets, scholars and cultural researchers can be invited to reside at the park. Internet facility in the rooms is a must. It does not matter if the lobby and the public areas are bit old, but access to the computer is required to facilitate the public ready access to the Internet. Then there is the set up of studios for artistic creation. This design should be conducted after the decisions of the internal conditions are done and then an open competition between major internal or external or young architects. The so-called conditions are those such as area of the studios, area of the residential rooms, gas, water and electricity, bathroom and kitchen equipment. For example, if 15 studios/exhibition rooms are set up, the overall facility will look like a general architectural museum. As a result, this facility will not only attract those people who are interested in art but will even attract those people who are interested in building constructions. It will be much more interesting if these people can join in the conversation with the artists and the local residents.

In order to stabilize the operation of the Art Village, a Foundation can be established. However, the operation of such an organization cannot operate in a bureaucratic manner because such a way would become meaningless. Therefore, it is necessary to plan a set of operating system to allow for flexible operation. Or perhaps even consider outsourcing the operation, and also needs to employ personnel to deal with the artists. If these centers can at the same time attract students as well as the local youth, then it will become an Art Village with much more dynamic and vitality. By frequently holding the latest exhibitions at the Gallery, it will not only be the nutrients for the resident artists, but will also gather audiences both internally and externally. In the smaller exhibition rooms, solo exhibitions of the resident artists can be conducted on application. The library will offer plenty of art books to provide nourishment for the resident artists, and also provide easy access for the expert academics to research on. Furthermore, if possible, an information center can be set up for those budding new artists by gathering and maintain the information about the applicants and the artists. Invite famous artists to give lectures at the facility. These activities do not only involve the resident artists but also allow the students and the local public to participate. As a result, the Art Village will become an Arts University with a high standard, or it will take on the responsibility of nurturing artists. There may still be other ideas, but for now, the above are my thoughts. If an Arts Village like this can be set up, this will become a vibrant place where all kinds of talented personnel congregate. This way, we will be able to cultivate talented personnel who will be responsible for the development of the future cultural arts.

Through Fumio Nanjo's description of his ideal Arts Village, my blueprint for the upcoming plan for the "Chrysanthenmum Island Cultural Park" just vividly appeared on paper. However, unlike Fumio Nanjo's dream of an ideal Arts Village, "Chrysanthemum Island Cultural Park" was more of a grand garden. The County Government had already many vision plans for this place. It did not allow for free imagination like Fumio Nanjo's did.

This learning journey that was about to set sail, I had no idea of what kind of scenery I will encounter in this journey. All I could do is fantasize this as a Don Quixote styled adventure and a journey of imagination, a journey from Kaohsiung on Taiwan Main Island, across the Taiwan Strait to Penghu in the middle. If it were not for my reading of the story of Don Quixote's adventurous journey whilst I was in University, and that the story has rooted deeply in my heart as I aged, I did not think I would be brave enough to cross the ocean to go to such a wonderful and strange island.

3.2. *Traveling to the Islands of Fisherman*

Like a surfer, before he can freely ride on the crest of the waves, he must go through a series of practices (Ming-De Wei, 2008). Therefore, in order to be able to leisurely ease into the next journey, I must have some understanding of the Penghu Islands. This will also assist the readers in visualizing and thinking about my travel.

Like a string of pearls scattered in the Taiwan Strait of the Pacific Ocean, Penghu Islands is comprised of nearly 100 large and small islands. It is situated between Mainland China and Taiwan, in the middle of the Strait slightly toward the East. In the past when the Portuguese navigated here, they gave it the name "Pescadores," which meant "the Islands of the Fishermen." The local residents relied primarily on the life of marine stocks for living. Penghu's historical characteristic had always been fishery. During the process of globalization and post-industrialization, "Pescadores" declined after failing to catch up with the transitional change of the industry. As a result, its economy was marginalized.

The gale wind in Penghu not only seriously affected the trading of the merchant fishermen, but also caused a great deal of restrictions and damage to the local agricultural production. The northeast monsoon that is often rampant for up to six months long made the sea surface surging with turbulent waves and water droplets spatter everywhere at the turn of the wind. With every passing, the formation of the salty rain on plant growth has made Penghu almost barren. The adverse natural conditions such as scarce rainfall, unfertile soil, gale wind plus salty rain have resulted in a weak economic production in this area, severely limiting the progress of its development (Yu Huang Zhang, 1998). The result is a large amount of migration of its population.

How is regional development possible in Penghu Islands? How can the problems of aging population, severe migration of population, and a declining economy and loss be solved? Using idle land space to introduce new industry so as to attract Penghu locals to return back to their hometown to join in the development seemed to be a pivotal opportunity.

3.3. *Nothing is impossible — I just wanted to give it a try*

When developing the "Chrysanthemum Island Cultural Park" in 2011, it was planned in the context of promotional development of Penghu tourism. Most of the park's resources came from the Tourism Bureau's budget funding for Appealing Tourist Attractions. If we looked in detail at the plan of the whole Chrysanthemum Cultural Park, and compared that with Fumio Nanjo's vision of an Arts Village, it is plain to see that this entire park is one which was under the support of tourism resources. Unfortunately, County Government's vision for this cultural park was limited only to the Chu Kuang New Village's "Chu Kuang New Village Phase 2 Cultural and Creative Industry Plan — Secondhand Featured Product District" and the "Chiang Kai-Shek Hall Art Exhibition District" with an area of 1,200 m^2. The County Government wished that the management of these two bases could be outsourced. Hence, the focus of our team's work was on promoting and carrying out Reconstruction, Operation, Transfer (ROT) pre-planning and investment plans.

"Chu Kuang New Village Phase 2 Cultural and Creative Industry Plan — Secondhand Featured Product District" and the "Chiang Kai-Shek Hall Art Exhibition District" were based within the Chu Kuang New Village. The Chu Kuang New Village was established by the National Women's League in three batches, completed in 1960, 1962 and 1965. The gray tiles and the basalt stone wall structured military-dependent housing quarters had about 80 families altogether. The whole housing community was divided into three levels (B, C, D) that were distinguished according to ranking. Most of the residents were families of the officers and men in the Department of Defense. The military-dependent housing quarters were later adjusted and merged and currently there are only 71 families still living there. In the 1960s and 1970s, the Chiang Kai-Shek Hall next to the housing quarters was the best leisure premise for the residents in the Chu Kuang New Village. The youngsters dated and watched movies there, and the elders considered the Chiang Kai-Shek Hall as the best location to meet and chat. The billiard room and the canteen inside the hall and the street vendor positioned around it before and after the screening of a movie, was a paradise that made the children of Chu Kuang New Village lingered on. From day to night, people strolled around the hall to look for friends to chat, to visit, to play mahjong, to drink tea and play chess.... By standing in the alley, one could smell the aroma of food coming out from neighboring houses, a simple push of the screen window and the faces of the family could be seen... This Chrysanthemum Island Cultural Park within the Chu Kuang New Village meant half a century of life memory for some Penghu locals. For a local public official, John, and Yang architect's team, they all had a dream that they wished to fulfill.

This large Chu Kuang New Village is situated in Penghu's most lively city, Magong City, which has a great scenic view because of its situation close to Penghu's inland seas. Originally, some influential locals planned on building a 5 star hotel using the method of Build, Operation, Transfer (BOT) and hoped to demolish this whole military-dependent housing quarters. A local public official, John, wished to retain this area and tried to persuade the higher level official and the influential locals, but was without much luck. Fortunately, with the improved cross-straits relationship and frequented visits between the two sides, that when some deputy major of Mainland China came and praised on how if Chu Kuang New Village was able to be retained that it should attract tourists from Mainland China to pay visits. This gave the high level officials the idea of retaining the area. John applied to the Central Government for budget funding for becoming one of Taiwan's top 10 tourist location. Hence, the funding for structure reinforcement and renovation was achieved. Through the tendering procedures of public construction procurement, architect Yang who specialized in the retention of cultural assets obtained the case was responsible for the renovation of the military-dependent housing quarters. Originally, according to the contract, architect Yang should complete the renovation and the planning design within six months. However, John thought the government lacked the ability to operate this on its own, since first, the government was not good at managing cultural parks, and second, the government's finance does not allow for subsequent maintenance funding support. This place needed to adopt ROT and appoint private company to operate the place, that is, finding an investing company through outsourcing. In order not to let Yang's work become a waste, John knew that he needed to find potential investors, because if the structural reinforcement and the preliminary planning and design can meet the operational needs of the potential investors, that would be the reasonable procedure. The romantic and imaginative Yang actively brought up in the meeting of his hope that the County Government can find an artist team, and then design and renovate to meet the needs of the artists. The architect team's work came to a halt. Finding potential investors and the artist team became the challenge of our team.

Most locals or the general public were not very optimistic about John's tendering idea for the "Chu Kuang New Village Phase 2 Cultural Industry

Plan — Secondhand Featured Product District" and the "Chiang Kai-Shek Hall Art Exhibition District." This was due to the fact that in the past, the locals did not take on much interest with those free cultural performances held by the Department of Cultural Affairs. With only a population of just more than 60,000 people, it was unable to support the so-called cultural consumer market. No Penghu locals would invest in a non-profitable cultural industry. Furthermore, it was almost impossible to attract tourist performing groups to perform in Chiang Kai-Shek Hall. Penghu's local university only offered departments of aquaculture, food processing and tourism and recreation. How is it able to support the works of artistic activities and the function of cultivation of performing talents without even a cultural performance or arts departments? Many were waiting to see how John's plan will work. They think that he was just day dreaming. It was just fortunate that John met me, a person who liked to dream as well. I thought to myself, that if outsourcing did not work, and since my own company was newly set up for experimentation, it can cope with some loss and still be bearable. So I dived in and joined John in his dreams.

I just wanted to give it a try, and that nothing is impossible. I knew John did not do the cultural park for himself. Cultural creation is a new industry. If you want the young people to return to Penghu, then it needs to develop new industries, creating work opportunities for them. Although the focus of our team's work was to promote and conduct ROT pre-planning scheme, to put it bluntly, this was just an assessment plan for the County Government to assess whether outsourcing is feasible or not. However, for me, completing the commissioned project for the government was just one of the goals. What I wanted to focus on is how to construct the "Chrysanthemum Cultural Park" so that it can become a cultural park, and whether this park land is able to become the base for promoting the development of Penghu's cultural industry? If the answer is yes, then the "Chu Kuang New Village Phase 2 Cultural Industry Plan — Secondhand Featured Product District" and the "Chiang Kai-Shek Hall Art Exhibition District" that I am currently working on, would become the control center for the future cultural park. With this in mind, how should the spatial plan of this control center be designed, how should the management system be planned and who should be the future potential investors? What role should my team and I play among all these? I knew these are the challenges that I have to face.

My first challenge was to find out the possible inducement for developing the cultural industry in outlying islands. I knew that without a market inducement, I would not be able to find any investor. And so back to the bookstore I went for more inspirations.

3.4. *Finding all kinds of possibilities from body movement*

In recent years, cultural or creative industry has become a familiar term among all walks of life in Taiwan. There are all sorts of books on the topic of culture and creation — books describing the development of cultural industry, the types of subsidy policy adopted by the government, the activation policy of the industry or of the cultural heritage, and how Britain and Scandinavia developed their cultural industry, and so on. What lacked was a book that tells me how to foster a place's cultural industry from scratch, especially for a place on the border, an outlying island that not even the locals are optimistic about. How to accomplish this? It was a huge challenge. After some thought, I decided to do some traveling first. I wanted to visit some of the cultural parks constructed by the Council for Cultural Affairs. Altogether, I visited four cultural and creative parks, from Tainan, Taichung, Chiayi and Hualien. Some thoughts came up during the process. These Central Government funded parks where they paid a great amount of money to renovate the place. Apart from the one in Tainan, the other three cultural parks in Taichung, Chiayi and Hualien were all renovated from idle industrial production spaces of old factories. I realized that these cultural parks were not situated in the downtown area. It was such a shame that when I visited them, they were mostly empty without many visitors. Whilst traveling in Hualien, I lived in a bed and breakfast guesthouse. The local artists and guesthouse owners complained about how Hualien's culture and creative appeared to be one which belongs to a consortium and not the people. The locals have no opportunity or the possibility of participating in it. I thought about how cultural or creative entrepreneurs are all micro-enterprises where they used ROT or BOT methods to operate the idle spaces. Of course, only a consortium has the financial means and the personnel required to operate such a place. However, in the future, I would like to get the investors and the young people to work together combing the financial capital of an investor with the creative capital of the young people.

Should Penghu introduce modern arts performances or traditional performing arts? Because of my own preferences and prejudice, this choice of whether the West or the East had truly confounded me for a long time.

I never watched the performance of traditional oriental arts. I preferred the Western performing arts like the opera, jazz and classical music. I thought that if even I do not like to watch it, then why other people would want to watch it. That was why I thought that there is no market for the local operas or the traditional arts performances. However, the date collected by the team all pointed out that Penghu was the birthplace for Nanguan and local traditional folk songs, Po-Kua. Po-Kua praise songs are Penghu local's folk songs with very rich traditional cultural resources. The Department of Cultural Affairs has deliberately cultivated their own local Chinese orchestra. My heart told me that to unearth those rich traditional stories and songs and present them with a new performing ways was the whole purpose for retaining the Chiang Kai-Shek Hall. This confusion was settled after a few trips to Ilan. The Lanyan Museum and Ilan's National Center for Traditional Arts gave me direction to my thinking. The role of the "Lanyan Museum" was oriented by the locals as an ecological museum. Through the collaborated efforts of the artists and the local community to develop Ilan's craft industry, finding new vitality for the local arts and crafts and the craftsmen. This was the initial planned positioning of Lanyan Museum and is one of the social values for its existence. Uni-President, the OT company for Ilan's "National Center for Traditional Arts," advanced Taiwan's traditional arts onto the stage of the cultural tourism. Through DIY education and primary and junior high school student excursions, the school students, families and general tourists are allowed the opportunity to learn about tradition arts and crafts with the traditional artists in the Center and participate in the teaching of the traditional performing arts. In the Center, one can watch and enjoy the various traditional arts performances and exhibitions such as Taiwanese opera, Nanguan, Beiguan, martial art and Hakka Songs. Ilan's National Center for Traditional Arts is a successful cooperation between a private enterprise and the government, a commercial fusion between the traditional arts and tourism. Finally, after nearly six months of reading, traveling, conversing and reflecting, I eventually found the market and the direction for the cultural and creative development in Penghu.

Penghu's near 700 years of culture and tradition can be the manifestation of the creative life industry. The exquisite stone carving technique of the local artists is an exhibition of the craft industry. The Chang Kai-Shek Hall can be exhibited using fixed performance play list during high tourist season and in off seasons, its main objective can be the cultivation of local performing arts talents. Although Penghu has only about just more than

60,000 resident population, but its annual tourists number can reach to more than 700,000 to 800,000 a year. Due to the travel conditions, Penghu's tourism market is one of planned travel where tourists usually stay for three days and two nights. With an average travel consumption of more than US$8,000, this makes the tourist output value at a conservative estimate of US$5 to 6 billion a year. Cultural and creative related consumption include dining, shopping and entertainment. This means that the cultural and creative market in Penghu has at least a market size of US$2 billion. Unlike the other cultural and creative parks in Taiwan where metropolitan cultural and creative parks rely on local consumption to support the cultural and creative market, the uniqueness of Penghu's development of cultural and creative industry is that it is supported by the tourism market. This is the vantage point for developing Penghu's cultural and creative industry! And so I have found the anchorage point to link up John and Yang's dreams. But what comes with a supporting point? Where are the investors and the entrepreneurs? This is my second challenge.

3.5.   *To dialogue and to going on...*

In the process of assisting the County Government with a BOT assessment program analyzing the feasibility of a senior resort in 2010, I discovered that Penghu folks have special attachment with their hometown. Every time I go visit the elders, they would thank me for helping for my effort in Penghu, tell me where their hometown in Penghu is, and how their childhood life was then? There have even been folks who told me that even though they are old now, but they dreamt of living in Penghu in their childhood. Due to the lack of job opportunity and harsh living environment in Penghu, many people leave their hometown after graduating from junior or senior high school. There are around 1.5 million Penghu people in Taiwan at a rough estimate. Because of Penghu folks' willingness to work hard, they stand out and prevail especially in the fisheries import and export, building construction, shipbuilding or shipping industries. Situating the Park at the heart of Penghu has great commercial value. However, I did not want to attract prospective business investors with the concept of land value. In my mind, only the hometown people would cherish the culture of their homeland. I wanted to find someone like a social capitalist to become the capitalist for the Park, who took developing the community as their objectives but whom also has the experience in business development. Thus, began my visits to potential folks for becoming a cultural and creative capitalist. The initial findings did not go smoothly. There were times when I wanted to give up. But then, perhaps I was motivated by the success of the Taiwan movie "Seediq Bale." It prompted me to continue the process in accomplishing the ideal inspiration. Like the director Te-Sheng Wei whose process in seeking investors did not go well, but his will to produce the film "Seediq Bale" was so strong that he did not give even if he underwent all conceivable hardship in the process. This attitude inspired me to go on. After in-depth interviews with prospective investors, in the end, I finally met a businessman, Boss, in "Café Astoria" in Taipei who just came back from Mainland China, an investor who was planning on returning to Penghu to settle down. Hence, I began the next process of matching young entrepreneur.

A young man whose hometown was in Penghu Tungchiyu, told me that every time he accompanied his father home, his father would keep looking back long after the ship has left the island. From my observation, he is an honest and reliable person who has been working along the line of cultural design for over 20 years, from graphic design, printing and packaging, website design to urban planning are all his strength. I asked him whether he would like to become the chief executive of a cultural and creative park where he could try to run a park. I have already found the investor and the architectural team will assist with the structural space part. Perhaps, Andy is like me who likes to take up challenges, and hence began the collaboration process of Andy and Boss. Andy is a hardworking man who, at time, can be very stubborn. However, he is talented and is a good partner in the process of execution. Boss was involved in the development of Hainan Island whilst he was in Mainland China. He is a businessman who is very particular about every digit. Therefore, Andy must be very specific about every cent and penny. He often reports the estimated amount of investment and the return on investment to Boss. Time and again, Boss would tell him pessimistically about how doubtful the cultural and creative market is, and that he should be more conservative and evaluate with more caution. Andy seemed very discouraged by this.

John was very worried about Andy's impulsiveness and discharges the hard to find investor. So he called me one day to ask me to talk with Andy. He felt Andy was like how he was when he was young, full of ideals. But ideals are often prone to failure. One needs a businessman like Boss to assist along side, who would grab hold of every dollar. This way, the project is more likely to succeed easily. I remember that day at the campus of the National Sun Yat-sen University. Andy and I sat down and discussed. We discussed the kind of resources required if this Park operates successfully. The conclusion we came up was that, first, we need creativity. The Government is already carrying most of the burden in the structural part of the Park. The most important investment of this Park is creativity — creativity is the soul of the Park. Second, we need a team. To have creativity, we must have a team that made up by a combination of different people, but the team members must have similar concept, common goals and ideals. And lastly, it would be financial affairs. Andy confessed that he wanted to go his own way, and not the way that Boss wanted, which would make the Park into just a commercial trading place by well-calculated businessman. He wanted to go his own way, setting up his own team. Perhaps, I was moved by his firmness in his belief; I gave Andy the book written by Director Wei which described how he looked for investors even under such a disheartened state, and how he motivated himself to complete the film with enthusiasm. It was not long after that Andy parted with the investor and went his way to find other partners.

This is the story of a journey between John, Yang, Boss, Andy and I in the development of Penghu's cultural industry. Life stories do not end. It is an ongoing life journey. We know that there will still be challenges ahead, and more perplexity. While our strength may be small, and lacks adequate resources, however, it is with the hope that Taiwan's cultural industry will gradually flourish because of our courage to walk our own path. This is a story that is still waiting for us to continue our efforts. On that account, the story is unfinished, to be continued. . . .

4. Reflection

Through the narrative of the planner (or the entrepreneur) on her process of entrepreneurship action, three themes emerged on how entrepreneurship is a venture on the boundary work. First, in Chapter 1 of the story, we saw a planner, who had been residing permanently in the city, was originally faced with the limitation of the urban space boundary. However, she was propelled to depart from the city to go to the outlying islands by an imagination and began a journey of learning. Through her description of her venture in Chapters 2 and 3, we also saw the fishery culture, which had long been the core of Penghu, because of its failure to integrate with the development of globalization and industrialization during the post-industrialization era, its economic development was somewhat restricted. In her narrative in Chapter 4, she described how her journey had induced her thoughts on the limitation of the cultural and economic boundary had guided her to discover the unique and advantageous development for the cultural and creative industry of Penghu that was unlike those in the metropolitan areas. In the last paragraph of the journey narrated in the story, is a dialogue between the narrator and the young entrepreneur, helping the two entrepreneurs to go beyond the boundaries of traditional thinking in enterprise capital.

After reading with us through the story of narrative inquiry, the following is the findings on the study of the founder's boundary work.

4.1. The imagination that led the entrepreneur to cross the limitation presented the boundaries of knowledge and space

The planner had long been living in the city. She knew that she had the enthusiasm to promote the cultural and creative industry, but lacked the experience in planning a cultural park in the outlying island district. She was left in speculation and "can only start from imagination." "Whenever I have something, I really wanted to do but did not know where to start, I would go to a bookstore to find inspiration..." Through reading Fumio Nanjo's description for an ideal Art Village, the planner was guided to form a sketch for the planning of the oncoming cultural park and questions such as: what kinds of hardware requirement are needed in the construction planning, how to configure the hardware within the planned space, and how to plan the park management and so forth, were answered. All these seemed to leap off the page.

"First, at the center of the park is a building with exhibition space, a library and a Customer Service Center. It can be a single building or a multiple linked buildings. Not far from there is the restaurant..." This paragraph which contained Fumio Nanjo's description of a setting for an art village, had assisted the planner in imagining the kind of spatial constructional requirements needed for the future cultural and creative park. The required plans included descriptions of a display area, a library and a service center. In addition to those, a separate and independent restaurant, and a unique styled bar is needed to allow the local residents and artists opportunities for interactive engagement and conversation. So, how to go about the operational management of the Park? This is what Fumio Nanjo had imagined — "In order to stabilize the operation of the Art Village, a Foundation can be established. However, the operation of such an organization cannot operate in a bureaucratic manner because such a way would become meaningless. Therefore, it is necessary to plan a set of operating system to allow for flexible operation. Or perhaps even consider outsourcing the operation . . . " The task of this entrepreneur was to assist the local government in the operation of outsourcing. By reading the imagination of Fumio Nanjo, the planner gained the confidence and the strength to progress forward.

The last paragraph set out Fumio Nanjo's expectation for an ideal Art Village — "As a result, the Art Village will become an Arts University with a high standard, or it will take on the responsibility of nurturing artists . . . If an Arts Village like this can be set up, this will become a vibrant place where all kinds of talented personnel congregate. This way, we will be able to cultivate talented personnel who will be responsible for the development of the future cultural arts." This seemed to have become the higher goal of the planner for the oncoming planned cultural and creative park. The Park will not just be any park. It could be planned into a university of the Arts where all kinds of talented people will gather. It would engage in the cultivation of talented personnel who will be responsible for the important task of cultural promotion. It would become a park that is full of vitality. With the assistance of Fumio Nanjo's vision, the planner went beyond the limitation imposed by the knowledge boundary where she originally had no knowledge on how to plan a cultural and creative park. It was also through Fumio Nanjo's vision that the planner formed her own imagination of the journey of which she was about to set off. "This learning journey that was about to set sail, I had no idea what kind of scenery I will encounter in this journey. All I could do is fantasize this as a Don Quixote styled adventure and a journey of imagination." Therefore, it is the vision that urged the planner to depart the city and head for the outlying islands to begin a journey of learning. This imagination also made the planner go beyond what was originally confined by the boundary of urban space, and propelled her "go to such a wonderful and strange islands."

4.2. Travel allowed the entrepreneur to find the supporting point to cross the limitation of culture and economic boundaries

Next, we come to Chapter 2 of the narrative. Penghu is a string of pearls on the Pacific Ocean. The local residents have long relied on the fishery culture as its core of development. The Portuguese had even named it the "Pescadores," the Islands of the Fishermen, during the Age of Discovery. However, with the evolution of times, because of its inability to smoothly transit with the industrial changes which was coupled with restrictions posed by the natural environment, the result was a large amount of migration of its population and a gradual marginalization of its economy. Through the narrative, we gained some understanding on the limitation in Penghu's cultural and economical boundaries.

Following the narrative of the planner, we also arrived with her at this planning base. In the 1960s, when the government's national military retreated to Taiwan during the Civil War, Penghu, with its location being mid-strait between Mainland China and Taiwan partially toward the East, was established as a military base. What was originally planned as a living compound for the families of the officers and men in the Department of Defense, under generations of changes, it had gradually become an unused idle area. However, with the major industry being the local traditional culture of fishery, it was a great challenge for the planner to foster the cultural and creative industry in the frontier. How the planner challenged the local traditional culture of fishery and the limitation in the economic development, and how she leaped over the restrictions presented in the boundary were the second challenge in her boundary work. This led us to Chapter 4 — a narrative on the process of finding all kinds of possibilities from a vision. The term "cultural and creative industry" had become a familiar term in Taiwan in recent years and many books had been written on this topic. However, this time, there was no one book that could tell the entrepreneur what to do, because "What lacked was a book that tells me how to foster a place's cultural industry from scratch, especially for a place on the border, an outlying island that not even the locals are optimistic about. How to accomplish this? It was a huge challenge." At that note, the planner set off on a journey after some thought.

The planner traveled northbound from South of Taiwan, then bypass to the East. She visited a total of four cultural and creative parks in Tainan, Taichung, Chiayi and Hualien. She saw evidence of the Central Government pouring a large amount of funding resources into these cultural heritages or into the renovation of the hardware in these old, idle industrial production spaces. Nevertheless, despite all those money that went into renovating the construction hardware, the result of such an industrial development seemed quite ineffective. It was a great pity when the planner visited these location to find that the Parks were mostly empty without much crowd. Most cultural and creative parks in metropolitan area relied on the local consumers to support the cultural and creative market. This was possible because there was a large enough population to support the consuming market needed for a cultural and creative park. This did not apply to the outlying islands. Penghu's consuming market required uniqueness to support the industry. This trip had raised this social entrepreneur's thoughts on the economical limitation faced in the frontier. Whilst traveling, her mind had been thinking: "Although Penghu has only about just more than 60,000 resident population, but its annual tourists number can reach to more than 700,000 to 800,000 a year. Due to the travel condition, Penghu's tourism market is one of planned travel where tourists usually stay for three days and two nights. With an average travel consumption of more than US$8,000, this makes the tourist output value at a conservative estimate of US$5 to 6 billion a year. Cultural and creative-related consumption include dining, shopping and entertainment. This means that the cultural and creative market in Penghu has at least a market size of US$2 billion. . ." Penghu was indeed different from other cultural and creative parks in Taiwan. During the travel, her thoughts on the economical limitation faced in the frontier had triggered the planner, who was originally residing in the urban area, with the thought of using the tourist market to support Penghu's cultural and creative market. This was the uniqueness and the advantage in developing Penghu's cultural and creative industry.

The personal cultural preference of the planner had also led her to rethink past her culture boundary limitation: "I never watched the performance of traditional oriental arts. I preferred the Western performing arts like the opera, jazz and classical music. I thought that if even I do not like to watch it, then why other people would want to watch it. That was why I thought that there is no market for the local operas or the traditional arts performances." Planner's own preference for Western culture had confined her cultural boundary. "Should Penghu introduce modern arts performances or traditional performing arts? Because of my own preferences and prejudice, this choice of whether the West or the East had truly confounded me for a long time." Such confusion was eased after several trips to Ilan. Through the travel which involved movement of the body and seeing "Lanyan Museum" and "Ilan's National Center for Traditional Arts" of the Ilan locals, new direction was triggered into her thinking. "Lanyan Museum" had been oriented as a local museum where the development of Ilan's local craft industry was conducted through the collaboration of artists and the community. Finding new vitality for the local traditional crafts and the traditional craftsmen was how Lanyan Museum was initially positioned during planning. This was one of the social values in its existence. Looking at Penghu with its nearly 700 years of culture and traditions and superb and exquisite stone carvings by the local artists, Penghu's cultural and creative park should be oriented to be a base for the promotion of local traditional culture. The planner had seen how a government-outsourced vendor had presented Taiwan's traditional arts on the culture and tourism stage in Ilan's National Center for Traditional Arts. With the use of DIY teaching and school excursions, elementary and junior high school students, families and the general tourists can learn about traditional arts and crafts with the traditional craftsmen, and participate in the teaching of the traditional performing arts. "Ilan's National Center for Traditional Arts" was a successful cooperation example between an enterprise and the government. This was also a successful illustration of how the traditional arts and the tourism business can be integrated together. This was back-upped by planner's "data collected by the team all pointed out that Penghu was the birthplace for Nanguan and local traditional folk songs, Po-Kua. Po-Kua praise songs are Penghu local's folk songs with very rich traditional cultural resources.... My heart told me that to unearth those rich traditional stories and songs and present them with a new performing ways was the whole purpose for retaining the Chiang Kai-Shek Hall." Thus, from what the planner saw, thought and felt during these trips had assisted her to go beyond the confines of the cultural boundaries, and had allowed her to find an orientation for developing the cultural and creative industry in Penghu.

4.3. Dialogue allowed the entrepreneurs to cross the confines of the thinking boundary on the venturing capital

Whilst traveling in Hualien, the planner lodged in a bed and breakfast guesthouse. Some of the local artists and the guesthouse owner complained about how Hualien's cultural and creative seemed to belong to a corporation and not to the people. The locals did not have any opportunity or the possibility of participating in it. This led the entrepreneur to ponder — "I thought about how cultural and creative entrepreneurs are all micro-enterprises where they used ROT or BOT methods to operate the idle spaces. Of course only a consortium has the financial means and the personnel required to operate such a place. However, in the future, I would like to get the investors and the young people to work together combing the financial capital of an investor with the creative capital of the young people." Following the narrative, we came to the end of the story — the process of matching investors with the entrepreneur. The cultural and creative park is situated at the heart of Penghu possessing great commercial values. The planner did not want to rely on the concept of land value to attract potential commercial investors. She believed that only the native hometown people will cherish their homeland culture. "I wanted to find someone like a social capitalist to become the capitalist for the Park, who took developing the community as their objectives but whom also has the experience in business development." Thus, began visits to potential would-be investor hometown people. After a series of in-depth interviews with potential investors, she finally found an investor, Boss, who just came back from doing business on the Mainland China and wanted to settle down in Penghu. Hence, began the next process of matching young entrepreneur.

The planner was under the impression that capital asset is an important element in the process of starting an enterprise and that in order for the cultural and creative park to operate successfully, it was important to have an experienced professional in the area of commercial development. It would be beneficial to the management of the cultural and creative park if they could combine the investor with a young entrepreneur. This kind of awareness, however, became the limitation on the knowledge boundary in the development of cultural and creative industry. In the course of interactive conversation with the young entrepreneur, Andy, it had given this planner, who had been doing the doctoral degree of business administration in the university, a fresh look at what is the most important enterprise capital in a cultural and creative industry. It had made her rethink beyond her traditional MBA training. "I remember that day at the campus of the National Sun Yat-sen University. Andy and I sat down and discussed. We discussed the kind of resources required if this park operates successfully. . ." After a discussion with Andy, the conclusion they reached in terms of the resources for cultural and creative industry were the following: the first required resource was creativity; the second required resource was a team; and the last required resource was finance. Such an analysis and conversation prompted the founder to go beyond the boundary of what was traditionally conceived about business knowledge, and also allowed Andy to have the chance "to go his own way, and not the way that Boss wanted, which would make the park into just a commercial trading place by well-calculated businessman. He wanted to go his own way, setting up his own team."

Through the planner (also the entrepreneur's) narrative on her story about the process of entrepreneurial actions, we found that entrepreneurship is a venture on the boundary work. We also understood how entrepreneurs went about doing boundary works and how confronting the challenges presented in the boundaries of knowledge, space, cultural, economic, and entrepreneurial thinking meant challenging and extending the limitations presented by the boundaries. The imagination led the planner to cross the confines in the boundaries of knowledge and space. Travel allowed the planner to find the supporting point for crossing the confines in the boundaries of culture and economics. Dialogue allowed the planner to cross the limitations in the boundaries of enterprise capital thinking. It was through this imagination, travel and dialogue that propelled the entrepreneur to think outside the boundaries of knowledge, space, culture, economics and entrepreneurial thinking.

References

Cornwall, J. R. (1998). The Entrepreneur as a Building Block for Community, *Journal of Development Entrepreneurship*, 3(2), pp. 141–148.

Hjorth, D. & Johannisson, B. (2003). Conceptualising the Opening Phase of a Regional Development as the Enactment of a Collective Identity, *Concepts and Transformation*, 8, pp. 69–92.

Johannisson, B. (2005). *Entreprenörskapets väsen*. Lund: Studentlitteratur.

Johansson, A. W. (2008). Live Story Research and the Researcher's Life, *International Small Business Journal*, 22, pp. 273–293.

Polkinghorne, D. (1988). *Narrative Knowing and the Human Science. Albany*, NY: State University of New York Press.

Spinosa, C., Flores, F. & Dreyfus, H. L. (1997). *Disclosing New Worlds: Entrepreneurship, Democratic Action, and the Cultivation of Solidarity*, Cambridge, MA and London: MIT Press.

Wei, M. D. (2008). Cong Yangjuan Xiaocun Dao Diqiucun.

Zhang, Y. H. (1998). The History of MaoKao.

Index